PENGUIN P

PL14

ALTONA
MEN WITHOUT SHADOWS
THE FLIES

JEAN-PAUL SARTRE

*

JEAN-PAUL SARTRE

ALTONA
MEN WITHOUT SHADOWS
THE FLIES

PENGUIN BOOKS

IN ASSOCIATION WITH

HAMISH HAMILTON

Penguin Books Ltd, Harmondsworth, Middlesex, England
Penguin Books Australia Ltd, Ringwood, Victoria, Australia

—

Les Séquestres d'Altona first published by Gallimard 1960
This translation first published by Hamish Hamilton 1960
Copyright © Hamish Hamilton 1960

—

Morts sans sépulture first published by Gallimard 1946
This translation first published by Hamish Hamilton 1949

—

Les Mouches first published by Gallimard 1943
This translation first published by Hamish Hamilton 1946

—

These three plays first published together in Penguin Books 1962
Reprinted 1965, 1968

—

Made and printed in Great Britain by Cox & Wyman Ltd,
London, Reading and Fakenham
Set in Monotype Bembo

CONTENTS

ALTONA

CHARACTERS

LENI

JOHANNA

WERNER

THE FATHER

FRANZ

S.S. MAN

AMERICAN OFFICER

THE WOMAN

LIEUTENANT KLAGES

THE SERGEANT-MAJOR

Note by the Author

I thought that I had invented the name Gerlach. I was mistaken. It was hidden in my memory. I regret my mistake even more because the name is that of one of the bravest and best known opponents of National-Socialism.

Hellmuth von Gerlach devoted his life to the struggle for rapprochement between France and Germany, and for peace. In 1933 his name was high up in the list of those proscribed by the Nazis. His property was seized, together with that of his family. He died in exile, two years later, having devoted his last efforts to providing help for his refugee compatriots.

It is too late to change the names of my characters, but I beg his friends and relatives to accept this as an earnest of my apology and my regret.

ACT ONE

A large room crowded with pretentious ugly furniture, most of which is in the German style of the end of the nineteenth century. An inside staircase leads to a small landing. On the landing, a closed door. Two french windows, right, lead to a thickly wooded park; the light filtering in through the trees has a greenish hue. Upstage, right and left, two doors. On the wall upstage, three enormous photos of Franz, mourning crêpe draped on the frames at the bottom and on the right.

> [LENI *is standing,* WERNER *is seated in an armchair, while* JOHANNA *is seated on a settee. They are silent. Then, after a moment, the large German clock strikes three.* WERNER *jumps up,* LENI *bursts into laughter.*]

LENI: Attention! [*Pause.*] At thirty-three! [*Annoyed.*] Oh, sit down!

JOHANNA: Why? Isn't it time?

LENI: Time? Now we start waiting, that's all. [WERNER *shrugs his shoulders. To Werner*] You know very well we shall have to wait.

JOHANNA: How should he know?

LENI: Because it's the rule. At all family conferences . . .

JOHANNA: Have there been many?

LENI: They were our big occasions.

JOHANNA: I hope you enjoyed them.

LENI [*continuing*]: Werner was always early, and old Hindenburg always late.

WERNER [*to Johanna*]: Don't believe a word of it. Father has always done things with military precision.

LENI: Absolutely! We used to wait here while he smoked a cigar in his office and looked at his watch. At three ten he

13

would make his entry, military fashion. Ten minutes; not a minute more, not a minute less. Twelve at staff meetings, eight when he presided at meetings of the directors.

JOHANNA: Why go to all that trouble?

LENI: To give us time to be afraid.

JOHANNA: And down at the shipyard?

LENI: The boss arrives last.

JOHANNA [*amazed*]: What? Who says that? [*She laughs.*] No one believes that any more.

LENI: Old Hindenburg believed it for fifty years of his life.

JOHANNA: Perhaps so, but now . . .

LENI: Now he no longer believes in anything. [*Pause.*] Nevertheless, he'll be ten minutes late. Principles may go, habits remain. Bismarck was still alive when our poor father acquired his habits. [*To Werner*] Don't you remember how we waited? [*To Johanna*] He used to tremble and wonder who was going to be punished.

WERNER: Didn't you tremble, Leni?

LENI [*laughing dryly*]: Me? I used to die of fright, but I used to say to myself: he'll pay for it.

JOHANNA [*ironically*]: Has he paid?

LENI [*smiling, but very harsh*]: He is paying. [*She turns to Werner.*] Who's going to be punished, Werner? Which of us two? How it makes us young again! [*Suddenly fierce*] I hate victims who respect their executioners.

JOHANNA: Werner is not a victim.

LENI: Look at him!

JOHANNA [*pointing to the mirror*]: Look at yourself!

LENI [*surprised*]: Me?

JOHANNA: You don't look so good. And you're talking a lot.

LENI: That's just to distract you. It's a long time since I've been afraid of father. Anyway, this time we know what he's going to say.

WERNER: I haven't the slightest idea.

LENI: Not the slightest? Hypocrite! Pharisee! You close your eyes to everything unpleasant! [*To Johanna*] Old Hindenburg is going to die, Johanna. Didn't you know?

JOHANNA: Yes, I did.

WERNER: It's not true. [*He starts to tremble.*] I tell you it's not true.

LENI: Stop trembling! [*Suddenly violent*] Die, yes, die! Like a dog! And you were told. The proof of that is that you told everything to Johanna.

JOHANNA: You're wrong, Leni.

LENI: Go on! He has no secrets from you.

JOHANNA: Oh, yes, he has some.

LENI: Then who told you?

JOHANNA: You.

LENI [*stunned*]: Me?

JOHANNA: Three weeks ago, one of the doctors came to see you in the Blue Room after the consultation.

LENI: Hilbert, yes. What of it?

JOHANNA: I met you in the corridor. He had just gone.

LENI: Well?

JOHANNA: Nothing. [*Pause.*] Your face gives you away, Leni.

LENI: I didn't know that. Thank you. Did I look elated?

JOHANNA: You looked terrified.

LENI [*shouts*]: That's not true! [*She regains control of herself.*]

JOHANNA [*gently*]: Go and look at your face in the glass. The terror is still there.

LENI [*curtly*]: I'll leave the looking-glasses to you.

WERNER [*striking the arm of his chair*]: That's enough! [*He looks at them angrily.*] If it's true that father is going to die, have the decency to keep quiet. [*To Leni*] What's the matter with him? [*She does not reply.*] I'm asking you what's the matter with him.

LENI: You know.

WERNER: That's not true.

LENI: You knew twenty minutes before I did.

JOHANNA: Leni, what are you trying to . . .?

LENI: Before going to the Blue Room, Hilbert went through the Rose Room. He met my brother and told him everything.

JOHANNA [*amazed*]: Werner! [*He slumps down into the armchair without replying.*] I . . . I don't understand.

LENI: You still don't know the Gerlachs, Johanna.

JOHANNA [*pointing to Werner*]: I knew one in Hamburg three years ago, and I fell in love with him right away. He was free, he was open and he was gay. How you have changed him!

LENI: Was he afraid of words in Hamburg, your Gerlach?

JOHANNA: No, he wasn't.

LENI: It's here that he's really himself.

JOHANNA [*turning to Werner sadly*]: You lied to me!

WERNER [*sharply*]: Not another word. [*Pointing to Leni*] Look at her smile. She's preparing the ground.

JOHANNA: For whom?

WERNER: For father. We are the chosen victims, and their first aim is to separate us. Whatever you may think, don't reproach me. You would be playing their game.

JOHANNA [*tender, but serious*]: I have nothing to reproach you with.

WERNER [*wildly*]: That's all right, then! That's all right, then!

JOHANNA: What do they want of us?

WERNER: Don't worry, they'll tell us. [*Pause.*]

JOHANNA: What's wrong with him?

LENI: Who?

JOHANNA: Father.

LENI: Cancer of the throat.

JOHANNA: Does one die of it?

LENI: Usually. [*Pause.*] He may drag on. [*Quietly*] You used to like him, didn't you?

JOHANNA: I still do.

LENI: He was always attractive to women. [*Pause.*] What a retribution! That mouth which was so loved. . . . [*She sees that Johanna does not understand.*] Perhaps you don't know, but cancer of the throat has this great disadvantage . . .

JOHANNA [*she understands*]: Be quiet!

LENI: You are becoming a Gerlach. Bravo!

    [*She goes to get the Bible, a thick, heavy, sixteenth-century volume, and carries it with difficulty over to the pedestal table.*]

JOHANNA: What's that?

LENI: The Bible. We put it on the table when we hold a family conference. [JOHANNA *looks at it, astonished.* LENI *adds, a trifle impatiently*] Yes, in case we have to take an oath.

JOHANNA: There's no oath to take.

LENI: You never know.

JOHANNA [*laughing to reassure herself*]:You believe neither in God nor the Devil.

LENI: That's true. But we go to church, and we swear on the Bible. I've already told you – this family has no longer any justification for living, but it has kept its good habits. [*She looks at the clock.*] Ten past three, Werner. You can stand up.

    [*At that moment the* FATHER *enters by the french windows.* WERNER *hears the door open and turns round.* JOHANNA *hesitates before standing, but at last decides to do so with bad grace. The* FATHER, *however, walks quickly across the room and places his hands on her shoulders to make her sit down again.*]

FATHER: Please, my child. [*She sits down again; he bows, kisses her hand, straightens up rather quickly and looks at Werner and Leni.*] Well, I don't need to tell you, do I? Very good! Let's get to the point, and without ceremony, eh? [*Brief silence.*] So, I am condemned. [WERNER *takes his arm, but he pulls away almost brutally.*] I said – without ceremony. [WERNER, *hurt turns away and sits down again. Pause. The* FATHER *looks at all three and speaks in a slightly harsh voice.*] How unconcernedly you all take my death! [*Keeping his eyes on them, as though to convince them*] I am going to die. I am going to die. There's no doubt about it. [*He recovers himself, almost playful.*] My children, Nature is playing me a shabby trick. Whatever my worth, this body of mine never harmed anyone. In six months I shall have all the disadvantages of a corpse without any of its advantages. [*At a gesture from* WERNER, *he laughs.*] Sit down! I shall go decently.

LENI [*politely interested*]: You are going . . . ?

FATHER: Do you think I shall submit to the extravagance of a few cells, I who set steel afloat on the seas? [*Short pause.*] Six months is more than I need to put my affairs in order.

WERNER: And after the six months?

FATHER: After? What do you think? Nothing.

LENI: Nothing at all?

FATHER: An industrial casualty. Nature finally redressed.

WERNER [*in a choked voice*]: Redressed by whom?

FATHER: By you, if you are capable of it. [WERNER *starts. The* FATHER *laughs.*] Don't worry, I'll take care of everything. You will only have to worry about the funeral arrangements. [*Pause.*] Enough of that. [*Long pause. To Johanna, pleasantly*] My child, I ask you to be patient just a little longer. [*To Leni and Werner, changing his tone*] You will have to swear an oath, one after the other.

JOHANNA [*anxious*]: What ceremony! And you said you didn't want any. What is there to swear?

FATHER [*good-humouredly*]: Nothing much, daughter-in-law. In any case, in-laws are exempt from the oath. [*He turns towards his son with a solemnity which could be taken as ironic or sincere.*] Werner, stand up! You were a lawyer, my son. When Franz died, I called on you for help, and you left the Bar without hesitation. That deserves a reward. You will be master of this house and head of the firm. [*To Johanna*] You see, nothing to worry about. I am making him one of the kings of this world. [JOHANNA *remains silent.*] Don't you agree?

JOHANNA: It's not for me to answer you.

FATHER: Werner! [*Impatiently*] You refuse?

WERNER [*gloomy and troubled*]: I shall do what you wish.

FATHER: Of course you will. [*He looks at him.*] But you are reluctant to do it?

WERNER: Yes.

FATHER: The largest shipbuilding firm is handed to you and that breaks your heart. Why?

WERNER: I . . . Let's say I'm not worthy of it.

FATHER: That's quite probable. But I can't help it. You are my sole male heir.

WERNER: Franz had all the necessary qualities.

FATHER: Except one, since he is dead.

WERNER: You see, I was a good lawyer. I shall find it hard to resign myself to being a bad employer.

FATHER: Perhaps you won't be such a bad one.

WERNER: When I look a man in the eyes, I become incapable of giving him orders.

FATHER: Why?

WERNER: I feel that he is my equal.

FATHER: Look at him above the eyes. [*Touches his forehead.*] There, for example. That's only bone.

WERNER: I should need your pride.

FATHER: Haven't you got it?

WERNER: Where could I have got it from? You spared nothing to mould Franz in your own image. Is it my fault that you taught me nothing but passive obedience?

FATHER: It's the same thing.

WERNER: What? What's the same thing?

FATHER: To obey and to command. In both cases you transmit orders you have received.

WERNER: You receive orders?

FATHER: Up to quite recently, I did.

WERNER: From whom?

FATHER: I don't know. Myself, perhaps. [*Smiling*] I'll give you the formula. If you want to command, think of yourself as someone else.

WERNER: I can't think of myself as anyone else.

FATHER: Wait till I die. At the end of a week you will think you are me.

WERNER: To decide! To decide! To be responsible for everything. Alone. On behalf of a hundred thousand men. And you have managed to live!

FATHER: It's a long time since I have decided anything. I sign the correspondence. Next year, you will sign it.

WERNER: Don't you do anything else?

FATHER: Nothing, for nearly ten years.

WERNER: Why are you needed? Wouldn't anyone do?

FATHER: Yes, anyone.

WERNER: Me, for example.

FATHER: You, for example.

WERNER: Nothing is perfect. There are so many cogs in the machine. Suppose one of them were to jam. . . .

FATHER: For repairs, Gelber will be there. A remarkable man, you know, who has been with us for twenty-five years.

WERNER: I'm lucky, in fact. He will give the orders.

FATHER: Gelber? You're mad! He is your employee. You pay him to let you know what orders to give.

WERNER [*after a pause*]: Oh, father, not once in your life have you trusted me. You thrust me at the head of the firm because I am your sole male heir, but you first made sure of turning me into an ornament.

FATHER [*laughing sadly*]: An ornament! And I? What am I? A hat on a flagpole. [*With a sad and gentle air, almost senile*] The greatest enterprise in Europe. . . . It's quite an organization, isn't it? Quite an organization.

WERNER: Perfect. If I find time hangs heavily, I'll go back to the Bar. And we shall travel too.

FATHER: No.

WERNER [*astonished*]: It's the best thing I could do.

FATHER [*imperious and crushing*]: Out of the question. [*He looks at Werner and Leni.*] Now listen to me. The estate is to remain intact. You are strictly forbidden to sell or hand over your share to anyone whatsoever. You are forbidden to sell this house. You are forbidden to leave it. You will live in it until you die. Swear! [*To Leni*] You first.

LENI [*smiling*]: To be honest, I must remind you that I am not bound by oaths.

FATHER [*also smiling*]: Go on, Leni, I rely on you. Be an example to your brother.

LENI [*approaches the Bible and raises her hand. She fights against an overwhelming desire to laugh*]: I . . . Oh, what does it matter! Excuse me, father, but I can't help laughing. [*Aside to Johanna*] It happens every time.

FATHER [*good-humouredly*]: Laugh, my child. I only ask you to swear.

LENI [*smiling*]: I swear on the Holy Bible to obey your last wishes. [*The* FATHER *looks at her laughingly, then turns to Werner.*] Your turn, head of the family.

[WERNER *appears lost in thought.*]

FATHER: Well, Werner?

[WERNER *raises his head sharply and faces his father with a haunted look.*]

LENI [*serious*]: Deliver us, brother. Swear, and all will be over.

[WERNER *turns towards the Bible.*]

JOHANNA [*courteously and quietly*]: One moment please. [*The* FATHER *looks at her, feigning amazement in order to intimidate her. She returns his gaze without emotion.*] Leni's oath was a farce. Everyone laughed. When Werner's turn comes, no one laughs any more. Why?

LENI: Because your husband takes everything seriously.

JOHANNA: One more reason to laugh. [*Pause.*] You were watching him, Leni.

FATHER [*with authority*]: Johanna . . .

JOHANNA: You too, father, you were watching him.

LENI: Well, you were watching me also.

JOHANNA: Father, I wish we were frank with each other.

FATHER: You and I?

JOHANNA: You and I. [*The* FATHER *smiles*, JOHANNA *takes the Bible and carries it with difficulty to another table, farther away.*] First, let's talk, then whoever wants to swear may do so.

LENI: Werner! Are you going to let your wife defend you?

WERNER: Am I being attacked, then?

JOHANNA [*to the Father*]: I should like to know why you dispose of my life.

FATHER [*pointing to Werner*]: I dispose of his because it belongs to me, but I have no power over yours.

JOHANNA [*smiling*]: Do you think we have two lives? You were married. Did you love their mother?

FATHER: I loved her as a husband should.

JOHANNA [*smiling*]: I see, and she died of it. We love each other more than that, father. We have always decided everything that concerned us, together. [*Pause.*] If he swears under constraint, if he shuts himself up in this house in order to remain faithful to his vow, he will decide without me and against me. You will separate us forever.

FATHER [*with a smile*]: Don't you like our house?

JOHANNA: Not in the least. [*Pause.*]

FATHER: What don't you like, daughter-in-law?

JOHANNA: I married a lawyer in Hamburg, who possessed only his talent. Three years later, I find myself in the solitude of this fortress, married to a shipbuilder.

FATHER: Is that such a miserable fate?

JOHANNA: For me, yes. I loved Werner for his independence, and you know very well that he has lost it.

FATHER: Who has taken it from him?

JOHANNA: You.

FATHER: Eighteen months ago, you both decided to come and settle here.

JOHANNA: You asked us to.

FATHER: Well, if a wrong has been done, you share the blame.

JOHANNA: I didn't want him to have to choose between you and me.

FATHER: You were wrong.

LENI [*amiably*]: He would have chosen you.

JOHANNA: An even chance. A hundred per cent chance that he would have hated his choice.

FATHER: Why?

JOHANNA: Because he loves you. [*The* FATHER *shrugs his shoulders irritably.*] Do you know what a hopeless love is like? [*The* FATHER'S *expression changes.* LENI *notices it.*]

LENI [*quickly*]: And you, Johanna, do you know?

JOHANNA [*coldly*]: No. [*Pause.*] Werner knows. [WERNER *gets up and walks towards the french windows.*]

FATHER [*to Werner*]: Where are you going?

WERNER: I'm going out. You'll be more comfortable.

JOHANNA: Werner! I am fighting for *us*.

WERNER: For us? [*Very curtly*] At the Gerlachs, the women keep quiet. [*He is about to go out.*]

FATHER [*softly, but imperiously*]: Werner! [WERNER *stops dead.*] Come back and sit down. [WERNER *slowly returns to his seat, turns his back on them and buries his head in his hands as though to indicate that he refuses to take part in the conversation.*]

WERNER: Talk to Johanna!

FATHER: Good! Well, daughter-in-law?

JOHANNA [*with an anxious look at Werner*]: Let us postpone this interview. I am very tired.

FATHER: No, my child. You began it. We must finish it. [*Pause.* JOHANNA, *at a loss, looks at Werner in silence.*] Am I to understand that you refuse to live here after my death?

JOHANNA [*almost pleading*]: Werner! [WERNER *remains silent. She abruptly changes her attitude.*] Yes, father, that's what I mean.

FATHER: Where will you live?

JOHANNA: In our old flat.

FATHER: You'll return to Hamburg?

JOHANNA: We shall return there.

LENI: If Werner wants to.

JOHANNA: He will.

FATHER: And the firm? Do you agree to his being its head?

JOHANNA: Yes, if that is your wish and if Werner has a taste for playing at being a figurehead.

FATHER [*as if thinking the matter over*]: Live in Hamburg. . . .

JOHANNA [*hopefully*]: We ask nothing else. Won't you make this single concession to us?

FATHER [*friendly, but adamant*]: No. [*Pause.*] My son will stay here, to live and die here as I am doing, and my father and grandfather did.

JOHANNA: Why?

FATHER: Why not?

JOHANNA: Does the house have to be lived in?

FATHER: Yes.

JOHANNA [*violently*]: Then let it collapse! [LENI *bursts into laughter.*]

LENI [*politely*]: Would you like me to set fire to it? It was one of my childhood dreams.

FATHER [*glancing round in amusement*]: Poor house, does it deserve such hatred? Is it Werner who finds it so horrible?

JOHANNA: Werner and me. How ugly it is!

LENI: We know that.

JOHANNA: There are four of us. At the end of the year there will be three. Do we need thirty-two cluttered rooms? When Werner is at the yard I am afraid.

FATHER: And so that's why you want to leave us? They are not serious reasons.

JOHANNA: No.

FATHER: Are there others?

JOHANNA: Yes.

FATHER: Let's have them.

WERNER [*shouting*]: Johanna, I forbid you . . .

JOHANNA: Well, speak for yourself!

WERNER: What's the good? You know very well I shall obey him.

JOHANNA: Why?

WERNER: He's my father. Oh, let's have done with it. [*He stands up.*]

JOHANNA [*placing herself in front of him*]: No, Werner, no!

FATHER: He is right, daughter-in-law. Let us have done with it. A family is a house. I ask *you* to live in this house because you have become part of our family.

JOHANNA [*laughing*]: The family has a broad back, and you are not sacrificing us to it.

FATHER: To whom, then?

JOHANNA: To your elder son!

[*Long pause.*]

LENI [*calmly*]: Franz died in the Argentine, nearly four years ago. [JOHANNA *laughs in her face.*] We received the death certificate in '56. Go to the Altona Town Hall. They will show it to you.

JOHANNA: Dead? I should think so. What else could you call the life he leads? One thing is sure, dead or alive, he is in this house.

LENI: No.

JOHANNA [*pointing to the door on the first floor*]: Up there. Behind that door.

LENI: What madness! Who told you that? [*Pause.* WERNER *rises quietly. From the time that the subject of his brother has come up, his eyes shine and he recovers his confidence.*]

WERNER: Who do you think? I did.

LENI: In bed?

JOHANNA: Why not?

LENI: Phew!

WERNER: She's my wife. She has the right to know what I know.

LENI: The right of love? How insipid you are! I would give my body and soul to the man I loved, but I would lie to him all my life if it were necessary.

WERNER [*violently*]: Listen to this blind woman who speaks of colours. Who would you lie to? To parrots?

FATHER [*in a commanding voice*]: Be quiet, all three of you. [*He strokes Leni's hair.*] The skull is hard, but the hair is soft. [*She pulls away brutally. He remains on the alert.*] Franz has lived upstairs for thirteen years. He does not leave his room, and no one sees him except Leni who looks after him.

WERNER: And you.

FATHER: I? Who told you that? Leni? And you believed her? How close the two of you get when anything is likely to hurt you, Werner. It is thirteen years since I last saw him.

WERNER [*stunned*]: But why?

FATHER [*very matter-of-fact*]: Because he won't see me.

WERNER [*taken aback*]: Good. [*Pause.*] Good. [*He returns to his seat.*]

FATHER [*to Johanna*]: Thank you, my child. In the family, you see, we have no objection to the truth. But whenever possible we contrive to have it spoken by a stranger. [*Pause.*] So, Franz lives up there, alone and ill. Does that change anything?

JOHANNA: Almost everything. [*Pause.*] Don't worry, father. An in-law, a stranger will speak the truth for you. This is what I know. A scandal broke out in '46. I don't know what it was, since my husband was a prisoner in France at the time. It appears there were legal proceedings. Franz disappeared, you say to the Argentine. In fact, he hid himself here. In '56, Gelber made a quick trip to South America and brought back a death certificate. Sometime after, you ordered Werner to give up his career, and you installed him here as your heir. Am I wrong?

FATHER: No. Continue.

JOHANNA: I have nothing more to say. Who Franz was, what he did, what has become of him, I do not know. The only thing I am certain of is that if we remain, it will be to become slaves to him.

LENI [*fiercely*]: That's not true! He only needs me.

JOHANNA: I can't believe that.

LENI: He won't see anyone but me!

JOHANNA: That may be, but in the background father protects him, and later, we shall have to protect him. Or guard him. Perhaps we shall be his slaves and his jailers.

LENI [*outraged*]: Am I his jailer?

JOHANNA: How do I know? Supposing the two of you had locked him up?

[*Pause.* LENI *takes a key from her pocket.*]

LENI: Go upstairs and knock. If he doesn't open the door, here's the key.

JOHANNA [*taking the key*]: Thank you. [*She looks at Werner.*] What should I do, Werner?

WERNER: What you like. One way or another, you will see that it is a booby-trap. . . .

[JOHANNA *hesitates, then slowly climbs the stairs and knocks at the door. Once, twice. A kind of nervous fury takes possession of her. A rain of blows against the door. She turns towards the room, and is about to descend.*]

LENI [*quietly*]: You have the key. [*Pause.* JOHANNA *hesitates. She is afraid.* WERNER *is anxious and agitated.* JOHANNA *masters herself, inserts the key in the lock and tries vainly to open the door, even though the key turns.*] Well?

JOHANNA: There is an inside bolt. It must be fastened. [*She starts to come down.*]

LENI: Who fastened it? Did I?

JOHANNA: Perhaps there is another door.

LENI: You know very well there is not. This lodge is isolated. If anyone has bolted it, it can only be Franz. [JOHANNA *has reached the foot of the staircase.*] Well, are we holding him prisoner?

JOHANNA: There are many ways of holding a man prisoner. The best is to get him to imprison himself.

LENI: How does one do that?

JOHANNA: By lying to him. [*She looks at Leni, who appears disconcerted.*]

FATHER [*to Werner, quickly*]: Have you acted as counsel in cases of this kind?

WERNER: What cases?

FATHER: Illegal restraint.

WERNER [*in a choked voice*]: Once.

FATHER: Good. Suppose the premises were searched. The court would institute proceedings, would it not?

WERNER [*trapped*]: Why should there be a search? There never has been one in thirteen years.

FATHER: I have been here. [*Pause.*]

LENI [*to Johanna*]: And then you've told me I drive too fast. I could crash into a tree. What would become of Franz?

JOHANNA: If he is in his right mind, he will call the servants.

LENI: He is in his right mind, but he will not call them. [*Pause.*] They will discover my brother's death by the smell! [*Pause.*] They will break down the door and find him on the floor among the shells.

JOHANNA: What shells?

LENI: He likes oysters.

FATHER [*to Johanna, in a friendly manner*]: Listen to her. If he dies, it will be the scandal of the century, Johanna. . . .

JOHANNA [*in a hard voice*]: Why should you care? You'll be under the ground.

FATHER [*smiling*]: I shall, yes. But not you. Let us go back to that affair in '46. Would there be legal prescription? Answer! It's your profession.

WERNER: I don't know the offence.

FATHER: At best, assault and battery; at the worst, attempted murder.

WERNER [*in a choked voice*]: There would be no prescription.

FATHER: You know what we can expect – complicity in attempted murder, forgery and the use of forged documents, and illegal restraint.

WERNER: Forgery? What forgery?

FATHER [*laughs*]: The death certificate, of course! It cost me plenty. [*Pause.*] What do you say, lawyer? The Assize Court? [WERNER *is silent.*]

JOHANNA: Werner, the game's up. It's up to us to choose. We shall either be servants of the madman whom they prefer to you, or we shall stand in the dock. What is your choice? Mine is made. The Assize Court. I'd rather a term in prison than penal servitude for life. [*Pause.*] Well?

[WERNER *says nothing. She makes a gesture of discouragement.*]

FATHER [*warmly*]: Children, I am thunderstruck. Blackmail! Traps! It all sounds false. It is all forced. My son, I am only asking for a little pity for your brother. There are situations that Leni cannot deal with alone. For the rest, you will be as free as air. You will see. Everything will turn out all right. Franz will not live very long, I fear. One night, you will bury him in the park. With him will disappear the last of the *true* von Gerlachs . . . [*At a gesture from* WERNER] . . .

29

I mean the last monster. You are both sane and normal. You will have normal children who will live where they wish. Stay, Johanna, for the sake of Werner's sons. They will inherit the firm. It is a fabulous power, and you haven't the right to deprive them of it.

WERNER [*starting, his eyes hard and glittering*]: Eh? [*They all look at him*]. Did you really say – for Werner's sons? [*The* FATHER, *astonished, nods.* WERNER *continues triumphantly.*] There it is, Johanna, there's the trick. Werner and his children. Father, you don't give a hang for them. You don't give a hang! You don't give a hang! [JOHANNA *goes up to him. Pause.*] Even if you were to live long enough to see my first son, he would loathe you because he would be flesh of my flesh, and because I have been filled with loathing for you from the day I was born. [*To Johanna*] Poor father! What a mess! He would have adored Franz's children.

JOHANNA [*urgently*]: Stop! You should hear yourself. We are lost if you pity yourself.

WERNER: On the contrary. I am freeing myself. What do you want me to do? Turn them down flat?

JOHANNA: Yes.

WERNER [*laughs*]: That's fine!

JOHANNA: Tell them *no*. Without shouting, without laughing. Just plain no.

[WERNER *turns towards the Father and Leni. They look at him in silence.*]

WERNER: They are looking at me.

JOHANNA: What of it? [WERNER *shrugs his shoulders and goes to sit down. With extreme weariness*] Werner! [*He does not look at her any more. Long silence.*]

FATHER [*discreetly triumphant*]: Well, daughter-in-law?

JOHANNA: He has not sworn.

FATHER: He will. The weak serve the strong. That's the law.

JOHANNA [*hurt*]: Who is strong according to you? The one upstairs, half mad and more helpless than a babe in arms, or my husband whom you abandoned, and who has managed quite well on his own?

FATHER: Werner is weak, Franz is strong. That can't be helped.

JOHANNA: What do the strong do on this earth?

FATHER: In general, they do nothing.

JOHANNA: I see.

FATHER: They are people who, by nature, live in close intimacy with death. They hold the destiny of others in their hands.

JOHANNA: Is Franz like that?

FATHER: Yes.

JOHANNA: What do you know about him after thirteen years?

FATHER: He holds the destiny of all four of us here in his hands without even thinking of it.

JOHANNA: What does he think of, then?

LENI [*ironic and brutal, but frank*]: Crabs.

JOHANNA [*ironic*]: All day long?

LENI: It is very absorbing.

JOHANNA: What old-fashioned nonsense! As old as your furniture. Go on! You don't believe in it.

FATHER [*smiling*]: I have only six months to live, daughter-in-law. It is too short a time to believe in anything. [*Pause.*] Werner believes it, though.

WERNER: You are mistaken, father. Those were your ideas, not mine, and you instilled them into me. But since you have lost them on the way, you shouldn't take it amiss that I have rid myself of them. I am like any other man. Neither strong nor weak, and like anyone else, I am trying to live. As for Franz, I don't know whether I'd still recognize him, but I'm sure he's like anyone else. [*He shows Franz's photos to Johanna.*] What has he got that I haven't got? [*He looks at them, fascinated.*] He's not even handsome.

LENI [*ironic*]: No! Not even!

WERNER [*still fascinated, weakening already*]: And suppose I had been born to serve him? There are slaves who revolt. My brother will not be my destiny.

LENI: Do you prefer that your wife should be?

JOHANNA: Do you consider me one of the strong?

LENI: Yes.

JOHANNA: What a strange idea! Why?

LENI: You were an actress, weren't you? A star?

JOHANNA: Yes, I was. But my career was a failure. What else?

LENI: What else? Well, you married Werner; since when you have done nothing, and you think of death.

JOHANNA: If you seek to humiliate him, you are wasting your time. When he met me, I had left the stage for good. I was out of my mind. He can be proud of having saved me.

LENI: I bet he isn't.

JOHANNA [*to Werner*]: What do you say?

    [*Pause.* WERNER *does not reply.*]

LENI: How you embarrass the poor man. [*Pause.*] Johanna, would you have chosen him if you hadn't failed? Some marriages are funerals.

    [JOHANNA *is about to reply, but the* FATHER *intervenes.*]

FATHER: Leni. [*He strokes her hair. She dodges away angrily.*] You surpass yourself, my girl. If I were vain, I should believe that my death upset you.

LENI [*quickly*]: You needn't doubt that, father. You can see very well that she'll throw a spanner in the works.

FATHER [*starting to laugh, to Johanna*]: Don't be angry with Leni, my child. She means that we are of the same species: you, Franz and I. [*Pause.*] I like you, Johanna, and at times I have felt that you would mourn my death. You will certainly be the only one. [*He smiles at her.*]

JOHANNA [*bluntly*]: If you still care about life, and if it is my good fortune that you like me, how do you dare humiliate my husband in front of me? [*The* FATHER *shakes his head without replying.*] Are you on this side of death?

FATHER: This side, the other side. It makes no difference any more. Six months – I am an old man with no future. [*He looks into space and speaks to himself.*] The firm will continue to grow. Private investment won't be enough. The State will have to poke its nose in. Franz will remain upstairs for ten years, twenty years. He will suffer . . .

LENI [*dogmatically*]: He does not suffer.

FATHER [*not hearing her*]: Death for me is now merely the continuation of my life without me. [*Pause. He sits down, huddled in his chair, staring fixedly into space.*] He will have grey hair . . . the unhealthy fat of prisoners . . .

LENI [*fiercely*]: Be quiet!

FATHER [*not hearing*]: It is intolerable. [*He appears to be suffering.*]

WERNER [*slowly*]: Would you feel any happier if we stayed here?

JOHANNA [*quickly*]: Take care!

WERNER: Of what? He's my father. I don't want him to suffer.

JOHANNA: He is suffering for the other one.

WERNER: I don't care.

[*He goes for the Bible and brings it back to the table on which Leni had placed it before.*]

JOHANNA [*quickly*]: He's putting it on for your benefit.

WERNER [*ill-natured, his voice full of innuendo*]: And you? Aren't you doing the same thing? [*To the Father*] Answer. . . . Would you be any happier . . .?

FATHER: I don't know.

WERNER [*to the Father*]: We'll see. [*Pause. The* FATHER *and* LENI *make no sign. They wait, watching keenly.*]

JOHANNA: One question. Just one question, and you can then do what you wish.

[WERNER *looks at her gloomily and obstinately.*]

FATHER: Wait a moment, Werner. [WERNER *moves away from the Bible with a grunt which could pass for acquiescence.*] What question?

JOHANNA: Why did Franz lock himself up?

FATHER: That's a good many questions in one.

JOHANNA: Tell me what happened.

FATHER [*with light irony*]: Well, there was the war.

JOHANNA: Yes, for everybody. Are the others hiding?

FATHER: You don't see those who are hidden.

JOHANNA: He fought, didn't he?

FATHER: Right to the end.

JOHANNA: On what front?

FATHER: In Russia.

JOHANNA: When did he come back?

FATHER: In the autumn of '46.

JOHANNA: That's late. Why?

FATHER: His regiment was wiped out. Franz came back on foot all the way through Poland and occupied Germany, hiding as he went. One day the doorbell rang. [*Distant, muffled ring.*] It was he.

[FRANZ *appears upstage, behind his Father, in the shadow. He is in civilian clothes, twenty-three or twenty-four years of age. Johanna, Werner, and Leni, during this flashback scene and the next, do not see the character evoked. Only those who recall him – the* FATHER *in these first two memory scenes,* LENI *and the* FATHER *in the third – turn towards those whom they evoke when they speak to them. The voice and actions of the characters who play a memory scene must bear an air of unreality, a far away quality which, even in the more violent action, distinguishes the past from the present. For the moment, no one sees Franz, not even the Father.*

FRANZ *holds an uncorked bottle of champagne in his right hand. It can only be seen when he takes a drink. A champagne glass*

34

placed near him on a console table is hidden by ornaments. He takes it when he wants to drink.]

JOHANNA: Did he shut himself up right away?

FATHER: Right away, in the house; a year later, in his room.

JOHANNA: Did you see him every day during that year?

FATHER: Almost every day.

JOHANNA: What did he do?

FATHER: He drank.

JOHANNA: And what did he say?

FRANZ [*in a distant and mechanical voice*]: Good morning. Good evening. Yes. No.

JOHANNA: Nothing more?

FATHER: Nothing, except one day. A flood of words. I understood none of it. [*Bitter laugh.*] I was in the library listening to the radio.

[*Crackling of radio, a repeated station call-sign. All these sounds muffled.*]

VOICE FROM THE LOUDSPEAKER: Good evening, listeners, Here is the news. In Nuremberg, the International Court has sentenced Marshal Goering . . .

[FRANZ *switches off the radio. He remains in shadow even while he moves. The* FATHER *turns with a start.*]

FATHER: What are you doing? [FRANZ *looks at him dully.*] I want to know the sentence.

FRANZ [*his voice is cynical and gloomy right through the scene*]: To be hanged by the neck until he is dead. [*He drinks.*]

FATHER: How do you know? [FRANZ *is silent.* FATHER *turns to Johanna.*] Didn't you read the newspapers at the time?

JOHANNA: Hardly. I was only twelve.

FATHER: They were all in the hands of the Allies. 'We are Germans, therefore we are guilty: we are guilty because we are Germans.' Every day, on every page. What an obsession! [*To Franz*] Eighty million criminals. What a filthy trick! At the most there were three dozen of them. Let them hang those and rehabilitate us. It would be the end of a nightmare. [*With authority*] Will you please turn on the radio. [FRANZ *drinks without moving. Dryly*] You drink too much. [FRANZ *gazes at him with such a hard expression that the* FATHER *is silent, abashed. A pause, then the* FATHER *resumes, with an ardent desire to understand.*] What do they gain by reducing a people to despair? What have I done to merit the contempt of the Universe? My opinions are well known. And you, Franz, you who fought to the end? [FRANZ *laughs coarsely.*] Are you a Nazi?

FRANZ: Hell, no!

FATHER: Then you must choose; either let those who were responsible be condemned or make the whole of Germany shoulder their crimes.

FRANZ [*without moving, bursts into a dry, savage laugh*]: Ha! [*Pause.*] It amounts to the same thing.

FATHER: Are you mad?

FRANZ: There are two ways of destroying a people. Either condemn them *en bloc* or force them to repudiate the leaders they adopted. The second is the worse.

FATHER: I repudiate no one, and the Nazis are not my leaders. I had to put up with them.

FRANZ: You supported them.

FATHER: What the devil did you expect me to do?

FRANZ: Nothing.

FATHER: As for Goering, I am his victim. Take a walk around our yards. A dozen air-raids – not a shed standing. That's how he protected them.

FRANZ [*brutally*]: I *am* Goering. If they hang him, they hang me.

FATHER: You loathed Goering!

FRANZ: I obeyed.

FATHER: Your military leaders, yes.

FRANZ: Who did they obey? [*Laughs.*] We hated Hitler, others loved him. What's the difference? You supplied him

36

with warships, and I with corpses. Tell me, could we have done more if we had worshipped him?

FATHER: Well? Is everyone guilty?

FRANZ: Good God, no! No one. Except the sleeping dogs who accept the judgement of the victors. Fine victors! We know them. They were the same in 1918, with the same hypocritical virtues. What did they do to us then? What did they do to themselves? Don't you tell me! It's the victors who take charge of history. They did so, and gave us Hitler. Judges? Have they never pillaged, massacred, and raped? Was it Goering who dropped the bomb on Hiroshima? If they judge us, who will judge them? They speak of our crimes in order to justify the crime they are preparing on the quiet – the systematic extermination of the German people. [*Smashing the glass against the table*] All are innocent before the enemy. All: you, me, Goering and the others.

FATHER [*shouts*]: Franz! [*The light dims and fades around Franz. He disappears.*] Franz! [*Short pause. He turns slowly to* JOHANNA *and laughs softly.*] I didn't understand a thing. Did you?

JOHANNA: Not a thing. What then?

FATHER: That's all.

JOHANNA: Wasn't it necessary to choose though – either all innocent or all guilty?

FATHER: He did not choose.

JOHANNA [*thinks a moment, then*]: That doesn't make sense.

FATHER: Perhaps it does . . . I don't know.

LENI [*quickly*]: Don't look too far, Johanna. My brother didn't care a rap for Goering and the Air Force, especially as he was in the infantry. For him, there were guilty and innocent, but they were not the same. [*To the* FATHER, *who is about to speak*] I know. I see him every day. The innocent were twenty years old, they were the soldiers; the guilty were fifty, they were the fathers.

JOHANNA: I see.

FATHER [*he has lost his relaxed good-humour. When he speaks of Franz, his voice assumes some passion*]: You see nothing at all. She is lying.

LENI: Father! You know perfectly well that Franz hates you.

FATHER [*forcefully, to Johanna*]: Franz loved me more than anyone.

LENI: Before the war.

FATHER: Before and after.

LENI: In that case, why do you say: he loved me?

FATHER [*taken aback*]: Oh, well, Leni . . . we were talking of the past.

LENI: Don't correct yourself, then. You've given yourself away. [*Pause.*] My brother joined up at eighteen. If father really wants to tell us why, you will understand the history of this family better.

FATHER: Tell it yourself, Leni. I won't deprive you of that pleasure.

WERNER [*forcing himself to be calm*]: Leni, I warn you. If you mention a single fact which reflects on my father, I shall leave this room instantly.

LENI: Are you so afraid of believing me?

WERNER: I won't have my father insulted in my presence.

FATHER [*to Werner*]: Calm down, Werner. I am going to speak. From the beginning of the war, the State gave us orders. We built the Navy. In the spring of '41, the Government gave me to understand that it wished to purchase a piece of land which we were not using. The land behind the hill – you know it.

LENI: The Government was Himmler. He was looking for a site for a concentration camp. [*Heavy silence.*]

JOHANNA: You knew that?

FATHER [*calmly*]: Yes.

JOHANNA: And you agreed?

FATHER [*in the same tone*]: Yes. [*Pause.*] Franz discovered the work going on. I had reports that he was always prowling along by the barbed wire.

JOHANNA: What happened?

FATHER: Nothing. Silence. It was he who broke it. One day in June '41. [*The* FATHER *turns towards Franz and looks at him closely while continuing the conversation with Werner and Johanna.*] I saw at once that he had put his foot in it. It couldn't have happened at a worse moment. Goebbels and Admiral Doenitz were in Hamburg, and were going to visit my new installations.

FRANZ [*youthful voice, softly, affectionate but worried*]: Father, I would like to speak to you.

FATHER [*looking at him*]: Have you been down there?

FRANZ: Yes. [*Abruptly and with horror*] Father, they are no longer men.

FATHER: The guards?

FRANZ: The prisoners. I am disgusted with myself, but it is they who fill me with horror. It's their squalor, their vermin, their sores. [*Pause.*] They look as if they are in fear all the time.

FATHER: They are what they have been made.

FRANZ: No one would make me like that.

FATHER: No?

FRANZ: I wouldn't give up.

FATHER: What proof have you that they have given up?

FRANZ: Their eyes.

FATHER: If you were in their place, yours would be the same.

FRANZ: No. [*With a fierce certainty*] No.
  [*The* FATHER *looks at him closely.*]

FATHER: Look at me. [*He raises Franz's chin and looks deep into his eyes.*] Where does it come from?

FRANZ: What?

FATHER: The fear of being a prisoner.

FRANZ: I'm not afraid of it.

FATHER: You want it to happen?

FRANZ: I . . . no.

FATHER: I see. [*Pause.*] You think I shouldn't have sold that land?

FRANZ: If you sold it, it was because you couldn't have done otherwise.

FATHER: But I could.

FRANZ [*stunned*]: You could have refused?

FATHER: Certainly. [FRANZ *makes a fierce movement.*] What of it? You no longer trust me.

FRANZ [*consciously mastering himself*]: I know that you will explain.

FATHER: What is there to explain? Himmler wanted somewhere to house his prisoners. If I had refused my land, he would have bought some elsewhere.

FRANZ: From others.

FATHER: Exactly. A little farther to the west, a little farther to the east, the same prisoners would suffer under the same guards, and I would have made enemies inside the Government.

FRANZ [*stubbornly*]: You shouldn't have got mixed up in this affair.

FATHER: Why not?

FRANZ: Because you are you.

FATHER: And to give you the Pharisee's joy of washing your hands of it, little puritan.

FRANZ: Father, you frighten me. You do not feel the sufferings of others enough.

FATHER: I shall allow myself to feel them when I have the means to put an end to them.

FRANZ: You never will have.

FATHER: Then I shall not feel their suffering. It is a waste of time. Do you suffer for them? Go on with you! [*Pause.*]

You do not love your neighbour, Franz, or you would not dare to despise these prisoners.

FRANZ [*hurt*]: I do not despise them.

FATHER: You do despise them. Because they are dirty, and because they are afraid. [*He gets up and walks over to Johanna.*] He still believed in human dignity.

JOHANNA: Was he wrong?

FATHER: I don't know anything about that. All I can tell you is that the Gerlachs are victims of Luther. That prophet filled us with an insane pride. [*He goes slowly back to his seat and points to Franz.*] Franz used to walk across the hills arguing with himself, and once his conscience said yes, you could have cut him into little pieces and you wouldn't have made him change his mind. I was like him when I was young.

JOHANNA [*with irony*]: You had a conscience?

FATHER: Yes. I lost it, out of modesty. It is a luxury for princes. Franz could afford it. When one does nothing, one believes oneself responsible for everything. I worked. [*To Franz*] What do you want me to say? That Hitler and Himmler are criminals? All right, then, I'll say it. [*Laughing*] A strictly personal opinion and of no value to anyone.

FRANZ: Then we are powerless?

FATHER: Yes, if we choose to be powerless. You can do nothing for mankind if you spend your time condemning it before God. [*Pause.*] Eighty thousand workers since March. I'm growing. My shipyards spring up overnight. I have the most formidable power.

FRANZ: Of course. You work for the Nazis.

FATHER: Because they work for me. They are the plebeian on the throne. But they are at war to find us markets, and I am not going to quarrel with them over a bit of land.

FRANZ [*stubbornly*]: You shouldn't have become mixed up in it.

FATHER: Little prince! Little prince! Do you want to carry the whole world on your shoulders? The world is heavy, and you don't know what it's like. Leave it alone. Take an interest in the firm. Today it's mine; tomorrow it will be yours. My flesh and blood, my power, my strength, your future. In twenty years you will be the master with ships on all the seas, and who will remember Hitler then? [*Pause.*] You're a dreamer.

FRANZ: Not as much as you think.

FATHER: Oh? [*He looks at Franz closely.*] What have you done? Something wrong?

FRANZ [*proudly*]: No.

FATHER: Something good? [*Long pause.*] My God! [*Pause.*] Well? Is it serious?

FRANZ: Yes.

FATHER: My little prince, don't worry, I'll fix it up.

FRANZ: Not this time.

FATHER: This time like every other time. [*Pause.*] Well? [*Pause.*] Do you want me to question you? [*He reflects.*] Does it concern the Nazis? Good. The camp? Good. [*Suddenly clear*] The Pole! [*He gets up and walks about agitatedly. He speaks to Johanna.*] He was a Polish rabbi. He had escaped the day before, and the camp commandant had notified us. [*To Franz*] Where is he?

FRANZ: In my room. [*Pause.*]

FATHER: Where did you find him?

FRANZ: In the park. He wasn't even hiding. He escaped through sheer madness. Now he is afraid. If they get their hands on him . . .

FATHER: I know. [*Pause.*] If no one has seen him, the matter can be settled. We can get him away by lorry to Hamburg. [FRANZ *is tense.*] Has anyone seen him? Well? Who?

FRANZ: Fritz.

FATHER [*to Johanna, in a conversational tone*]: He was our chauffeur, a real Nazi.

FRANZ: He took the car this morning, saying he was going to

the garage in Altona. He hasn't come back yet. [*With a glow of pride*] Am I such a dreamer?

FATHER [*smiling*]: More than ever. [*In a changed voice*] Why did you put him in your room? To redeem me? [*Silence.*] Answer! It is for me.

FRANZ: It is for us. You and I are one.

FATHER: Yes. [*Pause.*] If Fritz has denounced you. . . .

FRANZ [*continues*]: They'll come. I know.

FATHER: Go up to Leni's room, and bolt the door. It's an order. I'll settle everything. [FRANZ *looks at him defiantly.*] What is it?

FRANZ: The prisoner . . .

FATHER: I said – everything. The prisoner is under my roof. Go! [FRANZ *disappears. The* FATHER *sits down again.*]

JOHANNA: Did they come?

FATHER: Forty-five minutes later.

[*An* S.S. MAN *appears upstage. Two men behind him, motionless and silent.*]

S. S. MAN: *Heil Hitler.*

FATHER: *Heil.* Who are you and what do you want?

S. S. MAN: We have just found your son in his room with an escaped prisoner he has been hiding since last night.

FATHER: In his room? [*To Johanna*] Brave lad, he didn't want to lock himself up in Leni's room. He took all the risks. Good. Well?

S. S. MAN: Do you understand?

FATHER: Very well. My son has just committed a serious blunder.

S. S. MAN [*with stunned indignation*]: A what? [*Pause.*] Stand up when I speak to you.

[*Telephone rings.*]

FATHER [*without rising*]: No.

[*He lifts the receiver and, without even asking who the caller is, hands it to the* S.S. MAN, *who snatches it from him.*]

43

s. s. man [*into telephone*]: Hello? Oh! [*Clicks his heels.*] Yes. Yes. Yes. Very good, sir. [*He listens and looks at the Father with amazement.*] Right. Very good, sir. [*Clicks his heels and hangs up.*]

father [*hard and unsmiling*]: A blunder, isn't it?

s. s. man: That's all.

father: If you have touched a single hair of his head . . .

s. s. man: He threw himself at us.

father [*surprised and worried*]: My son? [*The s.s. man nods.*] Did you hit him?

s. s. man: No, I swear to you. We got hold of him . . .

father [*thoughtfully*]: He threw himself at you! That's not like him. You must have provoked him. What did you do? [*The s. s. man is silent.*] The prisoner! [*He stands up.*] Right in front of him? Right in front of my son? [*With cold but terrible anger.*] I think you have exceeded your duty. Your name?

s. s. man [*piteously*]: Hermann Aldrich.

father: Hermann Aldrich! I give you my word that you will remember the twenty-third of June 1941 all your life. Go.

   [*The s. s. man disappears.*]

johanna: Did he remember it?

father [*smiling*]: I think so. But his life wasn't very long.

johanna: And Franz?

father: Released at once. On condition that he enlisted. The following winter, he was a lieutenant on the Russian front. [*Pause.*] What's the matter?

johanna: I don't like this story.

father: I am not saying that it's pleasant. [*Pause.*] That was in '41.

johanna [*dryly*]: Well?

father: It was necessary to survive.

johanna: The Pole didn't survive.

FATHER [*indifferent*]: No. That's not my fault.

JOHANNA: I wonder.

WERNER: Johanna!

JOHANNA: You had forty-five minutes. What did you do to save your son?

FATHER: You know perfectly well.

JOHANNA: Goebbels was in Hamburg and you phoned him.

FATHER: Yes.

JOHANNA: You told him that a prisoner had escaped and you begged him to be indulgent to your son.

FATHER: I also asked him to spare the prisoner's life.

JOHANNA: Of course. [*Pause.*] When you phoned Goebbels...

FATHER: Yes.

JOHANNA: You couldn't have been *sure* that the chauffeur had denounced Franz.

FATHER: Go on! He spied on us constantly.

JOHANNA: Yes, but it is possible that he saw nothing and that he had taken the car for quite another reason.

FATHER: That's possible.

JOHANNA: Naturally, you didn't ask him anything.

FATHER: Who?

JOHANNA: This Fritz. [*The* FATHER *shrugs his shoulders.*] Where is he now?

FATHER: In Italy under a wooden cross.

JOHANNA [*after a pause*]: I see. Well, we shall never get to the bottom of the matter. If it wasn't Fritz who handed over the prisoner, it must have been you.

WERNER [*violently*]: I forbid you...

FATHER: Don't keep shouting, Werner. [WERNER *is silent.*] You are right, my child. [*Pause.*] When I took up the telephone, I said to myself, a fifty-fifty chance! [*Pause.*]

JOHANNA: A fifty-fifty chance to murder a Jew. [*Pause.*] Has that never kept you awake?

FATHER [*quietly*]: Never.

WERNER [to Father]: Father, I support you unreservedly. All lives are valuable. But, if one must choose, I think the life of a son must come first.

JOHANNA [softly]: We are not concerned with what you think, Werner, but with what Franz must have thought. What did he think, Leni?

LENI [smiling]: But you know the von Gerlachs, Johanna.

JOHANNA: He didn't say anything?

LENI: He left without opening his mouth and never wrote to us. [Pause.]

JOHANNA [to Father]: You told him that you would settle everything and he trusted you. As always.

FATHER: I kept my word. I had obtained an assurance that the prisoner would not be punished. Could I have imagined that they would kill him in front of my son?

JOHANNA: That was in '41, Father. In '41 it was prudent to imagine anything. [She approaches the photos and looks at them. Pause. She continues looking at the portrait.] He was a little puritan, a victim of Luther, who wanted to pay with his blood for the land you sold. [She turns towards the Father.] You wiped everything out. What remained was only a game for a rich playboy. With the risk of death to be sure - but for the partner . . . he understood that he could get away with everything because he counted for nothing.

FATHER [struck by an idea, pointing to her]: There's the wife he should have had.

[WERNER and LENI turn sharply to him.]

WERNER [furious]: What?

LENI: Father, what bad taste!

FATHER [to them]: She understood right off. [To Johanna] Didn't you? I ought to have compromised for two years in prison. What a blunder! Anything rather than that he should have gone unpunished.

[Pause. He is lost in thought. JOHANNA still looks at the

portraits. WERNER *stands up and, taking her by the shoulders,
turns her towards him.*]

JOHANNA [*coldly*]: What's the matter?

WERNER: Don't feel sorry for Franz. He wasn't the type to
suffer a setback.

JOHANNA: What do you mean?

WERNER [*pointing to the portrait*]: Look! Twelve decorations.

JOHANNA: Twelve more setbacks. He ran after death, no luck,
death ran quicker than he did. [*To Father*] Let's hear the rest.
He fought, he came back in '46 and then, a year later, there
was the scandal. What was it?

FATHER: One of our Leni's pranks.

LENI [*modestly*]: Father is too kind. I furnished the occasion.
Nothing more.

FATHER: Some American officers were billeted on us. She used
to lead them on and then, when they were well worked up,
she would whisper in their ear: 'I am a Nazi' and call them
dirty Jews.

LENI: To damp their ardour. Amusing, eh?

JOHANNA: Very. And did it work?

FATHER: Sometimes. Sometimes they exploded. One of them
took it very badly.

LENI [*to Johanna*]: An American is either a Jew, or an anti-
Semite, unless he is both at the same time. That one was not
a Jew. He was annoyed.

JOHANNA: What happened?

LENI: He tried to rape me. Franz came to my rescue. They
rolled on the floor, the American on top. I took a bottle and
gave him a terrific blow.

JOHANNA: Did it kill him?

FATHER [*very calm*]: What do you think? His skull broke the
bottle. [*Pause.*] Six weeks in hospital. Naturally, Franz took
the whole blame.

JOHANNA: The blow with the bottle, too?

47

FATHER: Everything. [*Two American officers appear upstage. The* FATHER *turns towards them.*] It was a mistake, pardon the word, a serious mistake. [*Pause.*] I beg you to thank General Hopkins on my behalf. Tell him my son will leave Germany as soon as he gets his visas.

JOHANNA: For the Argentine?

FATHER [*he turns towards her as the Americans disappear*]: That was the condition.

JOHANNA: I see.

FATHER [*carelessly*]: The Americans were really very good.

JOHANNA: Like Goebbels in '41.

FATHER: Better! Much better! Washington was counting on re-establishing our enterprise and giving us the job of building up the merchant fleet.

JOHANNA: Poor Franz!

FATHER: What could I do? There were big interests at stake, which weighed more heavily than a captain's skull. Even if I had not intervened, the occupying forces would have hushed up the scandal.

JOHANNA: It is quite possible. [*Pause.*] Did he refuse to leave?

FATHER: Not at first. [*Pause.*] I had obtained the visas. He was to have left us on the Saturday. On the Friday morning, Leni came to tell me that he would never come down again. [*Pause.*] At first I thought he was dead. Then I saw my daughter's eyes. She had won.

JOHANNA: Won what?

FATHER: She never said.

LENI [*smiling*]: Here, you know, we play loser wins.

JOHANNA: What happened after that?

FATHER: We lived for thirteen years.

JOHANNA [*turns towards the portrait*]: Thirteen years.

WERNER: What a nice job! Believe me, as an amateur, I have appreciated everything. How you have twisted her round. To begin with, she hardly listened. In the end, she couldn't stop asking questions. The picture is complete. [*Laughing*] 'You are the wife he should have had!' Bravo, Father! That's genius!

JOHANNA: Stop, or we shall be lost!

WERNER: We are lost. What is there left? [*He seizes her arm above the elbow, draws her to him and looks at her.*] Where are you? You have the eyes of a statue: blank. [*Pushing her away from him abruptly*] Such common flattery and you walked right into the trap! You disappoint me, my dear. [*Pause. They all look at him.*]

JOHANNA: Now is the moment.

WERNER: What?

JOHANNA: To stake everything, my love.

WERNER: Who?

JOHANNA: You. [*Pause.*] They've caught us. When they were talking to me of Franz, they contrived to make the words ricochet on you.

WERNER: Then perhaps it is I who have been taken in?

JOHANNA: No one has. They wanted to make you think I had been taken in.

WERNER: Why, if you please?

JOHANNA: To remind you that nothing belongs to you, not even your wife. [*The* FATHER *softly rubs his hands. Pause. Abruptly*] Take me away from here! [*Short pause.*] I beg you! [*WERNER laughs. She becomes cold and hard.*] For the last time, I ask you, let us leave. For the last time, do you hear?

WERNER: I hear. Have you any further questions to ask me?

JOHANNA: No.

WERNER: Then I do as I wish? [*JOHANNA nods, exhausted.*] Very well. [*On the Bible*] I swear to abide by the last wishes of my Father.

FATHER: You will stay here?

WERNER [*his hand still on the Bible*]: Since you demand it. This house is mine to live in and to die in.
[*He lowers his head.*]

FATHER [*rises and goes to him, with affectionate pride*]: Well done. [*He smiles at him.* WERNER *frowns an instant then ends by smiling in humble gratitude.*]

JOHANNA [*looking at everyone*]: So that's a family conference! [*Pause.*] Werner, I am leaving. With or without you. Choose.

WERNER [*not looking at her*]: Without.

JOHANNA: Very well. [*Short pause.*] I hope you will not miss me too much.

LENI: You will miss us. Especially Father. When are you leaving us?

JOHANNA: I don't know yet. When I am sure I have lost.

LENI: Aren't you sure?

JOHANNA [*with a smile*]: Well, no. Not yet. [*Pause.*]

LENI [*thinks she understands*]: If the police come, all three of us will be arrested for illegal restraint. And, in addition, I shall be charged with murder.

JOHANNA [*unmoved*]: Do I look like the sort of person to inform the police? [*To the Father*] May I leave?

FATHER: Good night, my child. [*She bows and goes out.* WERNER *begins to laugh.*]

WERNER [*laughing*]: Well . . . well . . . [*He stops abruptly, approaches his Father and touches him timidly on the arm, looking at him with anxious affection.*] Are you pleased?

FATHER [*in horror*]: Don't touch me! [*Pause.*] The conference is over, go and join your wife. [WERNER *gives him a despairing look, then turns and goes out.*]

LENI: All the same, don't you think you were too hard?

FATHER: With Werner? If it were necessary, I would be soft. But I have found that hardness pays.

LENI: You shouldn't drive him too far.

FATHER: Bah!

LENI: His wife is planning something.

FATHER: Theatrical threats. Resentment brought out the actress and the actress had to have her exit.

LENI: I hope to God you're right . . . [*Pause.*] See you this evening, Father. [*She waits for him to go out. He does not move.*] I have to close the shutters and then it will be time for Franz. [*Insistent*] See you this evening.

FATHER [*smiling*]: I'm going, I'm going! [*Pause. Somewhat timidly*] Does he know what is wrong with me?

LENI [*astonished*]: Who? Oh! Franz! Goodness no.

FATHER: Ah! [*With painful irony*] You wish to spare him?

LENI: As far as he's concerned, you could throw yourself under a train . . . [*Indifferently*] To tell you the truth I forgot to tell him.

FATHER: Make a knot in your handkerchief.

LENI [*taking her handkerchief in order to make a knot*]: There!

FATHER: You won't forget?

LENI: No, but I'll have to wait for an opportune moment.

FATHER: When it comes, try also to ask him to see me.

LENI [*wearily*]: Again! [*Hard, but without anger*] He will not see you. Why force me to repeat every day what you have known for thirteen years?

FATHER [*furiously*]: What do I know, you hussy? What do I know? You can't open your mouth without lying. I don't know if you give him my letters and pass on my requests, and I sometimes wonder whether you haven't convinced him that I have been dead for ten years.

LENI [*shrugs her shoulders*]: What do you expect to get out of it?

FATHER: I want the truth or an end to your lies.

LENI [*pointing to the first floor*]: The truth is up there. Go up, and you will find it. Go up! Go on!

FATHER [*his anger subsides. He seems frightened*]: You are mad!

LENI: Question him. You will set your mind at rest.

FATHER [*still apprehensively*]: I don't even know . . .

LENI: The signal! [*Laughing*] Oh yes, you know it. I've caught you spying on me a hundred times. I have heard your step and I have seen your shadow. I haven't said anything but I could hardly keep myself from laughing. [*The* FATHER *tries to protest.*] Am I wrong? Well, I shall have the pleasure of giving it to you myself.

FATHER [*dully and in spite of himself*]: No.

LENI: Give four knocks, then five, then three knocks twice. What's holding you back?

FATHER: What should I find? [*Pause. In a dull voice*] I couldn't bear it if he drove me away.

LENI: You'd rather convince yourself that I am preventing him from falling into your arms.

FATHER [*painfully*]: You must excuse me, Leni. I am often unjust. [*He strokes her hair; she stiffens.*] Your hair is soft. [*He caresses her more absent-mindedly as if he were thinking.*] Have you any influence over him?

LENI [*proudly*]: Naturally.

FATHER: Couldn't you, little by little, by handling it cleverly . . . I beg you to stress the main thing; that my first visit will also be my last. I will only stay an hour. Less, if that tires him. And above all, be sure to tell him that I am not in any hurry. [*Smiling*] There, that's not too much.

LENI: One meeting only.

FATHER: One only.

LENI: One only and then you will die. What's the good of seeing him again?

FATHER: Just to see him again. [*She laughs insolently.*] And to take leave.

LENI: What difference would it make if you took French leave?

FATHER: For me? Everything. If I see him again, I close the account and make out the bill.

LENI: Do you have to take so much trouble? The bill will be made out in any case.

FATHER: Do you think so? [*Short pause.*] I must draw it up myself, otherwise everything will be at a loose end. [*With a smile that is almost timid*] After all, I have lived this life, I don't want it to be wasted. [*Pause. Almost timidly*] Will you speak to him?

LENI [*brutally*]: Why should I? After thirteen years of mounting guard, should I relax my vigilance with only six months to go?

FATHER: Do you mount guard against me?

LENI: Against all those who want to destroy him.

FATHER: I want to destroy Franz?

LENI: Yes.

FATHER [*violently*]: Are you mad? [*He calms himself. With a strong desire to convince, almost pleadingly*] Listen, our opinions may differ as to what is best for him. But I am only asking to see him once. How would I have the time to harm him, even if I wanted to? [*She laughs coarsely.*] I give you my word . . .

LENI: Have I asked you for it? I want none of your gifts!

FATHER: But let's get things clear.

LENI: The von Gerlachs don't give explanations.

FATHER: You think you've got me, don't you?

LENI [*same voice, same smile*]: I have, in a way, haven't I?

FATHER [*ironic grimace, disdainful*]: That's what you think!

LENI: Which of us two, father, needs the other?

FATHER [*softly*]: Which of us two, Leni, is afraid of the other?

LENI: I am not afraid of you. [*Laughing*] What bluff! [*She looks at him defiantly.*] Do you know what makes me invulnerable? I am happy.

FATHER: You? What can you know of happiness?

LENI: And you? What do you know of it?

FATHER: I see you. If he has given you those eyes, it is the most refined of tortures.

LENI [*almost distraught*]: Yes! The most refined! The most refined! I am dizzy! If I stop, I shall crack up. That's happiness. [*Triumphantly and wickedly*] I see Franz! I! I have all I want. *The* FATHER *laughs softly. She stops suddenly and stares at him.*] No. You never bluff. I suppose you have a master card. All right. Show it.

FATHER [*good-humoured*]: Right away?

LENI [*hardening*]: Right away. You are not going to keep it up your sleeve to bring out when I am not expecting it.

FATHER [*still good-humoured*]: And if I don't want to show it?

LENI: I shall force you to.

FATHER: How?

LENI: I stick. [*She takes the Bible with an effort and places it on a table.*] Franz will never see you, I swear it. [*Placing her hand on the Bible*] I swear on this Bible that you will die without seeing him again. [*Pause.*] There. [*Pause.*] Lay down your cards.

FATHER [*calmly*]: Well, I never! You didn't have one of your laughs. [*He strokes her hair.*] When I stroke your hair, I think of the earth: covered in silk on top, in a ferment underneath. [*He rubs his hands softly. With a gentle, inoffensive smile*] I'll leave you, my child.

> [LENI *remains with her eyes fixed on the door upstage left, through which her Father has just gone out. She then pulls herself together, goes to the french windows on the right, opens them, closes the large shutters, then closes the glass doors. The room is plunged in semi-darkness. She slowly mounts the stairs leading to the first floor and knocks at Franz's door: four knocks, then five, then three knocks twice.*
>
> *Just as she knocks the two series of three, the door, right, opens and* JOHANNA *appears noiselessly. She is spying.*
>
> *The sounds can be heard of a bolt being drawn and an iron bar being lifted. The door above is opened, letting out a shaft of electric light from Franz's room. But he does not appear.* LENI *enters and closes the door. The bolt is fastened and the iron bar lowered.*

JOHANNA *enters the room, approaches a console table and taps out the two series of three with her index finger as though to commit them to memory. She has obviously not heard the series of five and four. She begins again. At that moment, all the lights of the chandelier light up and she starts, stifling a cry. It is the* FATHER *who appears left and who has switched them on.* JOHANNA *protects her eyes with her hand and forearm.*]

FATHER: Who's there? [*She lowers her hand.*] Johanna! [*Going towards her*] I am very sorry. [*He is in the middle of the room.*] In police interrogations they train spotlights on the accused. What must you think of me for shining all this light into your eyes?

JOHANNA: I think you ought to turn it out.

FATHER [*without moving*]: And?

JOHANNA: And that you are not the police but that you intend to subject me to a police interrogation. [*The* FATHER *smiles and lets his hands fall in mock surrender. Quickly*] You never enter this room. What were you doing if you were not spying on me?

FATHER: But you never come here either, my child. [JOHANNA *does not reply.*] The interrogation will not take place. [*He turns on two lamps – with rose muslin shades – and goes to turn out the chandelier.*] Here we have the rosy light of half-truths. Are you more comfortable?

JOHANNA: No. Do you mind if I go?

FATHER: You may go when you have heard my answer.

JOHANNA: I haven't asked anything.

FATHER: You asked me what I was doing here and I must tell you even though I have no reason to be proud of it. [*Short pause.*] For years, almost every day, when I am sure that Leni will not catch me, I have sat here in this armchair and have waited.

JOHANNA [*interested in spite of herself*]: What for?

FATHER: In case Franz should walk about in his room and I

should be lucky enough to hear him walk. [*Pause.*] That is all they have left me of my son – the sound of his two shoes on the floor. [*Pause.*] At night, I get up. Everyone is asleep. I know that Franz is awake. He and I suffer from the same insomnia. It is a way of being together. And you, Johanna, who are you spying on?

JOHANNA: I was not spying on anyone.

FATHER: Then it is a coincidence, a most extraordinary and fortunate coincidence. I was hoping to speak to you alone. [JOHANNA *is irritated. Quickly*] No, no, no secrets, no secrets, except from Leni. You can tell Werner everything, I promise you.

JOHANNA: In that case, the simplest thing would be to call him.

FATHER: I only ask for two minutes. Two minutes and I shall call him myself. If you still want me to.

[*Surprised by his last sentence,* JOHANNA *stops and faces him.*]

JOHANNA: All right. What do you want?

FATHER: To talk to my daughter-in-law about the young Gerlach household.

JOHANNA: The young Gerlach household is in pieces.

FATHER: What are you saying?

JOHANNA: Nothing new. You've smashed it.

FATHER [*distressed*]: Oh dear! I must have been clumsy. [*Solicitously*] But I thought you had a way of patching it up. [*She goes rapidly upstage left.*] What are you doing?

JOHANNA [*turning on all the lights*]: The interrogation has begun. I am turning on the spotlights. [*Coming back and standing under the chandelier*] Where should I stand? Here? Good. Now, under the cold light of whole truths and perfect lies, I declare that I will not make any confessions for the simple reason that I have none to make. I am alone, without strength and completely aware of my powerlessness. I am going to leave. I shall wait for Werner in Hamburg. If he doesn't come back . . . [*Despairing gesture*]

FATHER [*gravely*]: Poor Johanna, we have brought you nothing but misfortune. [*In a changed voice, suddenly confidential and jolly*] And above all, make yourself beautiful.

JOHANNA: I beg your pardon?

FATHER [*smiling*]: I say, make yourself beautiful.

JOHANNA [*almost outraged, violently*]: Beautiful!

FATHER: That won't be any trouble.

JOHANNA [*still angry*]: Beautiful! The day we say good-bye, I suppose: to leave you with pleasanter memories.

FATHER: No, Johanna. The day you go and see Franz. [JOHANNA *is transfixed.*] The two minutes are up. Shall I call your husband? [*She shakes her head.*] Very well. This will be our secret.

JOHANNA: Werner will know everything.

FATHER: When?

JOHANNA: In a few days. Yes, I'll see him, your Franz, I'll see this domestic tyrant, but it would be better to address yourself to God than to his saints.

FATHER [*after a pause*]: I am glad you will try your luck. [*He begins rubbing his hands and then puts them in his pockets.*]

JOHANNA: I'm not so sure about it.

FATHER: Why?

JOHANNA: Because our interests are opposed. I hope that Franz will resume a normal life.

FATHER: I hope so too.

JOHANNA: You? If he puts his nose outside, the police will arrest him and the family will be dishonoured.

FATHER [*smiling*]: I don't think you realize my power. My son has merely to come down, and I will arrange everything at once.

JOHANNA: That would be the best way to make him run straight up into his room again and lock himself up in it for-ever. [*Pause. The* FATHER *looks down at the carpet.*]

FATHER [*dully*]: A ten to one chance that he'll open the door to you, a hundred to one that he'll listen to you, and a thousand to one that he'll answer you. If you had this thousand to one chance . . .

JOHANNA: Well?

FATHER: Would you agree to tell him that I am going to die?

JOHANNA: Hasn't Leni . . .?

FATHER: No.

[*He raises his head.* JOHANNA *looks straight at him.*]

JOHANNA: So that's how it is? [*She continues looking at him.*] You are not lying. [*Pause.*] A thousand to one chance. [*She shudders and pulls herself together immediately.*] Must I also ask him if he will see you?

FATHER [*quickly, frightened*]: No, no! Just the announcement, nothing more. The old man is going to die. Without comment. It's a promise!

JOHANNA [*smiling*]: Sworn on the Bible.

FATHER: Thank you. [*Her eyes have not left him. Under his breath, as though to explain his conduct, but in a dull voice that seems to be directed only to himself*] I would like to help him. Don't attempt anything today. Leni will be down late. He will no doubt be tired.

JOHANNA: Tomorrow?

FATHER: Yes. In the early afternoon.

JOHANNA: Where shall I find you if I need you . . .?

FATHER: You will not find me. [*Pause.*] I am leaving for Leipzig. [*Pause.*] If you fail . . . [*Gesture*] I shall be back in a few days. By that time you will either have won or lost.

JOHANNA [*distressed*]: You are leaving me alone? [*She pulls herself together.*] Why not? [*Pause.*] Well, I wish you a pleasant journey and I beg you to wish me nothing.

FATHER: Wait! [*With an apologetic smile, but seriously*] I'm afraid I don't want to upset you, my child, but I repeat, you must make yourself beautiful.

JOHANNA: Again!

FATHER: It's thirteen years since Franz has seen anyone. Not a soul.

JOHANNA [*shrugs*]: Except Leni.

FATHER: Leni doesn't count. I wonder if he even sees her. [*Pause.*] He will open the door, and what will happen? What if he is afraid? What if he should bury himself forever in solitude?

JOHANNA: What difference would it make if I were to paint my face?

FATHER [*gently*]: He used to love beauty.

JOHANNA: What did he know about it, this son of an industrialist?

FATHER: He will tell you tomorrow.

JOHANNA: Nothing of the kind. [*Pause.*] I am not beautiful. Is that clear?

FATHER: If you aren't, who is?

JOHANNA: No one. There are only ugly women in disguise. I will not disguise myself any more.

FATHER: Even for Werner?

JOHANNA: Not even for Werner. You can have him. [*Pause.*] Do you understand the meaning of words? They made me ... a beauty. A different one for each film. [*Pause.*] Excuse me, it's a sore point with me. If you touch it, I lose my head.

FATHER: It is I who must apologize, my child.

JOHANNA: Let's leave it. [*Pause.*] You couldn't have known. Or perhaps you did know. It doesn't matter. [*Pause.*] I was pretty, I suppose. . . . They came and told me I was beautiful and I believed them. Did I know what I was living for? We have to justify our lives. The worst of it is, they were wrong. [*Abruptly*] Ships? Does that justify it?

FATHER: No.

JOHANNA: I thought not. [*Pause.*] Franz will take me as I am.

With this dress and this face. Any woman is still good enough for any man.

[*A pause. Above their heads,* FRANZ *begins to walk. The steps are irregular, sometimes slow and hesitant, sometimes quick and rhythmic, and sometimes marking time. She looks anxiously at the Father as if asking 'Is that Franz!'*]

FATHER [*answering her look*]: Yes.

JOHANNA: And you remain here whole nights . . .

FATHER [*pale and tense*]: Yes.

JOHANNA: I give up.

FATHER: You think he is mad?

JOHANNA: Raving mad.

FATHER: It is not madness.

JOHANNA [*shrugs*]: What is it?

FATHER: Misfortune.

JOHANNA: Who can be more unfortunate than a madman?

FATHER: He is.

JOHANNA [*brutally*]: I shall not go and see Franz.

FATHER: Yes you will. Tomorrow, early in the afternoon. [*Pause.*] It is our only chance, yours, his and mine.

JOHANNA [*turning towards the staircase, slowly*]: I shall climb those stairs, I shall knock at that door. . . . [*Pause. The footsteps have ceased.*] Very well. I shall make myself beautiful. To protect myself.

[*The* FATHER *smiles as he rubs his hands.*]

CURTAIN

ACT TWO

Franz's room.

On the left, in a recess, a door which leads to the landing, and which is secured with a bolt and an iron bar.

Two doors upstage, one on either side of the bed; one leading to the bathroom, and the other to the lavatory. An enormous bed without sheets or mattress. A blanket folded on the bed-springs. A table against the wall on the right. One chair.

On the left is a jumble of broken furniture and bric-à-brac. This pile of rubbish is all that remains of the room's furnishings.

On the wall at the back a large portrait of Hitler above and to the right of the bed. Also on the right, some shelves, on which are tape-recorder reels.

Placards on the walls, with texts in printed letters done by hand: DON'T DISTURB. FEAR IS FORBIDDEN! *On the table, oysters, bottles of champagne, champagne glasses, a ruler, etc. Mildew on the walls and on the ceiling.*

> [FRANZ *is wearing a tattered uniform, his skin showing in places through the tears. He is seated at the table, his back turned to Leni, and three-quarters turned away from the audience. The tape-recorder is hidden under the table.*
>
> LENI *is facing the audience, a white apron over her dress, sweeping the floor. She is working quietly, and without undue haste, like a good housewife, her face void of all expression, almost trance-like while Franz is speaking. From time to time, however, she glances quickly at him. It is clear that she is watching him and waiting for the speech to end.*]

FRANZ: Masked inhabitants of the ceilings, your attention, please! Masked inhabitants of the ceilings, your attention, please! They are lying to you. Two thousand million false witnesses! Two thousand million lies a second! Listen to the plea of mankind: We were betrayed by our deeds. By our words, by our lousy lives! Decapods, I bear witness that they didn't think what they were saying, and that they didn't do what they wished. We plead not guilty. And above all, don't condemn on the basis of statements, even signed statements. They said at the time: 'The accused has made a statement, therefore he is innocent.' Dear listeners, my century was a jumble-sale, in which the liquidation of the human species was decided upon in high places. They began with Germany, right to the bone. [*He pours himself a drink.*] One alone speaks the truth: the shattered Titan, the eye-witness, ageless, regular, secular, in saecula saeculorum. Me. Man is dead, and I am his witness. Centuries, I shall tell you how my century tasted, and you will acquit the accused. To hell with the facts; I leave them to the false witnesses. I leave to them the relevant causes and the fundamental reasons. This was how it tasted. Our mouths were full of it. [*He drinks.*] And we drank to get rid of it. [*Dreamily*] It was a queer taste, wasn't it? [*He stands up quickly in a kind of horror.*] I'll come back to it later.

LENI [*thinking that he has finished*]: Franz, I have to talk to you.

FRANZ [*shouts*]: Silence, in the presence of the Crabs!

LENI [*in a calm voice*]: Listen to me! It's serious.

FRANZ [*to the Crabs*]: You've chosen to wear shells? Bravo! Farewell nakedness! But why have you kept your eyes? That was the ugliest thing about us. Eh? Why? [*He pretends to wait. A click. He starts. In a different voice, dry, quick and raucous*] What's that? [*He turns towards Leni and looks at her angrily and defiantly.*]

LENI [*calmly*]: The reel. [*She stoops down, picks up the tape-recorder, and places it on the table,*] Finished. . . . [*She presses the button, and the spool re-winds, giving Franz's speech in reverse.*] Now you're going to listen to me. [FRANZ *sinks*

62

*into the chair, clutching his breast. She stops speaking suddenly
and turns to him, seeing him tense and apparently in pain, but
shows no emotion.*] What's the matter?

FRANZ: What do you think?

LENI: Your heart?

FRANZ [*painfully*]: It's thumping away.

LENI: What do you want, master-singer? Another reel?

FRANZ [*suddenly calm*]: Certainly not! [*He stands up and laughs.*]
I'm dead. Dead tired, Leni. Take that away! [*She goes to take
off the reel.*] Wait! I want to hear myself.

LENI: From the beginning?

FRANZ: Anywhere you like. [LENI *starts the machine, and
Franz's voice is heard: 'One alone speaks the truth', etc.* FRANZ
*listens for a moment to his recorded voice, his face intense, then he
speaks above the recorded voice.*] I didn't mean to say that. But
who's speaking? Not a word of truth. [*He listens again.*] I
can't stand that voice any more. It's dead. For God's sake,
stop it! Stop it! You're driving me mad . . . [LENI, *with no
undue haste, stops the machine. She re-winds the reel, takes it off,
writes a number on it and places it on the shelf near the others.*
FRANZ *looks at her, downcast.*] Good, I'll have to begin again.

LENI: As usual.

FRANZ: Not at all. I'm making progress. One day the words
will come by themselves, and I shall say what I want to. Then
I'll have some rest. [*Pause.*] Do you think there is such a thing?

LENI: What?

FRANZ: Rest?

LENI: No.

FRANZ: That's what I thought. [*A short pause.*]

LENI: Will you listen to me?

FRANZ: Eh?

LENI: I'm afraid.

FRANZ [*with a start*]: Afraid? [*He looks at her in some concern.*]
Did you say afraid?

LENI: Yes.

FRANZ [*brutally*]: Then get out!

[*He takes a ruler from the table, and taps the placard which reads:* FEAR IS FORBIDDEN!]

LENI: Right. I'm no longer afraid. [*Pause.*] Please listen to me.

FRANZ: That's what I'm doing. You're making my head split. [*Pause.*] Well?

LENI: I don't exactly know what they're planning. . . .

FRANZ: They're planning something? Where? Washington? Moscow?

LENI: Under your very feet.

FRANZ: On the ground floor? [*Suddenly aware*] Father's going to die.

LENI: Who's talking about father? He'll bury the lot of us.

FRANZ: Good.

LENI: Good?

FRANZ: Good, bad, to hell with it. Well? What's going on?

LENI: You're in danger.

FRANZ [*with conviction*]: Yes – after my death. If the centuries lose trace of me, I'll be devoured. And who'll save Mankind, Leni?

LENI: Whoever wants to. Franz, your life has been in danger since yesterday.

FRANZ [*indifferently*]: Then defend me. That's your job.

LENI: Yes, if you help me.

FRANZ: Haven't the time. [*Peevishly*] I'm writing History, and you come and worry me with your tales.

LENI: It would be a fine tale if they killed you.

FRANZ: Yes.

LENI: If they killed you too soon?

FRANZ [*frowning*]: Too soon? [*Pause.*] Who wants to kill me?

LENI: The Occupation Forces.

FRANZ: I see. [*Pause.*] They silence my voice, and they are confounding the thirtieth century with faked documents.

[*Pause.*] Have they someone in the house?

LENI: I think so.

FRANZ: Who?

LENI: I don't know yet. I think it's Werner's wife.

FRANZ: The hunchback?

LENI: Yes. She ferrets about everywhere.

FRANZ: Give her some rat-poison.

LENI: She's suspicious.

FRANZ: What a nuisance! [*Worried*] I need ten years.

LENI: Give me ten minutes.

FRANZ: You bore me.

> [*He goes to the upstage wall and passes his hand over the reels on the shelf.*]

LENI: Suppose they stole them?

FRANZ [*turning suddenly*]: What?

LENI: The reels.

FRANZ: You're losing your head.

LENI [*dryly*]: Suppose they came when I wasn't here – or, even better, after they had killed me?

FRANZ: Well? I wouldn't open the door. [*Amused*] Do they want to kill you too?

LENI: They're thinking of doing so. What would you do without me? [FRANZ *does not reply.*] You would die of hunger.

FRANZ: I've not time to be hungry. I shall die; that's all. I speak. Death will take my body, but I won't even notice it; I shall continue to speak. [*Pause.*] One advantage is that you won't blindfold me. My eyes pierce the door, and what do they see? The corpse of murdered Germany. [*Laughing*] I shall stink like a bad conscience.

LENI: They won't pierce anything. They'll knock, you will still be alive, and you will open the door.

FRANZ [*with amused surprise*]: I?

LENI: You. [*Pause.*] They know the signal.

FRANZ: They can't know it.

LENI: You can be sure they've picked it up since they started spying on me. I'm sure father knows it.

FRANZ: Ah! [*Pause.*] Is he in the plot?

LENI: Who knows? [*Pause.*] I tell you, you will open the door.

FRANZ: What then?

LENI: They'll take the reels.

[FRANZ *opens a drawer of the table, takes out a service revolver and shows it to Leni.*]

FRANZ [*smiling*]: What about that?

LENI: They won't take them by force. They'll persuade you to give them up. [FRANZ *bursts into laughter.*] I beg you, Franz; let's change the signal. [FRANZ *stops laughing. He looks at her in a cunning and hunted way.*] Well?

FRANZ: No. [*He improvises reasons for refusing.*] Everything is in place. History is sacred. If you change a single comma, nothing will be left.

LENI: Splendid. Let's leave History alone. You'll make them a present of your reels, and your tape-recorder into the bargain.

[FRANZ *goes up to the reels and looks at them in a hunted way.*]

FRANZ [*at first hesitant and torn with conflict*]: The reels . . . the reels. . . . [*Pause. He considers a moment, then with a swift gesture of his left hand he sweeps them on to the floor.*] That's what I do with them. [*He speaks in a kind of exultation, as though confiding an important secret to Leni. In fact, he is improvising as he goes along.*] It was only a precaution, in case the thirtieth hadn't discovered the window.

LENI: A window? That's something new. You've never mentioned it before.

FRANZ: I don't tell you everything, little sister. [*He rubs his hands happily, like the Father in Act One.*] Imagine a black window. Finer than ether. Ultrasensitive. It records the slightest breath. The *slightest* breath. All History is engraved on it, from the beginning of time up to this snap of my fingers. [*He snaps his fingers.*]

LENI: Where is it?

FRANZ: The window? Everywhere. Here. It's the day in reverse. They will invent machines to make it vibrate, and everything will come back to life. You see? [*In a sudden transport*] All our actions. [*He resumes his savage and inspired tone.*] Like a film, I tell you. The Crabs sitting round watching Rome burn and Nero dance. [*To the photo of Hitler*] They see you, little Father. For you danced, didn't you? [*He kicks the reels.*] Burn them! Burn them! What the hell do I want with them? Take them away! [*Suddenly*] What were you doing on the sixth of December 1944 at 8.30 p.m.? [LENI *shrugs her shoulders.*] You don't remember? They know. They've got your whole life spread out, Leni. I'm discovering the horrible truth. We're under observation all the time.

LENI: We are?

FRANZ [*facing out front*]: You, me, all the dead, mankind. [*He laughs.*] Be on your guard. They're watching you. [*Darkly, to himself*] No one is alone. [LENI *gives a short laugh.*] Laugh while you can, my poor Leni, the thirtieth will arrive like a thief in the night; the turn of a handle, the vibrating Night. You'll land in the middle of them.

LENI: Living?

FRANZ: A thousand years dead.

LENI [*with indifference*]: Pooh!

FRANZ: Dead and revived. The window will reveal everything, even our thoughts. See? [*Pause. With an anxiety which may or may not be sincere*] What if we are already there?

LENI: Where?

FRANZ: In the thirtieth century. Are you sure this comedy is being played for the first time? Are we living, or reincarnated? [*He laughs.*] Be on your guard! If the decapods are watching us, you may be sure they find us very ugly.

LENI: How do you know?

FRANZ: Crabs only like Crabs. It's only natural.

LENI: Suppose they are men?

FRANZ: In the thirtieth century? If there is a man left, he'll be preserved in a museum. . . . Do you think they'll still have our nervous system?

LENI: And will Crabs do that?

FRANZ [*curtly*]: Yes. [*Pause.*] They'll have different bodies, and therefore different ideas. What ideas, eh? What? Can you grasp the importance of my task, and its exceptional difficulty? I am defending you before judges whom I haven't the pleasure of knowing. Working blind. You drop a word here to the judge, and it tumbles down the centuries. What will it mean up there? Do you know I sometimes say 'white' when I mean to say 'black'? [*He suddenly slumps into his chair.*] Good God!

LENI: Now what?

FRANZ [*overcome*]: The window!

LENI: Well?

FRANZ: It's all direct transmission now. We have to be on our guard all the time. It was a good thing I found out about it. [*Savagely*] Explain! Justify! Not a moment's respite. Men, women, hunted executioners, relentless victims, I am your martyr.

LENI: If they see everything, why do they need your commentaries?

FRANZ [*laughing*]: Ha! But they are Crabs, Leni. They don't understand anything. [*He wipes his brow with his handkerchief, looks at the handkerchief and throws it with disgust on to the table.*] Salt water!

LENI: What did you expect?

FRANZ [*shrugging his shoulders*]: Blood. I've earned it. [*He stands up, alert and with false gaiety.*] Follow my orders, Leni. I'll get you to speak directly to them. Testing for voice. Speak loudly and pronounce clearly. [*Very loud*] Testify before the judges that the Crusaders of Democracy don't want to let us

rebuild the walls of our houses. [LENI, *annoyed, remains silent.*]
Go on; if you obey me, I'll listen to you.

LENI [*to the ceiling*]: I declare that everything is in ruins.

FRANZ: Louder!

LENI: Everything is in ruins.

FRANZ: What's left of Munich?

LENI: A few bricks.

FRANZ: Hamburg.

LENI: A no-man's-land.

FRANZ: Where are the last Germans?

LENI: In the cellars.

FRANZ [*to the ceiling*]: Well, do you grasp that? After thirteen
years! Grass covers the streets, our machines are tangled
among the weeds. [*Pretending to listen*] A punishment? What
a filthy lie! No competition in Europe; that's the principle
and the doctrine. Say what's left of the firm.

LENI: Two slipways.

FRANZ: Two! Before the war, we had a hundred! [*He rubs his
hands, and speaks to Leni in his natural voice.*] Enough for today.
Your voice is weak, but it would do if you let it go. [*Pause.*]
Now speak! Well? [*Pause.*] So they want to sap my morale?

LENI: Yes.

FRANZ: A bad move. My morale is like steel.

LENI: My poor Franz; he'll do as he likes with you.

FRANZ: Who?

LENI: The representative of the Occupation Forces.

FRANZ: Ha! Ha!

LENI: He'll knock, you'll open up, and do you know what he'll
say?

FRANZ: I don't care a damn!

LENI: He'll say: you imagine you're the witness, but you're
the accused. [*Short pause.*] What will you reply?

FRANZ: Get out! You're in their pay. You're the one who's
trying to demoralize me.

LENI: What will you reply, Franz? What will you reply? For twelve years now you've been prostrating yourself before this tribunal of the future, and you have conceded it every right. Why not the right to condemn you?

FRANZ [*shouting*]: Because I'm a witness for the defence.

LENI: Who appointed you?

FRANZ: History.

LENI: It has happened, hasn't it, that a man believed himself appointed by History, only to find it was someone else.

FRANZ: That won't happen to me. You'll all be acquitted. Even you. That'll be my revenge. I'll put History into a mousehole. [*He stops, worried.*] Ssh! They're listening. You egg me on; you egg me on until I forget myself. [*To the ceiling*] I beg your pardon, listeners; my words have betrayed my thoughts.

LENI [*savage and ironic*]: There he is; the man with morale like steel! [*Contemptuously*] You spend your time begging pardon.

FRANZ: I'd like to see you in my place. They're going to grind tonight.

LENI: Do the Crabs grind, then?

FRANZ: They do, up there. It's very unpleasant. [*To the ceiling*] Please take note of my correction, listeners. . . .

LENI [*bursting out*]: Stop it! Stop it! Send them packing!

FRANZ: Are you out of your mind?

LENI: Challenge their competence, I beg you, it's your only weakness. Tell them: 'You are not my judges,' and you'll have no one else to fear; neither in this world nor the next.

FRANZ [*angrily*]: Get out!

[*He takes two oyster-shells, and rubs them together.*]

LENI: I haven't finished clearing up.

FRANZ: Very well. I'm going to the thirtieth. [*He stands up, still keeping his back to her, and goes over to the placard which reads:* DON'T DISTURB. *He turns it round, so that it reads:* BACK AT 12 O'CLOCK. *He sits down again and rubs the shells together.*] You're looking at me. I can feel my neck burning. I forbid you to look at me! If you stay, keep working. [LENI *does not move.*] Will you take your eyes off me!

LENI: I will if you speak to me.

FRANZ: You're driving me mad! Mad! Mad!

LENI [*with a mirthless laugh*]: You'd like me to.

FRANZ: You want to look at me? Then do so! [*He stands up, and does the goose-step.*] Left, right, left, right!

LENI: Stop!

FRANZ: Left, right, left, right!

LENI: Please, stop!

FRANZ: What's the matter, my beauty? Afraid of a soldier?

LENI: I'm afraid of despising you.

[*She takes off her apron, throws it on the bed, and goes towards the door.* FRANZ *stops abruptly.*]

FRANZ: Leni! [*She is at the door. He speaks with a rather bewildered gentleness*] Don't leave me alone!

LENI [*she turns, speaking passionately*]: Do you want me to stay?

FRANZ [*in the same gentle voice*]: I need you, Leni.

LENI [*she goes towards him, overcome*]: My dear!

[*She is close to him. She raises her hand hesitantly and caresses his face. He allows her to do so for a moment, then jumps back.*]

FRANZ: Keep your distance! Keep a respectful distance! And no emotion.

LENI [*smiling*]: Puritan!

FRANZ: Puritan? [*Pause.*] You think so? [*He comes close to her, and caresses her shoulders and neck. Ill at ease, she allows him to do so.*] Puritans don't know how to caress. [*He caresses her breasts. She shudders and closes her eyes.*] But I do. [*She lets herself go against him. He suddenly breaks free.*] Get away! You disgust me!

LENI [*with icy calm, taking a step backwards*]: Not always!

FRANZ: Always! Always! From the very first day!

71

LENI: Down on your knees! Why aren't you begging their pardon?

FRANZ: Pardon for what? Nothing has happened?

LENI: What about yesterday?

FRANZ: Nothing, I tell you! Nothing at all!

LENI: Nothing except incest.

FRANZ: You always exaggerate.

LENI: Aren't you my brother?

FRANZ: Yes, of course.

LENI: Haven't you slept with me?

FRANZ: Not very often.

LENI: Even if you only did it once. . . . Are you so afraid of words?

FRANZ [*shrugging his shoulders*]: Words! [*Pause.*] If we had to find words for all the tribulations of this rotting flesh! [*He laughs.*] Are you trying to say that I make love? Oh, little sister! You are there, and I clasp you. Kind sleeps with kind – as it does a thousand million times every night upon this earth. [*To the ceiling*] But I swear to you that Franz, the eldest son of the Gerlachs, has never desired his younger sister, Leni.

LENI: Coward! [*To the ceiling*] Masked inhabitants of the ceiling, the witness of the centuries is a false witness. I, Leni, incestuous sister, love Franz, and I love him because he is my brother. No matter how little you care for family ties, you will condemn us outright, but I don't care a rap. [*To Franz*] That's the way to talk to them, you poor lost sheep. [*To the Crabs*] He desires me, but he doesn't love me. He dies of shame, and he sleeps with me in the dark. . . . So? I win. I wanted to have him, and I have him.

FRANZ [*to the Crabs*]: She's mad. [*He winks at them.*] I'll explain to you, when we're alone.

LENI: I forbid you! I shall die; I am already dead, and I forbid you to plead my cause. I have only one judge – myself – and

72

I acquit myself. Oh, witness for the defence, testify before yourself. You will be invuinerable if you dare to state: 'I have done what I wanted, and I want what I have done.'

FRANZ [*his face suddenly petrified, cold, filled with hatred and threatening. He speaks harshly and defiantly*]: What have I done, Leni?

LENI [*crying out*]: Franz! They'll have the hide off you if you don't defend yourself.

FRANZ: Leni, what have I done?

LENI [*worried, giving ground*]: Well . . . I've already told you.

FRANZ: Incest? No, Leni, it wasn't the incest you were talking about. [*Pause.*] What have I done?

[*A long silence. They look at each other.* LENI *turns away first.*]

LENI: All right; I've lost. Forget it. I'll protect you without your help. I'm used to it.

FRANZ: Get out! [*Pause.*] If you don't obey, I'll go on a silence strike. You know I can hold out for two months.

LENI: I know. [*Pause.*] I can't. [*She goes to the door, lifts the bar and draws the bolt.*] I'll bring your dinner this evening.

FRANZ: No use. I shan't open the door.

LENI: That's your business. Mine is to bring your dinner. [*He does not reply. Going out, she speaks to the Crabs.*] In case he doesn't open the door; good night, my pretty ones!

[*She goes out and closes the door.* FRANZ *turns, waits a moment, then lowers the bar and draws the bolt, his face set. He relaxes as soon as he feels safe, and appears reassured and almost gay, but it is now that he seems most mad. During the following speech, he speaks to the Crabs. It is not a monologue, but a dialogue carried on with invisible persons.*]

FRANZ: Doubtful witness. To be examined in my presence and according to my instructions. [*Pause. Reassured, weary, very softly*] Eh? Tiresome? In a way, yes – rather tiresome. But what a fuss! [*He yawns.*] Her main job is to keep me awake. It has been midnight for twenty years this century. It's not very easy to keep your eyes open at midnight. No, no; just dozing, that's all. It comes over me when I'm alone. [*He becomes increasingly sleepy.*] I shouldn't have sent her away. [*He sways, then quickly straightens up and marches in military style to the table. He bombards the portrait of Hitler with oyster-shells, shouting*] Sieg! Heil! Sieg! Heil! Sieg! [*Standing to attention and clicking his heels*] Führer, I am a soldier. If I fall asleep, it's serious, *very* serious. Abandoning my post. I swear to remain awake. Put on the searchlights, you! Full in my face, right in the eyes. That wakes you up. [*He waits.*] You lousy scum! [*He goes to his chair, and speaks in a soft and conciliatory voice.*] Well, I'll sit down a while. . . . [*He sits down, his head nodding, his eyes blinking.*] Roses. . . . Oh, isn't it lovely . . . [*He jumps up so quickly that he knocks over the chair.*] Roses? And if I take the bouquet, they will make me the highlight of their Carnival. [*To the Crabs*] A brazen Carnival! Help me, friends! I know too much; they want to get me out of the way. That's the Great Temptation. [*He goes to the bedside table, takes some tablets from a tube and chews them.*] Ugh! Listeners, take note of my new call-sign: *De profundis clamavi.* D. P. C. Listen, everyone! Grind! Grind away! If you don't listen to me, I'll fall asleep. [*He pours himself some champagne, drinks, spills half of it over his tunic, then lets his hand fall to his side, the glass hanging from his fingers.*] Meanwhile the century gallops on. . . . They've put cotton-wool in my head. Fog. It's white. [*His eyes blink.*] It's spreading over the fields . . . giving them cover. They're creeping up. There'll be bloodshed tonight.

[*The sound of distant shots, noises, galloping. He dozes off, and his eyes close.* SERGEANT-MAJOR HERMANN *opens the door of the lavatory and comes towards* FRANZ, *who is facing the audience, with his eyes closed.* HERMANN *salutes, standing to attention.*]

FRANZ [*in a thick, dull voice, without opening his eyes*]: Partisans?

SERGEANT-MAJOR: About twenty.

FRANZ: Anyone killed?

SERGEANT-MAJOR: No. Two wounded.

FRANZ: Ours?

SERGEANT-MAJOR: Theirs. We put them in the barn.

FRANZ: You know my orders, Dismiss!

[*The* SERGEANT-MAJOR *looks at Franz, hesitant, but angry.*]

SERGEANT-MAJOR: Very good, lieutenant.

[*Salute. About-turn. He goes out through the lavatory door, closing it behind him. Pause.* FRANZ'*s head falls on to his chest. He utters a terrible cry, and wakes up with a start, facing the audience.*]

FRANZ: No! Heinrich! Heinrich! I said no! [*He rises painfully, takes a ruler from the table and strikes himself on the fingers of his left hand, as though hammering in a lesson.*] Of course I did! [*Blows with the ruler*] I take full responsibility. What was it she said? [*Taking up Leni's words in his own terms*] I do what I like, and I like what I do. [*Harried*] Hearing of May 20th, 3059, Franz Von Gerlach, lieutenant. Don't throw my century into the dustbin. Not without hearing me. Evil, your lordships, Evil was the only material we had. We worked on it in our refineries, and the finished product became Good. Result: the Good turned bad. And don't run away with the idea that the Evil turned out well. [*He smiles, debonair; his head droops.*] Eh? [*Shouts.*] Falling asleep? Come on! Senile decay. They want to get at my head. Take care, you judges; if I rot, my century will be engulfed. The flock of the centuries needs a black sheep. What will the fortieth say, Arthropods, if the twentieth has wandered from the fold? [*Pause.*] No help? Never? Thy will be done. [*He returns to the front of the stage, and goes to sit down.*] Ah! I should never have let her go. [*Sound of knocking at the door. He listens, and straightens up. It is the agreed signal. He cries out in joy*] Leni! [*He runs to the door, raises the bar, and draws the bolt with strong and decisive movements. He is suddenly wide-awake. Speaking as he opens the door*] Come in quickly! [*He takes a step back to allow her to pass.* JOHANNA *appears in the doorway, looking very beautiful, made up and wearing a long dress.* FRANZ *takes a step backwards.*]

FRANZ [*with a hoarse cry*]: Ha! [*He draws back.*] What's this? [*She is about to reply, but he stops her.*] Not a word! [*He retreats and sits down. He looks at her, fascinated, sitting astride his chair. He nods agreement, and speaks with a restrained voice.*] Yes. [*Brief pause.*] She will come in… [*As he says this, she comes in.*] … and I shall still be alone. [*To the Crabs*] Thank you, comrades; I needed your help. [*In a kind of trance*] She will say nothing, and it will only be a vision. I shall look at her. [JOHANNA *has also appeared to be fascinated by this. She recovers, and smiles as she speaks in order to overcome her fear.*]

JOHANNA: Nevertheless, I have to talk to you.

FRANZ [*retreating from her slowly, without taking his eyes off her*]: No! [*He strikes the table.*] I knew she would spoil everything. [*Pause.*] It's *someone* now. In my room. Get out! [*She does not move.*] I'll have you thrown out like a tramp.

JOHANNA: By whom?

FRANZ [*shouting*]: Leni! [*Pause.*] You're a shrewd one, you've found the weak spot; I'm alone. [*He turns round suddenly. Pause.*] Who are you?

JOHANNA: Werner's wife.

FRANZ: Werner's wife? [*He stands up and looks at her.*] Werner's wife? [*He looks at her in amazement.*] Who sent you?

JOHANNA: No one.

FRANZ: How did you know the signal!

JOHANNA: From Leni.

FRANZ [*with a short laugh*]: From Leni? I can well believe that!

JOHANNA: She was knocking. I… surprised her at it and counted the knocks.

FRANZ: I was warned that you have your nose in everything. [*Pause.*] Well, madam, you have risked killing me. [*She*

laughs.] Laugh! Laugh! I could have had a seizure. What
would you have done? I've been ordered not to have visitors
– because of my heart. It's liable to conk out without any
warning. As luck would have it, you are beautiful. Oh! One
moment. It's over now. I took you for God knows what . . .
perhaps a vision. Take advantage of that salutary error to
disappear before you commit a crime.

JOHANNA: No.

FRANZ [*shouts*]: I'm going to . . . [*He goes towards her, threateningly, then stops. He slumps into his chair and feels his pulse.*]
A hundred and forty at least. For God's sake, if you don't
clear out you'll certainly see me pass out.

JOHANNA: That would be the best solution.

FRANZ: What? [*He takes his hand from his chest and looks at
Johanna in surprise.*] She was right. You're in their pay! [*He
stands up and walks easily.*] They won't get me so quickly.
Take it easy! Take it easy! [*He turns quickly back to her.*] The
best solution? For whom? For all the false witnesses of this
earth?

JOHANNA: For Werner and me. [*She looks at him.*]

FRANZ [*dumbfounded*]: Am I in your way?

JOHANNA: You tyrannize over us.

FRANZ: I don't even know you.

JOHANNA: You know Werner.

FRANZ: I have even forgotten what he looks like.

JOHANNA: They are keeping us here by force. Because of you.

FRANZ: Who?

JOHANNA: Father and Leni.

FRANZ [*amused*]: Do they beat you? Do they chain you up?

JOHANNA: Oh, no.

FRANZ: Well?

JOHANNA: Blackmail.

FRANZ: That, yes. That is like them. [*Dry laugh. His astonishment returns.*] Because of me? What do they want?

JOHANNA: To keep us in reserve. We will take over in case of accident.

FRANZ [*gaily*]: Your husband will make my soup and you will sweep out my room? Do you know how to darn?

JOHANNA [*pointing to the uniform in rags*]: The needlework will not be very interesting.

FRANZ: Don't fool yourself! These holes are consolidated. If it weren't that my sister has fairy fingers... [*Suddenly serious*] No changes. Take Werner to the devil and don't let me see you any more! [*He goes to his chair. Just as he is about to sit down, he turns.*] Still there?

JOHANNA: Yes.

FRANZ: You didn't understand me. I give you your freedom.

JOHANNA: You give me nothing at all.

FRANZ: I tell you, you are free.

JOHANNA: Words! Hot air!

FRANZ: You want deeds?

JOHANNA: Yes.

FRANZ: Well, what shall I do?

JOHANNA: The best thing would be to do away with you.

FRANZ: Again! [*Laughs shortly.*] Don't bank on it. Out of the question.

JOHANNA [*after a pause*]: Then help us.

FRANZ [*choked*]: Eh?

JOHANNA [*with warmth*]: You must help us, Franz!
   [*Pause.*]

FRANZ: No! [*Pause.*] I don't belong to this century. I will save the world as a whole but I will not help any one in particular. [*He paces agitatedly.*] I forbid you to draw me into your affairs. I am ill, do you understand? They take advantage of it to force me to live in the most abject dependence and you ought to be ashamed, you who are young and healthy, to ask someone who is weak and oppressed to help you. [*Pause.*] I am delicate, Madam, and my peace of mind comes before everything. Doctor's orders. You could be strangled before my very eyes, and I would not lift a finger. [*Complacently*] Do I disgust you?

JOHANNA: Intensely.

FRANZ [*rubbing his hands*]: Very good.

JOHANNA: But not enough to make me go.

FRANZ: Good. [*He takes the revolver and aims it at her.*] I shall count three. [*She smiles.*] One! [*Pause.*] Two! [*Pause.*] Phut! No one here. Vanished! [*To the Crabs*] What calm! She is quiet. It's all there, comrades: 'Be beautiful and keep quiet!' A vision. Is it inscribed on your window? Oh no! What could be inscribed on it? Nothing has changed; nothing has happened. The trick brought nothing into the room, that's all. Nothing, a diamond which cuts no glass, a vision, Beauty. You'll see nothing but the blaze there, poor Crustaceans. You took our eyes to examine what exists, while we, living in man's epoch, have seen with those same eyes what does not exist.

JOHANNA [*quietly*]: Father is going to die. [*Pause.* FRANZ *throws the revolver on to the table and quickly gets up.*]

FRANZ: Not a chance! Leni has just told me that he is as strong as an oak.

JOHANNA: She lies.

FRANZ [*with assurance*]: To everybody except me. It's the rule of the game. [*Quickly*] Go and hide yourself, you ought to die of shame. A ruse so vulgar and so quickly exposed! Eh? Two wonderful opportunities in less than an hour – and you cannot even take advantage of such unheard-of luck! You are a common type, my young sister-in-law, and I am no longer surprised that Werner married you.

[*He turns his back on her, sits down, and knocks two shells against each other. His face gloomy and withdrawn, he ignores Johanna.*]

JOHANNA [*disconcerted for the first time*]: Franz! [*Silence.*] . . . He will die in six months! [*Silence. Overcoming her fear, she approaches him and touches him on the shoulder. No reaction. Her hand falls back. She looks at him in silence.*] You are right, I did not know how to take advantage of my luck. Good-bye! [*She is about to leave.*]

FRANZ [*quickly*]: Wait! [*She turns slowly. He still has his back to her.*] The tablets, over there, in the tube. On the bedside table. Hand them to me!

JOHANNA: [*She goes to the bedside table.*] Benzedrine, is that it? [*He nods. She throws the tube to him and he catches it in flight.*] Why are you taking benzedrine?

FRANZ: To put up with you. [*He swallows four tablets.*]

JOHANNA: Four at a time?

FRANZ: And four in a little while, which makes eight. [*He drinks.*] They have designs on my life, Madam, I know it. You are the tool of a murderer. This is the moment to think clearly, eh? And to the point? [*He takes another tablet.*] There were mists . . . [*Finger on his forehead*] . . . there. I'm letting some sunshine in. [*He drinks, makes a violent effort to control himself and turns round, his face hard and set.*] This dress, these jewels, these gold chains, who advised you to put them on? To put them on *today*? Father sent you.

JOHANNA: No.

FRANZ: But he gave you his advice. [*She tries to speak.*] Useless! I know him just as if I had made him. To tell you the truth, I am no longer sure which of us made the other. When I want to know what trick he is up to, I begin by emptying my brain and it always works – the first thoughts which are born are his. Do you know why? He created me in his image – that is, unless he has become the image of what he created. [*He laughs.*] You don't understand a thing? [*Sweeping everything away with a tired gesture*] Tricks with a mirror. [*Imitating his Father*] 'And be sure to make yourself beautiful!' I can hear it from here. He loves Beauty, mad old fool: therefore he knows that I set it above everything. Except my own madness. Are you his mistress? [*She shakes her head.*] He must have aged! His accomplice, then?

JOHANNA: Until now, I was his enemy.

FRANZ: Switching sides? He loves that. [*Abruptly serious*] Six months?

JOHANNA: Not more.

FRANZ: The heart?

JOHANNA: The throat.

FRANZ: Cancer? [JOHANNA *nods.*] Thirty cigars a day! The idiot! [*A pause.*] Cancer? Then he will kill himself. [*Pause. He gets up, takes some shells and bombards the portrait of Hitler.*] He will kill himself, the old Führer, he will kill himself! [*Silence.* JOHANNA *looks at him.*] What's the matter?

JOHANNA: Nothing. [*Pause.*] You love him.

FRANZ: As much as I do myself and less than cholera. What does he want? To see me?

JOHANNA: No.

FRANZ: It's just as well he doesn't. [*Shouting*] I don't care whether he lives or dies! Look at what he has made of me! [*He takes the tube of tablets and begins to unscrew the cap.*]

JOHANNA [*gently*]: Give me that tube.

FRANZ: Why are you meddling?

JOHANNA [*holding out her hand*]: Give it to me!

FRANZ: I have to dope myself. I hate having my habits changed. [*She still holds out her hand.*] I'll give it to you but you're not to mention this stupid business any more. Agreed? [JOHANNA *makes a vague sign which could pass for a nod of agreement.*] Good. [*He gives her the tube.*] As for me, I am going to forget the whole thing. At once. I forget what I want to forget. An asset, eh? [*Pause.*] There, *Requiescat in pace.* [*Pause.*] Well? Talk to me!

JOHANNA: About whom? About what?

FRANZ: About anything, except the family. About yourself.

JOHANNA: There is nothing to tell.

FRANZ: That's for me to decide. [*He looks at her closely.*] A beauty snare, that's what you are. [*He runs his eyes over her.*] It's so good, it's professional. [*Pause.*] Actress?

JOHANNA: I was.

FRANZ: And then?

JOHANNA: I married Werner.

FRANZ: You didn't succeed?

JOHANNA: Not enough.

FRANZ: An extra? Starlet?

JOHANNA [*with a gesture which denies the past*]: Pooh!

FRANZ: Star?

JOHANNA: If you like.

FRANZ [*with ironic admiration*]: Star! And you didn't succeed? What did you want?

JOHANNA: What does one want? Everything.

FRANZ [*slowly*]: Everything, yes. Nothing else. All or nothing. [*Laughing*] Turned out badly, eh?

JOHANNA: Always does.

FRANZ: And Werner? Does he want *everything*?

JOHANNA: No.

FRANZ: Why did you marry him?

JOHANNA: Because I loved him.

FRANZ [*gently*]: You didn't.

JOHANNA [*bristling*]: What?

FRANZ: Those who want everything . . .

JOHANNA [*still bristling*]: Well?

FRANZ: . . . can't love.

JOHANNA: I don't want anything now.

FRANZ: Except his happiness, I hope!

JOHANNA: Except that. [*Pause.*] Help us!

FRANZ: What do you expect me to do?

JOHANNA: Come back to life.

FRANZ: Well, I'm damned! [*Laughing*] You are proposing my suicide.

JOHANNA: It's one or the other.

FRANZ [*with a sneering laugh*]: It's all becoming clear! [*Pause.*] I am charged with murder and it was the announcement of my death which put an end to the proceedings. You knew that, didn't you?

JOHANNA: I knew it.

FRANZ: And you want me to come back to life?

JOHANNA: Yes.

FRANZ: I see. [*Pause.*] If the brother-in-law can't be killed, then he must be put into safe custody. [*She shrugs her shoulders.*] Must I wait here for the police or should I give myself up?

JOHANNA [*on edge*]: You will not go to prison.

FRANZ: No?

JOHANNA: Of course not.

FRANZ: Then it's because he'll fix it up for me. [JOHANNA *nods.*] He hasn't given up then? [*With an irony full of resentment*] What hasn't he done for me, the good man! [*Gesture pointing to the room and to himself*] And here is the result. [*Fiercely*] You can all go to the devil!

JOHANNA [*overwhelmed with disappointment*]: Oh Franz! You're a coward!

FRANZ [*bridling up*]: What? [*He recovers himself, and speaks with deliberate cynicism.*] Yes, I am. So what?

JOHANNA: What about those? [*She flicks his medals with her fingers.*]

FRANZ: Those? [*He takes off a medal, and removes its silver-paper wrapping. It is made of chocolate. He eats it.*] Oh, I won them all. They're all mine, so I have the right to eat them. Heroism is my business. But heroes. . . . Do you know what they are?

JOHANNA: No.

FRANZ: Well, there are all kinds. Policemen and thieves, soldiers and civilians – not many civilians – cowards, and even brave men; the whole caboodle. They've one thing in common – medals. I'm a cowardly hero, and I wear chocolate

medals. It's more decent. Do you want one? Don't be shy;
I've got over a hundred in my drawer.

JOHANNA: Gladly. [*He tears off a medal and gives it to her. She
eats it.*]

FRANZ [*in sudden violence*]: No!

JOHANNA: What's the matter?

FRANZ: I won't allow myself to be judged by the wife of my
younger brother. [*Emphatically*] I'm not a coward, Madam,
and I'm not afraid of prison. I live in one. You wouldn't
stand three days of the life which I have to endure.

JOHANNA: What does that prove? It's of your own choosing.

FRANZ: Mine? But I never choose, my dear girl! I am chosen.
Nine months before my birth, they had chosen my name, my
career, my character and my fate. I tell you that this prison
routine has been forced upon me, and you should understand
that I would not submit myself to it unless it were vitally
necessary.

JOHANNA: Why is it so vital?

FRANZ: [*He steps back a pace. Short silence.*] Your eyes are
shining. No, Madam, I shall make no confessions.

JOHANNA: You are cornered, Franz. Either your reasons are
valid, or your younger brother's wife will judge you without
mercy. [*She comes up to him, intending to pull off a medal.*]

FRANZ: Are you death? No, take a cross. They're made of Swiss
chocolate.

JOHANNA [*taking a cross*]: Thanks. [*She draws slightly away from
him.*] Death? Do I look like it?

FRANZ: At times.

JOHANNA [*glancing into the mirror*]: You amaze me. When?

FRANZ: When you are beautiful. [*Pause.*] They're using you,
Madam. You're a tool in their hands, to get me to talk, and
if I tell you anything, I risk my neck. [*Pause.*] I don't care. I'll
risk everything. Carry on!

JOHANNA [*after a pause*]: Why are you hiding here?

FRANZ: First of all, I'm not hiding. If I had wanted to escape prosecution, I would have gone to the Argentine long ago. [*Pointing to the wall*] There was a window. Here. It over-looked what was our park.

JOHANNA: *Was?*

FRANZ: Yes. [*They look at each other for a moment.*] I had it walled up. [*Pause.*] Something is happening. Outside. Something I don't want to see.

JOHANNA: What?

FRANZ [*looking at her challengingly*]: The murder of Germany. [*He is still looking at her, half pleadingly, half threateningly, as though to prevent her from speaking. They have reached the danger-point.*] Be quiet! I've seen the ruins.

JOHANNA: When?

FRANZ: Coming back from Russia.

JOHANNA: That was fourteen years ago.

FRANZ: Yes.

JOHANNA: And you believe nothing has changed?

FRANZ: I *know* that everything is getting worse every hour.

JOHANNA: Is it Leni who tells you?

FRANZ: Yes.

JOHANNA: Do you read the papers?

FRANZ: She reads them for me. The razed towns, the smashed machines, the looted industry, the steep rise in unemploy-ment and tuberculosis and the sharp fall in the birth-rate. Nothing escapes me. My sister copies out all the statistics. [*Pointing to the drawer of the table*] They are all filed in this drawer. The finest murder in History. I have all the proofs. If not in twenty years, then in fifty at the most, the last German will be dead. Don't think I am complaining. We were defeated, and they are strangling us. It's impeccable. Perhaps you can understand that I have no desire to witness the butchery. I shall not make a tour of the destroyed cathe-drals and the burnt-out factories. I shan't visit the families huddled in the cellars. I shan't wander among the invalids, the slaves, the traitors, and the prostitutes. I imagine you are used to the sight, but I tell you frankly, I couldn't stand it. And the cowards, in my opinion, are those who can stand it. We should have won the war. By any means. I mean *any*, or vanish. Believe me, I would have had enough military courage to blow my brains out, but since the German people accepts the abject agony imposed on it, I have decided that one voice shall remain to cry No. [*He suddenly becomes excited.*] No! *Not guilty!* [*Shouting*] No! [*Pause.*] That's it.

JOHANNA [*slowly, undecided*]: The abject agony imposed on it . . .

FRANZ [*without taking his eyes off her*]: I said, that's it, that's all.

JOHANNA [*bewildered*]: Yes, that's it. That's all. [*Pause.*] Is that the only reason why you shut yourself up?

FRANZ: The only reason. [*Pause. She is lost in thought.*] What's the matter? Finish your work? Have I frightened you?

JOHANNA: Yes.

FRANZ: Why, my dear?

JOHANNA: Because you are afraid.

FRANZ: Of you?

JOHANNA: Of what I am going to tell you. [*Pause.*] I would rather not know what I know.

FRANZ [*defiantly, mastering his mortal anguish*]: What do you know? [*She hesitates, and they look at each other searchingly.*] Well? What do you know? [*She does not reply. Pause. They look at each other, and are both afraid. There is a knock at the door: five, four, then twice three.* FRANZ *smiles vaguely. He stands up and goes to open one of the doors upstage, revealing the bathroom. He speaks in a low voice.*] It won't be for long.

JOHANNA [*speaking normally*]: I won't hide.

FRANZ [*putting a finger to his lips*]: Ssh! [*In a low voice*] If you stand on your dignity, you'll lose the benefit of your little scheme. [*She hesitates, then decides to enter the bathroom. The knock is repeated.*]

[*He opens the door and* LENI *enters carrying a tray.*]

LENI [*stunned*]: Didn't you bolt the door?

FRANZ: No.

LENI: Why?

FRANZ [*curtly*]: Are you questioning me? [*Quickly*] Give me that tray and stay there.

[*He takes the tray from her and starts to carry it to the table.*]

LENI [*dumbfounded*]: What's come over you?

FRANZ: It's too heavy. [*He turns round and looks at her.*] Are you reproaching me for my good deeds?

LENI: No, but I am afraid of them. When you are good, I expect the worst.

FRANZ [*laughing*]: Ha! Ha! [*She enters and closes the door behind her.*] I did not tell you to come in. [*Pause. He takes a wing of chicken and eats.*] Well, I am going to have my dinner. See you tomorrow.

LENI: Wait. I want to ask you to forgive me. It was I who picked the quarrel.

FRANZ [*his mouth full*]: Quarrel?

LENI: Yes, when I was here before.

FRANZ [*vaguely*]: Oh yes! When you were here . . . [*Quickly*] Well, I forgive you. There!

LENI: I told you that I was afraid of despising you. I didn't mean it.

FRANZ: Perfect! Perfect! Everything is perfect. [*He eats.*]

LENI: I accept your Crabs. I submit to their judgement. Shall I tell them? [*To the Crabs*] Crustaceans, I worship you.

FRANZ: What's come over you?

LENI: I don't know. [*Pause.*] There is something else I want to tell you. I need you, you, the heir to our name, the only one whose caresses stir me without humiliating me. [*Pause.*] I don't amount to anything, but I was born a Gerlach, which means I am mad with pride – and I cannot make love to anyone but a Gerlach. Incest is my law and my fate. [*Laughing*] In a word, it's my way of strengthening the family ties.

FRANZ [*imperiously*]: Enough. Psychology tomorrow. [*She starts. She is defiant again, and observes him closely.*] We are reconciled, I give you my word. [*Pause.*] Tell me, the hunchback . . .

LENI [*taken by surprise*]: What hunchback?

FRANZ: Werner's wife. Is she pretty at least?

LENI: Ordinary.

FRANZ: I see. [*Pause. Seriously.*] Thank you, little sister. You have done what you could. Everything you could. [*He leads her back to the door. She allows herself to be led but remains anxious.*] I have not been a very easy patient, eh? Good-bye!

LENI [*trying to laugh*]: How solemn you are! I'll see you tomorrow, you know.

FRANZ [*softly, almost tenderly*]: I hope so with all my heart.

[*He opens the door. He bends and kisses her forehead. She raises her head and quickly kisses him on the mouth and goes out. He closes the door, bolts it, takes out his handkerchief and wipes his lips. He goes back to the table.*]

FRANZ: Don't be taken in, comrades, Leni *cannot* lie. [*Pointing to the bathroom*] The liar is in there. I am going to tie her up in knots, eh? Don't worry, I know more than one trick. This evening you will see the downfall of a false witness. [*He notices that his hands are trembling, and makes a violent effort to control himself as he continues to gaze at his hands.*] Come on, boys, come on! There! There! [*His hands gradually stop trembling. With a quick glance in the mirror, he straightens his tunic and adjusts his Sam Browne belt. He has changed. For the first time since the beginning of the scene, he is fully master of himself. He goes to the bathroom door, opens it, and bows.*] To work, Madam!

[*JOHANNA enters. He closes the door and follows her, hard, on the alert. Throughout the following scene, it is obvious that he is trying to dominate her. He goes and places himself in front of Johanna, who has take a step towards the entrance. She stops.*]

88

FRANZ: Don't move. Leni hasn't left the drawing-room.

JOHANNA: What is she doing there?

FRANZ: Tidying up. [*She takes another step.*] Your heels. [*He imitates the noise of a woman's heels with little blows against the door. As he speaks, his eyes never leave her face. One feels that he is measuring the risk he is running, and that his words are calculated.*] You wanted to leave, but wasn't there something you wanted to tell me?

JOHANNA [*she seems ill at ease since she has come out of the bathroom*]: No, there wasn't.

FRANZ: Oh. [*Pause.*] Haven't you anything to say?

JOHANNA: No, I haven't.

FRANZ [*gets up abruptly*]: No, my dear sister-in-law, that would be too easy. She was going to set me free, and now she has changed her mind and is going away for ever, leaving behind her carefully planted doubts to poison me. I'll have none of that! [*He goes to the table, takes two champagne glasses and a bottle. As he pours the champagne into the glasses*] Is it Germany? Has she recovered? Are we swimming on the tide of prosperity?

JOHANNA [*exasperated*]: Germany . . .

FRANZ [*very quick, covering his ears*]: Useless! Useless! I will not believe you. [JOHANNA *looks at him, shrugs her shoulders and is silent. He walks about airily and quite at ease.*] In fact it has failed.

JOHANNA: What has?

FRANZ: Your escapade.

JOHANNA: Yes. [*Pause. In a gloomy voice*] It was kill or cure.

FRANZ: Oh yes! [*Amiably*] You will find something else. [*Pause.*] At any rate, you have given me the pleasure of looking at you, and I must thank you for your generosity.

JOHANNA: I am not generous.

FRANZ: What would you call all the trouble you have taken? All that work in front of the mirror? That must have taken you several hours. What a lot of preparation for one man!

JOHANNA: I do it every evening.

FRANZ: For Werner.

JOHANNA: For Werner, and sometimes for his friends.

FRANZ [*he shakes his head and smiles*]: No.

JOHANNA: Do I drag around like a slattern in my room? Do I neglect myself?

FRANZ: Not that either. [*He stops looking at her and turns his eyes to the wall, describing what he imagines.*] You stand very straight. Very straight. To keep your head above water. Hair drawn back. Lips unpainted. Not a grain of powder. Werner has the right to be looked after, to tenderness, to kisses – to smiles, never. You do not smile any more.

JOHANNA [*smiling*]: Visionary!

FRANZ: A recluse has special powers of vision which enable him to recognize his kind.

JOHANNA: They cannot meet each other very often.

FRANZ: Well, you see, it does happen sometimes.

JOHANNA: You recognize me?

FRANZ: We recognize each other.

JOHANNA: Am I a recluse? [*She gets up and looks at herself in the glass, then turns round, very beautiful, provocative for the first time.*] I would not have believed it. [*She goes to him.*]

FRANZ [*quickly*]: Your heels!

[JOHANNA *takes off her shoes, smiling as she does so, and throws them, one after another, at the portrait of Hitler.*]

JOHANNA [*near Franz*]: I saw the daughter of one of Werner's clients – chained up, weighing about eighty pounds, covered in lice. Do I look like her?

FRANZ: Like a sister. She wanted everything, I suppose. That's a losing game. She lost everything, and locked herself up in her room so that it would look as if she refused everything.

JOHANNA [*irritated*]: Are we going to talk about me for long? [*She steps back and points to the floor.*] Leni must have left the drawing-room.

FRANZ: Not yet.

JOHANNA [*with a quick glance at her wrist watch*]: Werner will be back. It's eight o'clock.

FRANZ [*violently*]: No! [*She looks at him in surprise.*] Never mention the time here – Eternity. [*He calms down.*] Patience. You will soon be free. [*Pause.*]

JOHANNA [*with a mixture of defiance and curiosity*]: So I lock myself up?

FRANZ: Yes.

JOHANNA: Through pride?

FRANZ: Certainly!

JOHANNA: What's missing?

FRANZ: You were not beautiful enough.

JOHANNA [*smiling*]: Flatterer!

FRANZ: I am saying what you think.

JOHANNA: And you? What do you think?

FRANZ: Of myself?

JOHANNA: Of me.

FRANZ: That you are possessed.

JOHANNA: Mad?

FRANZ: Raving.

JOHANNA: What are you telling me? Your life-story, or mine?

FRANZ: Ours.

JOHANNA: What possessed you?

FRANZ: Has it a name? Emptiness. [*Pause.*] Let's say – grandeur ... [*He laughs.*] It possessed me, but I didn't possess it.

JOHANNA: So that's it!

FRANZ: You watched yourself, eh? You tried to surprise yourself? [JOHANNA *nods.*] Did you catch yourself?

JOHANNA: What do you think? [*She glances at the mirror uneasily.*] I saw that. [*She points to her reflection. Pause.*] I used to go to the local cinemas. When the star Johanna Thies slid on to the end wall, I used to hear a little murmur. They were moved, each one by the other's emotion. I would look ...

FRANZ: And then?

JOHANNA: Then nothing. I never saw what they saw. [*Pause.*] What about you?

FRANZ: I was the same as you. I was a failure. I was decorated in front of the whole army. Does Werner find you beautiful?

JOHANNA: I certainly hope not. Just think! One man. Does that count?

FRANZ [*slowly*]: I find you beautiful.

JOHANNA: Well, I hope you enjoy it, but don't talk about it. No one, you understand, no one, since the public rejected me . . . [*She calms down a little and laughs.*] You take yourself for a whole army corps.

FRANZ: Why not? [*He does not take his eyes from her.*] You must believe me. It's your chance. If you believe me, I become invulnerable.

JOHANNA [*laughing nervously*]: It's a bargain. 'Share my madness, and I will share yours.'

FRANZ: Why not? You have nothing more to lose. As for my madness, you have been sharing that for a long time. [*Pointing to the door of the room*] When I opened the door to you, it wasn't me that you saw; it was a reflection in the depths of my eyes.

JOHANNA: Because they are empty.

FRANZ: For that very reason.

JOHANNA: I no longer remember what the photo of a faded star was like. Everything disappeared when you spoke.

FRANZ: You spoke first.

JOHANNA: I couldn't stand it. I had to break the silence.

FRANZ: To break the spell.

JOHANNA: In any case, it turned out all right. [*Pause.*] What's the matter with you? [*She laughs nervously.*] It's like the lens of a camera. Stop! You're dead.

FRANZ: At your service. Death mirrors death. My grandeur reflects your beauty.

JOHANNA: I wanted to please the living.

FRANZ: The downtrodden mob that dreams of dying? You showed them the pure and tranquil face of Eternal Rest. The cinemas are cemeteries, my dear. What is your name?

JOHANNA: Johanna.

FRANZ: Johanna, I do not desire you, I do not love you. I am your witness and that of all mankind. I bear witness before the centuries, and I say – you are beautiful.

JOHANNA [*as though spellbound*]: Yes.
   [*He strikes the table violently.*]

FRANZ [*in a hard voice*]: Confess that you have lied. Say that Germany is on its deathbed.

JOHANNA [*she starts almost painfully*]: Ha! [*She shudders, her face tensed. She suddenly becomes almost ugly.*] You have spoilt everything.

FRANZ: Everything – I have shattered the image. [*Abruptly*] And you would like to bring me back to life? You would smash the mirror for nothing. I would go down among you. I would have my meals with the family, and you would go to Hamburg with your Werner. Where will that lead us?

JOHANNA [*she has gained control of herself. Smiling*]: To Hamburg.

FRANZ: You will never be beautiful again there.

JOHANNA: No. Never again.

FRANZ: Here you will be beautiful every day.

JOHANNA: Yes, if I come to see you every day.

FRANZ: You will come.

JOHANNA: Will you open the door?

FRANZ: I shall open it.

JOHANNA [*imitating him*]: Where will that lead us?

FRANZ: Here, to Eternity.

JOHANNA [*smiling*]: *Folie à deux* . . . [*She is thinking. The spell has gone. One feels that she has returned to her original plans.*] Good. I shall come back.

FRANZ: Tomorrow?

JOHANNA: Perhaps tomorrow.

FRANZ [*softly. Johanna is silent*]: Say that Germany is on its deathbed. Say it, or else the mirror is in pieces. [*He gets excited, his hands begin to tremble again.*] Say it! Say it! Say it!

JOHANNA [*slowly*]: *Folie à deux* – very well. [*Pause.*] Germany is on its deathbed.

FRANZ: Is it really true?

JOHANNA: Yes.

FRANZ: They are strangling us?

JOHANNA: Yes.

FRANZ: Right. [*He cocks his ear.*] She has gone. [*He goes to pick up Johanna's shoes, kneels down in front of her and puts them on her feet. She stands up. He gets up again and bows, clicking his heels.*] See you tomorrow! [JOHANNA *goes as far as the door. He follows her, draws the bolt and opens the door. She nods to him, with the hint of a smile on her lips. She is about to leave, when he stops her.*] Wait! [*She turns round, and he looks at her with sudden defiance.*] Who has won?

JOHANNA: Won what?

FRANZ: The first round.

JOHANNA: Guess.

[*She goes out. He closes the door, bolts and bars it. He seems relieved. He goes back to the middle of the room and stops.*]

FRANZ: Ah! [*The smile remains a moment, then his features become tense. He is afraid.*] *De profundis clamavi!* [*He is overwhelmed by suffering.*] Grind! Grind! Grind away! [*He begins to tremble.*]

CURTAIN

ACT THREE

Werner's study. Modern furniture. A mirror. Two doors.
  [There is a knock at the door. The stage is empty. Another knock, then the FATHER *enters. He is carrying a briefcase in his left hand, and his raincoat is folded over his right arm. He closes the door, places his raincoat and briefcase on an armchair, then, as an afterthought, goes back to the door and reopens it.]*

FATHER *[calling offstage]*: I can see you. *[A short silence.]* Leni!
  *[*LENI *appears after a moment.]*

LENI *[with a touch of defiance]*: Here I am!

FATHER *[stroking her hair]*: Hallo. You were hiding?

LENI *[drawing back slightly]*: Hallo, father. Yes, I was hiding.
  [She looks at him.] Look at you!

FATHER: The journey has made me flushed. *[He coughs. A short dry cough which hurts.]*

LENI: Is there flu in Leipzig?

FATHER *[not understanding]*: Flu? *[He understands.]* No. I'm coughing. *[She looks at him in a kind of fear.]* What's that to do with you?

LENI *[turning and looking into space]*: Nothing at all, I hope.
  [Pause.]

FATHER *[jovially]*: So, you were spying on me?

LENI *[amiably]*: Yes, I was spying on you. It's my turn.

FATHER: You don't lose any time. I've only just arrived.

LENI: I wanted to know what you'd do when you arrived.

FATHER: You can see, I'm visiting Werner.

LENI *[glancing at her wrist-watch]*: You know very well that Werner is down at the yard.

FATHER: I'll wait for him.

LENI *[pretending amazement]*: You?

FATHER: Why not? [*He sits down.*]

LENI: Of course, why not? [*She sits down also.*] Shall I wait with you?

FATHER: I'll wait alone.

LENI: All right. [*She stands up.*] What have you been up to?

FATHER [*astonished*]: In Leipzig?

LENI: Here.

FATHER [*astonished again*]: What have I been up to?

LENI: That's what I'm asking you.

FATHER: I've been away for six days, my child.

LENI: What did you do on Sunday evening?

FATHER: You get on my nerves. [*Pause.*] Nothing. I had dinner and I went to bed.

LENI: Everything has changed. Why?

FATHER: What has changed?

LENI: You know.

FATHER: I've just come from the plane. I know nothing, and I've seen nothing.

LENI: You can see me.

FATHER: Exactly. [*Pause.*] You'll never change, Leni, no matter what happens.

LENI [*pointing to the mirror*]: Father! I can see myself too. [*She goes over to the mirror.*] Of course, you've spoilt my hair. [*She smoothes back her hair.*] When I see myself . . .

FATHER: You don't recognize yourself any more?

LENI: Not any more. [*She lets her arms fall, surprised as she looks at herself without illusions.*] How futile! [*Without turning from the mirror*] At dinner last night Johanna was wearing make-up.

FATHER: Ah? [*His eyes glitter for a moment, but he recovers.*] Well?

LENI: That's all.

FATHER: All women use make-up these days.

LENI: But she never does.

FATHER: She probably wants to win her husband back.

LENI: Her husband! [*With a sneer*] You didn't see her eyes.

FATHER [*smiling*]: What of them?

LENI [*pointedly*]: You'll see. [*Pause. With a short laugh*] Ah, you won't recognize anyone. Werner talks in a loud voice, and he eats and drinks enough for four men.

FATHER: It's not I who have changed you all.

LENI: Who else?

FATHER: No one. The vagaries of this old windpipe of mine. Well, when a father departs . . . But what are you complaining about? I've given you six months' warning. You'll have time to make the best of it, and you ought to thank me.

LENI: Thank you. [*Pause. In a changed voice*] On Sunday evening you planted a time-bomb in our midst. Where is it? [*The* FATHER *shrugs his shoulders and smiles.*] I'll find it.

FATHER: A bomb! Why should you . . .?

LENI: The great ones of this world can't bear to die alone.

FATHER: Am I going to blow up the whole family?

LENI: The family – no. You don't love it enough for that. [*Pause.*] Franz.

FATHER: Poor Franz! Would I carry just him with me to my grave when the whole universe will survive me? Leni, I hope that you will stop me.

LENI: You can count on me. [*She takes a step towards him.*] If anyone attempts to go near him you'll depart right away, and alone.

FATHER: Good. [*Pause. He sits down.*] Have you nothing more to tell me? [*She shakes her head. He speaks with authority, but without changing his tone.*] Go!

[LENI *looks at him for a moment, bows her head and goes out. The* FATHER *gets up, goes to the door and opens it, glances into the corridor as though to make sure that Leni is not hiding there, closes the door, turns the key in the lock and places his handkerchief over the key in order to cover the keyhole. He crosses the room, goes to the door at the other end, opens it and calls in a loud voice*]

FATHER: Johanna!

[*He is interrupted by a fit of coughing. He turns round. Now that he is alone, he no longer keeps a firm hand on himself, and he is visibly suffering. He goes to the desk, takes a carafe, pours himself a glass of water and drinks it.* JOHANNA *enters by the upstage door behind him.*]

JOHANNA: What is it? [*He turns round.*] Oh, it's you?

FATHER [*in a choking voice*]: Yes, it is. [*He kisses her hand. His voice becomes firmer.*] Weren't you expecting me?

JOHANNA: I had forgotten about you. [*She recovers herself and laughs.*] Have you had a good trip?

FATHER: Excellent. [*She looks at the handkerchief covering the key.*] That's nothing. Just to blind someone. [*Pause. He looks at her.*] You're not wearing make-up.

JOHANNA: No.

FATHER: Aren't you going to see Franz?

JOHANNA: I'm not going to see anyone; I'm waiting for my husband.

FATHER: But you have seen him?

JOHANNA: Who?

FATHER: My son.

JOHANNA: You have two sons, and I don't know which one you are talking about.

FATHER: The elder. [*Pause.*] Well, my child?

JOHANNA [*with a start*]: Father?

FATHER: What of our agreement?

JOHANNA [*with an air of amused surprise*]: That's true; you have your rights. What a farce. [*Almost in confidence*] Everything is a farce on the ground floor, even you who are going to die. How do you manage to keep that rational expression? [*Pause.*] I'm sure you will understand nothing.

FATHER [*he was expecting this, but is unable to avoid a certain anguish on hearing it*]: You saw Franz? [*Pause.*] When? Monday?

JOHANNA: Monday, and every day since.

FATHER: Every day! [*Astounded*] Five times?

JOHANNA: I suppose so. I haven't counted.

FATHER: Five times. [*Pause.*] It's a miracle. [*He rubs his hands.*]

JOHANNA [*authoritatively, but without raising her voice*]: Please! [*The* FATHER *puts his hands in his pockets.*] Don't look so pleased.

FATHER: You must excuse me, Johanna. Coming back on the plane, I was in a cold sweat. I thought everything was lost.

JOHANNA: Well?

FATHER: And now I hear that you see him every day.

JOHANNA: It is I who have lost everything.

FATHER: Why? [*She shrugs her shoulders.*] My child, since he opens his door to you, you must get on well with each other.

JOHANNA: We get on well. [*In a hard and cynical voice*] We're as thick as thieves.

FATHER [*disconcerted*]: What? [*Pause.*] At least you're good friends?

JOHANNA: Anything but friends.

FATHER: Anything? [*Pause.*] You mean ...

JOHANNA [*surprised*]: What? [*She bursts into laughter.*] Lovers? Would you believe it; we haven't even thought of it. Was it necessary for your plans?

FATHER [*with some irritation*]: Excuse me, daughter-in-law, but it's your fault. You explain nothing to me because you have made up your mind that I wouldn't understand.

JOHANNA: There's nothing to explain.

FATHER [*worried*]: He isn't ... ill, is he?

JOHANNA: Ill? [*She understands. With crushing contempt*] Oh, mad? [*Shrugging her shoulders*] How should I know?

FATHER: You see him in the flesh.

JOHANNA: If he's mad, so am I. And why shouldn't I be?

FATHER: In any case, you can tell me if he is unhappy.

JOHANNA [*amused*]: Oh, that! [*In confidence*] Words don't have the same meaning up there.

FATHER: I see. How do you say that you're suffering up there?

JOHANNA: Nobody is suffering.

FATHER: Oh?

JOHANNA: One is kept busy.

FATHER: Franz is kept busy? [JOHANNA *nods.*] At what?

JOHANNA: At what? You mean by whom?

FATHER: Yes, that's what I mean. Well?

JOHANNA: That's none of my business.

FATHER [*gently*]: Don't you want to talk to me about him?

JOHANNA [*with a profound weariness*]: In what language? I have to translate all the time, and that makes me tired. [*Pause.*] I'm going away, father.

FATHER: Will you abandon him?

JOHANNA: He doesn't need anyone.

FATHER: Naturally, you have the right, you are free. [*Pause.*] You made me a promise.

JOHANNA: I've kept it.

FATHER: He knows . . . [JOHANNA *nods.*] What did he say?

JOHANNA: That you smoked too much.

FATHER: What else?

JOHANNA: Nothing else.

FATHER [*deeply hurt*]: I knew it! She lies to him all along the line, the bitch. What she must have told him during these thirteen years . . .

[JOHANNA *laughs softly. He stops short and looks at her.*]

JOHANNA: Now you see that you don't understand! [*He looks at her sternly.*] What do you think I do with Franz? I lie to him.

FATHER: You?

JOHANNA: I lie to him every time I open my mouth.

FATHER [*amazed and almost disarmed*]: But . . . you always hated lying.

JOHANNA: I still do.

FATHER: Well?

JOHANNA: Well, so I lie. To Werner in silence, to Franz in words.

FATHER [*curtly*]: That's not what we agreed upon.

JOHANNA: No, it isn't.

FATHER: You were right; I . . . I don't understand. You're working against your own interests.

JOHANNA: Against Werner's.

FATHER: Which are yours.

JOHANNA: I no longer know.

[*Silence. The* FATHER, *bewildered for a moment, recovers.*]

FATHER: Have you gone over to the other side?

JOHANNA: There are no sides.

FATHER: Good. Then listen to me. Franz is greatly to be pitied, and I can understand that you wanted to spare him. But you can't go on like that. If you allow yourself to be affected by the pity you feel for him . . .

JOHANNA: We have no pity.

FATHER: We?

JOHANNA: Yes, Leni and I.

FATHER: Leni is another matter. But you, daughter-in-law, whatever you choose to call your feelings, don't lie to my son any more. You degrade him. [*She smiles. He speaks more sharply.*] He has only one desire; to run away. If you load him up with your lies, he'll allow himself to go under.

JOHANNA: I haven't time to do him much harm. I've told you, I'm going away.

FATHER: When and where?

JOHANNA: Tomorrow; anywhere.

FATHER: With Werner?

JOHANNA: I don't know.

FATHER: Running away?

JOHANNA: Yes.

FATHER: But why?

JOHANNA: Two languages, two lives, two truths; don't you think that's too much for one person? [*She laughs.*] The orphans of Düsseldorf, well I shall never get rid of them.

FATHER: What's that? A lie?

JOHANNA: A truth up there. They are abandoned children; they are dying of hunger in a camp. They must exist somehow or another, since they pursue me down to the ground floor. Yesterday evening I almost asked Werner if we couldn't save them. [*She laughs.*] That wouldn't mean anything. But up there . . .

FATHER: Well?

JOHANNA: I'm my own worst enemy. My voice lies, and my body contradicts it. I talk about the famine, and I say that we are dying of starvation. Look at me now! Do I look starved? If Franz saw me . . .

FATHER: Doesn't he see you, then?

JOHANNA: He hasn't got round to looking at me yet. [*As though speaking to herself*] A traitor. Inspired. Convincing. He speaks, and you listen. Then, suddenly, he sees himself in the glass; a placard across his chest with a single word on it, that can be read even when he says nothing: treachery. That's the nightmare waiting for me daily in your son's room.

FATHER: It's everybody's nightmare. Every day and every night. [*Pause.*]

JOHANNA: Can I ask you a question? [*The* FATHER *nods.*] What is all this to do with me? Why have you dragged me into it?

FATHER [*sharply*]: You're out of your mind, daughter-in-law. It was you who decided to become involved.

JOHANNA: How did you know I decided to?

FATHER: I didn't know.

JOHANNA: Don't lie, you who reproached me for lying. At any rate, don't lie too soon. Six days is a long time. You have given me time to think. [*Pause.*] The family conference was held especially for me.

FATHER: No, my child, for Werner.

JOHANNA: Werner? Pooh! You attacked him so that I could defend him. It was I who had the idea of talking to Franz, I agree. Or, rather, it was I who found the idea. You had hidden it in the room, and you guided me so skilfully that I eventually found it staring me in the face. Isn't that true?

FATHER: I did, in fact, wish that you would meet my son; for reasons which you well know.

JOHANNA [*vehemently*]: For reasons which I don't know. [*Pause.*] When you brought us together, I who know, and he who doesn't know, did you warn me that one word would be enough to kill him?

FATHER [*with dignity*]: Johanna, I know nothing about my son.

JOHANNA: Nothing except that he is trying to run away, and that we are helping him in it by our lies. Come on! You want to have it both ways. I tell you that one word is enough to kill him, and you don't even flinch.

FATHER [*smiling*]: What word, my child?

JOHANNA [*laughing in his face*]: Wealth.

FATHER: I beg your pardon?

JOHANNA: That or any other word which conveys the meaning that we are the richest nation in Europe. [*Pause.*] You don't seem very surprised.

FATHER: I'm not. Twelve years ago I became aware of my son's fears through certain remarks which he let fall. He believed that they wanted to wipe out Germany, and he shut himself up in order not to witness our extermination. If it had been possible at that time to reveal the future to him, he would have been cured at once. Today it will be more difficult to save him. He has acquired certain habits. Leni spoils him, and a cloistered life has certain advantages. But never fear, the only cure for his illness is the truth. He'll take it badly at first, for it will remove all his pretexts for sulking, but within a week he will be the first to thank you.

JOHANNA [*vehemently*]: What rubbish! [*Brutally*] I saw him yesterday; isn't that enough for you?

FATHER: No.

JOHANNA: Up there, Germany is more dead than the moon. If I bring it back to life, he will blow his brains out.

FATHER [*laughing*]: You don't say?

JOHANNA: I tell you that everything points that way.

FATHER: Does he no longer love his country?

JOHANNA: He worships it.

FATHER: Well then, Johanna, that doesn't make common sense.

JOHANNA: Oh no, it doesn't. [*Laughing a little wildly*] Common sense? [*Pointing to the Father*] That's what you have in your head. I have his eyes in my head. [*Pause.*] Stop everything! Your infernal machine is going to blow up in your hands.

FATHER: I can't stop anything.

JOHANNA: Then I shall go away without seeing him again, and for good. As for the truth; I shall tell it, don't worry, but not to Franz – to Werner.

FATHER [*quickly*]: No. [*Recovering himself*] You will only hurt him.

JOHANNA: What else have I been doing since Sunday? [*The sound of a car horn is heard in the distance.*] There he is. He will know everything within a quarter of an hour.

FATHER [*commandingly*]: Wait! [*She stops, taken aback. He goes to the door, removes the handkerchief and turns the key, then turns to face Johanna.*] I'll make you a proposition. [*She remains silent and tense. Pause.*] Say nothing to your husband. Go and see Franz one last time and tell him that I request an interview. If he accepts, I'll release Werner from his oath, and you shall *both* go whenever you wish. [*Pause.*] Johanna, I'm offering you freedom.

JOHANNA: I know. [*The car enters the park.*]

FATHER: Well?

JOHANNA: I don't want it at that price.

FATHER: What price?

JOHANNA: Franz's death.

FATHER: My child, what has happened to you? It's like listening to Leni.

JOHANNA: It is. We are twin sisters. Don't be surprised. It's you who have made us the same, and if all the women in the world paraded in your son's room, they would be so many Lenis all lined up against you. [*A sound of car brakes. The car stops in front of the steps.*]

FATHER: I beg of you, don't decide yet! I promise you . . .

JOHANNA: It's no use. For hired killers, apply to the other sex.

FATHER: Will you tell Werner everything?

JOHANNA: Yes.

FATHER: Very well. And suppose I tell Leni everything?

JOHANNA [*amazed and frightened*]: Tell Leni? You?

FATHER: Why not? The house would blow up.

JOHANNA [*on the edge of hysterics*]: Blow the house up! Blow the planet up! Then we should get some peace at last. [*She starts to laugh, a low mirthless laugh which increases in volume in spite of herself.*] Peace! Peace! Peace!

[*There is a sound of footsteps in the corridor. The* FATHER *goes rapidly over to Johanna, seizes her roughly by the shoulders and shakes her, looking hard at her.* JOHANNA *succeeds in calming herself. The* FATHER *releases her and steps away from her just as the door opens.* WERNER *enters quickly and sees his Father.*]

WERNER: Well!

FATHER: Hallo, Werner.

WERNER: Hallo, father. Pleased with your trip?

FATHER: Huh! [*He rubs his hands without being aware that he is doing so.*] Pleased, yes, pleased. Perhaps very pleased.

WERNER: You wanted to talk to me?

FATHER: To you? Oh, no. I'll leave you, children. [*At the door*] Johanna, my proposition still stands. [*He goes out.*]

WERNER: What proposition?

JOHANNA: I'll tell you.

WERNER: I don't want him to come nosing about in here. [*He takes a bottle of champagne and two glasses from a cupboard, places the glasses on the desk and begins to uncork the bottle.*] Champagne?

JOHANNA: No.

WERNER: Very well; I'll drink on my own. [JOHANNA *takes the glasses away.*]

JOHANNA: Not this evening. I need you.

WERNER: You surprise me. [*He looks at her. Sharply*] In any case, that doesn't prevent my drinking. [*He releases the cork.* JOHANNA *utters a short cry.* WERNER *laughs, fills both glasses and looks at her.*] My word, you're afraid!

JOHANNA: I'm a bit on edge.

WERNER [*with a kind of satisfaction*]: I say that you're afraid. [*Pause.*] Of whom? Father?

JOHANNA: Of him as well.

WERNER: And you want me to protect you? [*Laughing derisively; but a little more relaxed*] The roles are reversed. [*He drains his glass at one go.*] Tell me what's worrying you. [*Pause.*] Is it so difficult? Come on! [*She does not move, but remains tense: He pulls her towards him.*] Put your head on my shoulder. [*He almost forces Johanna's head on to his shoulder. Pause. He looks at himself in the mirror and smiles.*] Back to normal. [*A short silence.*] Speak, my dear!

JOHANNA [*raising her head to look at him*]: I've seen Franz.

WERNER [*pushing her away angrily*]: Franz! [*He turns away from her, goes to the desk, pours himself another glass of champagne, calmly drinks, then turns back to her, cool and smiling.*] That's good! Now you know the whole family. [*She looks at him uneasily.*] How do you find my elder brother? Quite a swell,

eh? [*She looks at him, bewildered, and shakes her head.*]Well!
[*Amused*] Well, well. Is he in a bad way? [*She has difficulty in
speaking.*] Eh?

JOHANNA: You're taller than he.

WERNER [*still amused.*]: Ha! ha! [*Pause.*] And does he still wear
his fine officer's tunic?

JOHANNA: It's no longer a fine tunic.

WERNER: Rags? But, I say, poor old Franz is pretty low, then.
·[JOHANNA *maintains a tense silence. He picks up the glass.*] To
his cure. [*He raises his glass, then, seeing that she has no glass,
he goes to get the other glass and holds it out to her.*] Let's drink a
toast. [*She hesitates. Commandingly*] Take this glass. [*Her
expression hardens as she takes the glass.*]

JOHANNA [*defiantly*]: I drink to Franz!

 [*She tries to clink her glass against Werner's but he quickly
 draws his glass away. They look at each other for a moment,
 nonplussed, then* WERNER *bursts out laughing and throws the
 contents of his glass on the floor.*]

WERNER [*with violent abandon*]: It's not true! It's not true!
[JOHANNA *is amazed. He goes towards her.*] You've never seen
him. You didn't take me in for a moment. [*Laughing in her
face*]What about the bolt, dear? And the iron bar? They
have a signal; you can be sure of that.

JOHANNA [*who has regained her icy calm*]: They have. I know it.

WERNER [*still laughing*]: You do! I suppose you asked Leni.

JOHANNA: I asked your father.

WERNER [*astounded*]: Ah! [*A long silence. He goes to the desk, puts
down his glass and thinks. Then he turns back to Johanna. He has
maintained his jovial manner, but it is clear that he is making a
great effort to control himself.*] Well, it was bound to happen.
[*Pause.*] Father never does anything without reason. What is
his interest in this affair?

JOHANNA: I'd like to know.

WERNER: What was it he proposed to you just now?

JOHANNA: He'll release you from your oath if Franz will grant him an interview.

WERNER [*he has become gloomy and suspicious, and his suspicion increases during the course of the ensuing dialogue*]: An interview … and will Franz grant it?

JOHANNA [*with assurance*]: Yes.

WERNER: And then?

JOHANNA: Nothing. We shall be free.

WERNER: Free to do what?

JOHANNA: To go away.

WERNER [*with a harsh laugh*]: To Hamburg?

JOHANNA: Wherever we please.

WERNER: Perfect! [*With a harsh laugh*] Well, my wife, that's the finest kick up the backside that I've received in all my life.

JOHANNA [*amazed*]: Werner, your father isn't thinking for a moment. …

WERNER: Of his younger son? You bet he isn't. Franz will take my desk, he will sit in my armchair and drink my champagne, he will throw his oyster-shells under my bed. Apart from that, who will think of me? Do I matter? [*Pause.*] The old man has changed his mind, that's all.

JOHANNA: But don't you understand anything?

WERNER: I understand that he wants to put my brother in charge of the firm. And I understand that you have deliberately acted as an intermediary for them. So long as you can clear out of here, you don't care if I'm kicked out. [JOHANNA *looks at him coldly. She lets him go on without attempting to put her own point.*] They break up my lawyer's practice to put me under house arrest in this frightful building, surrounded by the dear memories of my childhood. Then, one fine day, the prodigal son consents to leave his room. They kill the fatted calf, kick me out of doors, and everybody is satisfied, starting with my own wife! What a wonderful story, isn't it? You can retail it in Hamburg. [*He goes to the desk and pours himself a glass of champagne, and drinks it. He becomes increasingly drunk up to the end of the Act.*] All the same, it would be as well for you not to pack your bags yet, because, you see, I'm not sure that I'll let them get away with it. [*Loudly*] I have the firm, and I'm keeping it. They'll see what I'm made of. [*He sits down at the desk and speaks in a calm and malicious voice with a hint of self-importance.*] Now leave me alone. I have to think. [*Pause.*]

JOHANNA [*slowly and in a cold and calm voice*]: It's not a question of the firm. No one wants to take that from you.

WERNER: No one except my father and his son.

JOHANNA: Franz won't take charge of the firm.

WERNER: Why not?

JOHANNA: He doesn't want to.

WERNER: He doesn't *want* to, or is it because he *can't*?

JOHANNA [*against her will*]: Both. [*Pause.*] And your father knows it.

WERNER: Then why?

JOHANNA: Because he wants to see Franz again before he dies.

WERNER [*slightly relieved, but defiant*]: It sounds crooked.

JOHANNA: Very crooked, but it's no concern of yours.
[WERNER *stands up and goes right over to her. He looks straight into her eyes, and she returns his look.*]

WERNER: I believe you. [*He drinks.* JOHANNA *annoyed, turns her head away.*] Good for nothing. [*He laughs.*] And a weakling into the bargain. On Sunday Father spoke about unhealthy fat.

JOHANNA [*quickly*]: Franz is nothing but skin and bone.

WERNER: Yes, with a shrunken stomach, like all prisoners. [*He looks at himself in the mirror and, almost unconsciously, throws out his chest.*] Good for nothing. In rags. Half cracked. [*He turns towards Johanna.*] Have you seen him ... often?

JOHANNA: Every day.

WERNER: I wonder what you find to say to each other. [*He moves with new assurance.*] 'There's no tree without a rotten branch.' I can't remember who said that. Terrible, but true, eh? Only up to now I thought I was the rotten branch. [*Placing his hands on Johanna's shoulders*] Thank you, my dear wife, you have rescued me. [*He goes to take his glass, but she prevents him.*] You're right; no more champagne. [*He sweeps the two glasses off with his hand, and they break on the floor.*] Send him some bottles from me. [*He laughs.*] As for you, you won't see him again. I forbid you.

JOHANNA [*still icy*]: Very well. Take me away from here.

WERNER: I tell you that you've rescued me. I was imagining things, you know. From now on everything will be all right.

JOHANNA: Not for me.

WERNER: No? [*He looks at her. His face changes, and his shoulders slump slightly.*] Even if I swear to you that I'll turn over a new leaf and put them all in their place?

JOHANNA: Not even then.

WERNER [*sharply*]: You two have been making love! [*A short laugh*] Say it; I won't mind. He only had to whistle and he had all the women running after him. [*He looks at her angrily.*] I asked you a question.

JOHANNA [*very hard*]: If you were to force me to reply, I should never forgive you.

WERNER: Reply and don't forgive.

JOHANNA: No.

WERNER: You don't make love. Good. But you're dying to do so.

JOHANNA [*coldly, but with a touch of hatred*]: You're a rotter.

WERNER [*smiling and malicious*]: I'm a Gerlach. Answer.

JOHANNA: No.

WERNER: Then what are you afraid of?

JOHANNA [*still icy*]: Before I knew you, death and madness fascinated me. It's beginning all over again up there, and I don't want it to. [*Pause.*] I believe in his crabs more than he does.

WERNER: Because you love him.

JOHANNA: Because they're true. Madmen often speak the truth, Werner.

WERNER: Really? Which truth?

JOHANNA: There's only one: the horror of living. [*Recovering her warmth*] I can't stand it! I can't stand it! I prefer to lie to myself. If you love me, save me. [*Pointing to the ceiling*] That lid is crushing me. Take me to some town where everyone is the same, where they all lie to themselves. With a wind, a wind which comes from afar. We shall find each other again, Werner, I swear it.

WERNER [*with a sudden and savage violence*]: Find each other again? Ha! And how could I have lost you, Johanna? I have never had you. Enough of that! I didn't need your sympathy. You cheated me on the deal. I wanted a wife, and I've only possessed her corpse. I don't care if you do go mad; we shall stay here. [*He mimics her.*] 'Defend me! Save me!' How? By clearing out? [*He controls himself, and smiles coldly and maliciously.*] I was carried away just now. Forgive me. You will do your best to be a good wife; that's your part in life. But the pleasure will be all yours. [*Pause.*] How far would we have to go for you to forget my brother? How far would we have to run? Trains, ships, planes; what a business, and how dreary! You'll look at everything with those empty eyes – the tragic woman de luxe – and that won't be much of a change for you. As for me, have you considered what I shall be thinking all that time? That I gave up in advance, and that I ran away without raising a finger. A coward, eh? A coward. That's what you would like me to be, and then you could comfort me. Maternally. [*Violently*] We'll stay here! Until one of the three of us dies; you, my brother, or me.

JOHANNA: How you hate me!

WERNER: I shall love you when I have won you. And I'm going to fight, don't worry. [*He laughs.*] I shall win. You only like strength, you women. And I'm the one who has strength.
[*He takes her by the waist and kisses her brutally. She strikes him with her clenched fists, releases herself and bursts into laughter.*]

JOHANNA [*laughing heartily*]: Oh, Werner, do you think he bites?

WERNER: Who? Franz?

JOHANNA: The ruffian you're trying to ape. [*Pause.*] If we stay, I shall visit your brother every day.

WERNER: I don't doubt it. And you'll spend every night in my bed. [*He laughs.*] It'll be easy to make the comparison.

JOHANNA [*sadly and slowly*]: Poor Werner! [*She goes towards the door.*]

WERNER [*suddenly bewildered*]: Where are you going?

JOHANNA [*with a malicious laugh*]: To make the comparison.
[*She opens the door and goes out. He makes no effort to stop her.*]

CURTAIN

ACT FOUR

Franz's room. The same decor as in Act Two, but all the placards have disappeared, leaving only the portrait of Hitler. There are no longer any oyster-shells on the floor. There is a desk-lamp on the table. Franz is alone.

FRANZ: Masked inhabitants of the ceilings, your attention, please! Masked inhabitants of the ceilings, your attention, please! [*Pause. He looks at the ceiling.*] Eh? [*Under his breath*] I can't feel them. [*Loudly*] Comrades! Comrades! Germany is speaking to you. Martyred Germany. [*Pause. He becomes despondent.*] This audience is stone cold. [*He gets up and starts to walk about.*] Strange and unfounded impression. This evening History is going to stop. Contact! The explosion of the planet is on the agenda, and the scientists have their finger on the button. Good-bye! [*Pause.*] Still, it would have been nice to know what would have become of the human race if it had survived. [*Angrily and almost violently*] I prostitute myself to please them, and they don't even listen. [*Warmly*] Dear listeners, I beg you, if I no longer have your ear, if the false witnesses have led you astray. . . . [*Sharply*] Wait! [*He searches in his pocket.*] I have the culprit. [*He brings out a wrist-watch and holds it in disgust by the end of the leather strap.*] I was given this beast as a present, and I was foolish enough to accept it. [*He looks at it.*] Fifteen minutes! Fifteen minutes late! Unpardonable. I'll smash this watch. [*He puts it on his wrist.*] Fifteen minutes. Sixteen now. [*Bursts out.*] How can I preserve my ageless patience if they annoy me with pin-pricks? It will all come to a sticky end. [*Pause.*] It's quite simple; I won't open the door. I'll keep her waiting two solid hours on the landing. [*There is a triple knock at the door. He hurries to open it, then steps back to allow* JOHANNA *to enter. He points to his wrist-watch.*]

FRANZ: Seventeen!

JOHANNA: What?

FRANZ [*imitating the speaking clock*]: Four, seventeen, and thirty seconds. Have you brought my brother's photo? [*Pause.*] Well?

JOHANNA [*unwillingly*]: Yes.

FRANZ: Show it to me.

JOHANNA [*still hesitant*]: What are you going to do with it?

FRANZ [*with an insolent laugh*]: What does one usually do with a photo?

JOHANNA [*after some hesitation*]: Here it is.

FRANZ [*looking at it*]: Well, I wouldn't have recognized him. He's quite an athlete. Congratulations! [*He puts the photo in his pocket.*] And how are our orphans?

JOHANNA [*at a loss*]: Which orphans?

FRANZ: You know. In Düsseldorf.

JOHANNA: Oh.... [*Quickly*] They're dead.

FRANZ [*addressing the ceiling*]: Crabs, there were seven hundred of them. Seven hundred poor kids without hearth or home... [*He checks himself.*] I'm fed up with those orphans, dear. Let them be buried as soon as possible. Good riddance. [*Pause.*] You see! That's what I've become because of you – a bad German.

JOHANNA: Because of me?

FRANZ: I ought to have known that she would upset everything. It took me five years to drive time out of this room, and you only needed a moment to bring it back. [*He shows her the watch.*] This wheedling beast that purrs on my wrist, and that I stuff into my pocket when I hear Leni knock at the door, is Universal Time, the time of the speaking clock, of the timetables and the observatories. What am I supposed to do with it? Am I universal? [*Looking at the watch*] I find this gift suspect.

JOHANNA: Then give it back to me.

FRANZ: Oh no. I'm keeping it. Only, I wonder why you gave it to me.

JOHANNA: Because I'm still living, just as you used to live.

FRANZ: What is living? Waiting for you? I wasn't expecting anything more for a thousand years. That lamp never goes out. Leni comes when she likes. I used to sleep off and on, when sleep overcame me. In short, I never knew what time it was. [*Peevishly*] Now I have the bustle of days and nights. [*Glancing at the watch*] Four twenty-five; the shadows are lengthening, and daylight is fading. I hate the afternoons. When you leave, it will be night, with the light full on here, and I shall be afraid. [*Suddenly*] When are they going to bury the poor little things?

JOHANNA: On Monday, I believe.

FRANZ: They must have a memorial chapel in the open air, in the ruins of the church. Seven hundred little coffins mourned by a crowd dressed in rags! [*He looks at her.*] You haven't put on any make-up?

JOHANNA: You can see I haven't.

FRANZ: An oversight?

JOHANNA: No; I didn't intend to come.

FRANZ [*violently*]: What?

JOHANNA: It's Werner's day. [*Pause.*] Yes, Saturday.

FRANZ: Why does he need a day when he has you every night? Saturday . . .? Ah, yes; the weekend. [*Pause.*] And Sunday as well, of course.

JOHANNA: Of course.

FRANZ: If I understand you rightly, it's Saturday. Ah, madam, the watch doesn't say so. You must give me a calendar. [*He laughs harshly, then speaks sharply.*] Two days without you? Impossible!

JOHANNA: Do you think that I should deprive my husband of the only moments when we can be together?

FRANZ: Why not? [*She laughs, and does not reply.*] Has he got rights over you? I'm sorry, but so have I.

JOHANNA [*with some violence*]: You? None. Not in the least.

FRANZ: Did I seek you out? [*Shouting*] When will you understand that this trivial waiting about is keeping me away from my job. The crabs can't understand, and they're getting suspicious. The false witnesses are winning. [*Insultingly*] Delilah!

JOHANNA [*breaking into a sarcastic laugh*]: Phew! [*She goes to him and looks at him insolently.*] And is this Samson? [*Laughing more than ever*] Samson! Samson! [*She stops laughing.*] I imagined him to be quite different.

FRANZ [*in a formidable voice*]: I *am* Samson. I'm carrying the centuries on my back, and if I straighten up they will crash. [*Pause. He resumes his natural voice, and speaks with bitter irony.*] Besides, I'm convinced that he was a poor fellow. [*He walks across the room.*] To be so dependent! [*Pause. He sits down.*] You annoy me, madam. [*Pause.*]

JOHANNA: I shan't annoy you any more.

FRANZ: What have you done?

JOHANNA: I've told Werner everything.

FRANZ: Good heavens! Why?

JOHANNA [*bitterly*]: I wonder.

FRANZ: Did he take it well?

JOHANNA: He took it very badly.

FRANZ [*upset and nervous*]: Is he leaving us? Is he taking you away?

JOHANNA: He's staying here.

FRANZ [*reassured*]: That's all right. [*He rubs his hands.*] Quite all right.

JOHANNA [*with bitter irony*]: You never take your eyes off me! But what do you see? [*She goes over to him, takes his head between her hands, and forces him to look at her.*] Look at me! Yes, like that. Now dare to tell me that everything is quite all right.

FRANZ [*he looks at her and releases himself*]: I can see, yes, I can see. You miss Hamburg. The easy life. Being admired and desired by men. [*Shrugging his shoulders*] That's important to you.

JOHANNA [*sadly and dully*]: Samson was just a poor fellow.

FRANZ: Yes, yes, yes. A poor fellow.
    [*He starts to walk sideways.*]

JOHANNA: What are you doing?

FRANZ [*in a deep, harsh voice*]: I'm walking crab-wise. [*Amazed at what he has just said*] What's that? [*Coming back to her and speaking naturally*] Why am I a poor fellow?

JOHANNA: Because you don't understand anything. [*Pause.*] We shall go through Hell.

FRANZ: Who?

JOHANNA: Werner, you, and me. [*A short pause.*] He's staying here out of jealousy.

FRANZ [*amazed*]: What?

JOHANNA: Out of jealousy. Is that clear? [*Pause. She shrugs her shoulders.*] You don't even know what it is. [FRANZ *laughs.*] He'll send me to you every day – even Sunday. He'll make a martyr of himself at the yard in his huge ministerial office, and I'll pay for it every evening.

FRANZ [*genuinely surprised*]: Pardon me, my dear, but *who* is he jealous of? [*She shrugs her shoulders. He takes out the photo and looks at it.*] Of me? [*Pause.*] Have you told him . . . what has become of me?

JOHANNA: Yes, I have.

FRANZ: And what does he say?

JOHANNA: Well, he's jealous.

FRANZ: He's being completely unreasonable. I'm ill, mad perhaps. I'm in hiding. The war has broken me, madam.

JOHANNA: It hasn't broken your pride.

FRANZ: Is that enough to make him jealous of me?

JOHANNA: Yes.

FRANZ: Tell him that my pride is shattered. Tell him that I boast as a defence. Wait! I'll debase myself completely. Tell Werner that I'm jealous.

JOHANNA: Of him?

FRANZ: Of his freedom, of his muscles, of his smile, of his wife, of his clear conscience. [*Pause.*] Well? What a sop for his pride.

JOHANNA: He won't believe me.

FRANZ: That's his bad luck. [*Pause.*] What about you?

JOHANNA: Me?

FRANZ: Do you believe me?

JOHANNA [*uncertain and annoyed*]: No, I don't.

FRANZ: There have been some indiscretions, madam. I know every minute of your private life.

JOHANNA [*shrugging her shoulders*]: Leni lies to you.

FRANZ: Leni never talks about you. [*Pointing to his watch*] It's the chatterbox. It tells everything. It starts to talk as soon as you leave me. Half past eight, family dinner. Ten o'clock, everyone retires; cosy chat with your husband. Eleven o'clock, evening toilet. Werner goes to bed, you take a bath. Midnight, you get into his bed.

JOHANNA [*with an insolent laugh*]: Into his bed? [*Pause.*] No.

FRANZ: Twin beds?

JOHANNA: Yes.

FRANZ: In which one do you make love?

JOHANNA [*exasperated, insolently*]: Sometimes in one, sometimes in the other.

FRANZ [*growls*]: Huh! [*He looks at the photo.*] Twelve stone. The athlete must crush you. Do you like that?

JOHANNA: If I chose it, it's because I prefer athletes to weaklings.

FRANZ [*he looks at the photo with a growl, then replaces it in his pocket*]: I haven't slept a wink for sixty hours.

JOHANNA: Why?

FRANZ: You shan't make love while I'm asleep.

JOHANNA [*with a dry laugh*]: Then don't sleep any more.

FRANZ: I don't intend to. When he takes you tonight, you'll know that I'm awake.

JOHANNA [*angrily*]: I am sorry to deprive you of your disgusting, solitary pleasures. Sleep tonight. Werner won't touch me.

FRANZ [*disconcerted*]: Oh!

JOHANNA: Are you disappointed?

FRANZ: No.

JOHANNA: He won't touch me again while we remain here because of him. [*Pause.*] Do you know what he thinks? That you have seduced me. [*Insultingly*] You! [*Pause.*] You two are alike.

FRANZ [*looking at the photo*]: We are not.

JOHANNA: Yes, you are. Two Gerlachs, two brothers both living in a dream world. And what am I? Nothing. An instrument of torture. You each look for the other's caresses on me. [*She comes up to him.*] Look at this body. [*She takes his hand and makes him place it on her shoulder.*] Before, when I lived among men, they didn't need to indulge in black mass in order to desire it. [*She repulses him and breaks away. Pause; then she speaks abruptly*] Your father wants to speak to you.

FRANZ [*coldly*]: Oh!

JOHANNA: If you will meet him, he will release Werner from his oath.

FRANZ [*calmly and coldly*]: And what then? Will you go away?

JOHANNA: That will depend entirely on Werner.

FRANZ [*still coldly*]: Do you want me to meet him?

JOHANNA: Yes.

FRANZ [*in the same tone*]: And must I give up seeing you?

JOHANNA: Of course.

FRANZ [*maintaining his cold manner*]: What will happen to me?

JOHANNA: You will go back to Eternity.

FRANZ: All right. [*Pause.*] Go and tell my father . . .

JOHANNA [*quickly*]: No.

FRANZ: What?

JOHANNA [*heatedly*]: No, I'll tell him nothing.

FRANZ [*impassive, thinking that he has won*]: I must give him my reply.

JOHANNA [*still angry*]: It's no good. I shan't tell him.

FRANZ: Then why did you convey his request?

JOHANNA: I didn't intend to.

FRANZ: Didn't intend to?

JOHANNA [*she gives a short laugh, and looks at him in hatred*]: Just imagine. I wanted to kill you.

FRANZ [*amiably*]: Oh! For how long?

JOHANNA: For the past five minutes.

FRANZ: And have you got over it now?

JOHANNA [*smiling and calm*]: I still feel like scratching your face. [*She draws the fingers of both hands down his face, and he makes no attempt to prevent her.*] Like this. [*She drops her hands and breaks away from him.*]

FRANZ [*still amiably*]: Five minutes. You're lucky. My desire to kill you lasts all night.

[*A short pause. She sits on the bed and looks into space, talking to herself.*]

JOHANNA: I shan't ever go away again.

FRANZ [*watching her closely*]: Never again?

JOHANNA [*without looking at him*]: Never again.

[*She utters a short wild laugh, opens her hands as though to let something fall and looks at her feet. FRANZ watches her, and his manner changes. He again becomes the madman, stiff and aloof as in Act Two.*]

FRANZ: Stay with me, then – all the time.

JOHANNA: In this room?

FRANZ: Yes.

JOHANNA: And never leave it? [FRANZ *nods.*] Lock myself up?

FRANZ: Yes. [*He walks about while speaking, and* JOHANNA *watches him. As he continues speaking, she recovers and hardens. She understands that Franz is merely seeking to protect his delirium.*] I have lived for twelve years on a roof of ice above the summits. I had cast into the night the teeming baubles.

JOHANNA [*suspicious already*]: What baubles?

FRANZ: The world, dear madam. The world where you live. [*Pause.*] That jumble of iniquity lives again. Through you. When you leave me, it surrounds me because you are in it. You crush me at the feet of Saxon Switzerland. I rave in a hunting lodge twenty feet above sea-level. The water is reborn around your flesh. Now the Elbe is flowing and the grass is growing. Woman is a traitor, madam.

JOHANNA [*in a low and hard voice*]: If I am betraying anyone, it is not you.

FRANZ: Yes, me. Me as well, you double agent. For twenty hours out of twenty-four, you see, you feel and you think beneath the soles of my feet with all the others. You subject me to ordinary laws. [*Pause.*] If I have you under lock and key – absolute peace. The world will return to the abyss, and you will be nothing but what you are. [*Pointing at her*] That! The crabs will trust me again, and I shall speak to them.

JOHANNA [*sarcastically*]: Will you speak to me sometimes?

FRANZ [*pointing to the ceiling*]: We shall speak to them together. [JOHANNA *bursts out laughing, and he looks at her in bewilderment.*] You refuse?

JOHANNA: What is there to refuse? You're relating a nightmare, and I'm listening. That's all.

FRANZ: Won't you leave Werner?

JOHANNA: I've told you I won't.

FRANZ: Then leave me. Here is your husband's photo. [*He gives it to her, and she takes it.*] As for the watch, it will enter Eternity at the third stroke precisely. [*He undoes the strap and looks at the watch.*] Pip! [*He throws it on the floor.*] From now on it will always be four-thirty. In remembrance of you, madam. Good-bye. [*He goes to the door, draws the bolt, and lifts the bar. A long pause. He bows and shows her the door. She goes slowly to the door, pushes the bolt back and lowers the bar. Then she comes up to him, calm and unsmiling, with real authority.*] Good! [*Pause.*] What are you going to do?

JOHANNA: What I have been doing since Monday. A shuttle service.

FRANZ: And suppose I don't open the door?

JOHANNA [*calmly*]: You will.

[FRANZ *stoops down, picks up the watch and holds it to his ear. His face changes and his voice takes on a certain warmth. From this point a real complicity is established between them for a time.*]

FRANZ: We're in luck; it's going. [*He looks at the watch.*] Four thirty-one; a minute past Eternity. Turn, you little hands, turn. We have to live. [*To Johanna*] How?

JOHANNA: I don't know.

FRANZ: We shall be three raving lunatics.

JOHANNA: Four.

FRANZ: Four?

JOHANNA: If you refuse to meet your father, he'll tell Leni.

FRANZ: He's quite capable of it.

JOHANNA: What would happen?

FRANZ: Leni doesn't like complications.

JOHANNA: Well?

FRANZ: She'll simplify matters.

JOHANNA [*picking up the revolver which is on* FRANZ's *table*]: With this?

FRANZ: With that, or some other way.

JOHANNA: In such cases women shoot the woman.

FRANZ: Leni is only half a woman.

JOHANNA: Are you worried about dying?

FRANZ: Frankly, yes. [*Pointing to the ceiling*] I haven't yet found the words that they understand. What about you?

JOHANNA: I wouldn't want Werner to be left alone.

FRANZ [*summing up, with a short laugh*]: We can neither live nor die.

JOHANNA: We can neither see each other nor leave each other.

FRANZ: We're in a hell of a fix. [*He sits down.*]

JOHANNA: We are.

> [*She sits on the bed. Silence.* FRANZ *turns his back on her and rubs two oyster-shells together.*]

FRANZ: There must be a way out.

JOHANNA: There isn't.

FRANZ [*fiercely*]: There must be one. [*He rubs the shells together with a wild and desperate violence.*] Mustn't there?

JOHANNA: Put those shells down. I can't stand it.

FRANZ: Be quiet! [*He throws the shells against the portrait of Hitler.*] Look what an effort I'm making. [*He half turns towards her and shows her how his hands are trembling.*] Do you know what makes me afraid?

JOHANNA: The way out? [*He nods assent, still tense.*] What is it?

FRANZ: Take it easy. [*He stands up and walks about agitatedly.*] Don't hurry me. All roads are closed, there isn't even the choice of a lesser evil. But there is one road that's never closed, since it leads nowhere – the worst one. Shall we take it?

JOHANNA [*cries out*]: No!

FRANZ: You see; you *do* know the way out.

JOHANNA [*passionately*]: We've been happy.

FRANZ: Happy in Hell?

JOHANNA [*taking him up, passionately*]: Happy in Hell! Yes. In spite of ourselves. I beg you, I implore you, let us stay as we are. Let us wait, without a word or a sign. [*She takes him by the arm.*] Don't let's change.

FRANZ: The others change, Johanna; the others will change us. [*Pause.*] Do you think Leni will let us live?

JOHANNA [*violently*]: Leni! I'll take care of her. If there's any shooting to be done, I'll shoot first.

FRANZ: Let's forget about Leni. Here we are, alone and face to face. What will happen?

JOHANNA [*with the same passion*]: Nothing will happen. Nothing will change. We shall be . . .

FRANZ: What will happen is that you will destroy me.

JOHANNA [*still passionately*]: Never!

FRANZ: You will destroy me slowly and surely by your very presence. Already my madness is falling in ruins. It was my refuge, Johanna. What will become of me when I see the light of day?

JOHANNA [*passionately*]: You will be cured.

FRANZ [*bursts out*]: Ha! [*Pause. Harsh laugh*] I shall be in my dotage.

JOHANNA: I shall never hurt you. I'm not thinking of curing you. Your madness is my cage. I turn round and round in it.

FRANZ [*with a sad and bitter tenderness*]: You turn round, little squirrel? Squirrels have good teeth. You will bite through the bars.

JOHANNA: It's not true. I don't even want to. I bow to your whims.

FRANZ: Yes, you do, that's pretty obvious. But your lies give you away.

JOHANNA [*tense*]: I never lie to you.

FRANZ: You do nothing but. Generously, virtuously, like a good little soldier. Only you lie very badly. To lie well, you have to be a lie yourself. That's what I am. You, you're true. When I look at you, I know that truth exists, and that it's not on my side. [*Laughing.*] If there are any orphans in Düsseldorf, I'll bet they're as fat as pigeons.

JOHANNA [*in a set and mechanical voice*]: They are dead. Germany is dead.

FRANZ [*brutally*]: Be quiet! [*Pause.*] Well? Do you know the worst road now? You open my eyes by trying to close them,

and I become your accomplice every time I find you out,
because . . . because I rely on you.

JOHANNA [*recovering a little*]: So we do the opposite of what
we want to do.

FRANZ: Exactly.

JOHANNA [*abruptly and scornfully*]: Well? What's the way out?

FRANZ: Let us each want what we have to do.

JOHANNA: Then I must want to destroy you?

FRANZ: We must help each other to want the truth.

JOHANNA: You will never want that. You're a fake, right to
the marrow of your bones.

FRANZ [*dry and distant*]: I had to defend myself, my dear.
[*Pause. More warmly*] I shall renounce my illusions when . . .
[*He hesitates.*]

JOHANNA: When?

FRANZ: When I love you more than my lies, and when you
love me in spite of my truth.

JOHANNA [*ironically*]: Have you a truth? What is it? What you
tell the crabs?

FRANZ [*pouncing on her words*]: What crabs? Are you mad?
What crabs? [*Pause. He turns away.*] Ah, yes, yes . . . [*With a
sudden thought*] The crabs are men. [*Pause.*] What? [*He sits
down.*] Where did I discover that? [*Pause.*] I knew it . . .
once . . . Yes, yes, yes. But I've got so much on my mind.
[*Pause. In a decided tone*] Real men, good and handsome, on
all the balconies of the centuries. When I was crawling in the
yard, I thought I heard them saying: 'What's that, brother?'
And that . . . was me. [*He stands up, springs to attention, gives
a military salute and speaks in a loud voice.*] I, the Crab. [*He
turns towards Johanna, and speaks familiarly to her*] Well, I
said no; men won't judge my time. What will they be, after
all? The sons of our sons. Are brats allowed to condemn
their grandfathers? I turned the tables, and I cried: 'Here is
man; after me, the deluge; after the deluge, *you*, the crabs!'

All unmasked, the balconies swarming with arthropods.
[*Solemnly*] You must know that the human race started off
on the wrong foot, but I put the lid on its fabulous ill-fortune
by handing over its mortal remains to the Court of the
Crustaceans. [*Pause. He walks sideways slowly.*] Good. They
will be men. [*He laughs gently in an absent-minded way, and
walks backwards towards the portrait of Hitler.*] Men, you see
that! [*Bristling suddenly*] Johanna, I challenge their competence. I take the matter out of their hands, and I pass it over
to you. Judge me.

JOHANNA [*more resigned than surprised*]: Judge you?

FRANZ [*shouting*]: Are you deaf? [*His violence gives way to
anxious surprise.*] What's that? [*He recovers himself, with a dry,
sinister and almost conceited laugh.*] You shall judge me, by
Heaven, you shall judge me.

JOHANNA: Only yesterday you were the witness. The witness
for Mankind.

FRANZ: Yesterday was yesterday. [*He passes his hand across his
brow.*] The witness for Mankind ... [*Laughing*] And who
should that be? Come, madam, it's Mankind. A child could
guess that. The accused testifies for himself. I see that there
is a vicious circle. [*With sombre pride*] I am Mankind, Johanna,
I am every man, and all Mankind, I am the Century. [*A
brief clownish humility*] Like anyone.

JOHANNA: In that case, I shall be trying someone else.

FRANZ: Who?

JOHANNA: Anyone.

FRANZ: The accused promises to be exemplary. I ought to give
evidence for the defence, but I'll indict myself, if you wish.
[*Pause.*] Of course, you're free, but if you abandon me without hearing me and for fear of knowing me, you will have
passed sentence in any case. Decide. [*Pause. He points to the
ceiling.*] I tell them whatever comes into my head. Never any
reply. I tell them jokes as well, funny stories. I've got to the

point of wondering whether they swallow them, or whether they are holding them against me. A pyramid of silence over my head. A silent millennium. That's killing me. And what if they don't even know I exist? What if they have forgotten me? What is to become of me without a trial? What contempt! 'You can do what you like; nobody cares!' Well, don't I come into it? If a life is not sanctioned, the earth consumes it. That was the Old Testament. Here is the New. You shall be the future and the present; the world and myself. Beyond you there is nothing. You will make me forget the centuries. I shall live. You will listen to me, and I shall surprise your looks; I shall hear you reply to me. One day, perhaps, in years to come, you will recognize my innocence, and I shall know it. What a day of joyous celebration! You will be all to me, and all will acquit me. [*Pause.*] Johanna, is it possible? [*Pause.*]

JOHANNA: Yes.

FRANZ: Is it still possible to love me?

JOHANNA [*with a sad smile, but deeply sincere*]: Unfortunately, yes. [FRANZ *stands up. He appears relieved, almost happy. He goes to Johanna and takes her in his arms.*]

FRANZ: I shall never again be alone . . . [*He is about to kiss her, then he suddenly breaks away and resumes his hard and wild manner.* JOHANNA *looks at him, understands that he has again retreated into his solitude, and she in turn hardens, with a bitter irony, turned only against herself.*] I beg your pardon, Johanna; it's a little too soon to corrupt the judge whom I have appointed over myself.

JOHANNA: I'm not your judge. One doesn't judge those whom one loves.

FRANZ: And suppose you stop loving me? Won't that be a judgement? The final judgement?

JOHANNA: How could I?

FRANZ: By learning who I am.

JOHANNA: I already know.

FRANZ [*rubbing his hands with a cheerful air*]: Oh, no. Not at all! Not at all! [*Pause. He looks quite mad.*] A day will come, just like any other day, I shall talk about myself, and you will listen, then, suddenly, love will be shattered. You will look at me with horror, and I shall again become [*going down on his hands and knees and walking sideways*] . . . a crab.

JOHANNA [*looking at him in horror*]: Stop!

FRANZ [*on his hands and knees*]: You will look at me with those eyes, exactly like that. [*He stands up quickly.*] Condemned, eh? Condemned without right of appeal. [*In a changed voice, ceremonious and optimistic*] Of course, it is just as likely that I may be acquitted.

JOHANNA [*tense and contemptuous*]: I'm not sure that you want to be.

FRANZ: Madam, I want to get it over with, one way or the other. [*Pause.*]

JOHANNA: You've won. Hurray! If I go, I condemn you, and if I stay, you sow mistrust between us. I can already see it in your eyes. Well, let's carry on with it. Let's do our best to degrade ourselves together. Let us take great pains to debase each other. We shall make our love into an instrument of torture. We'll drink, shall we? You'll go back to your champagne; mine was always whisky. I'll bring some. Both of us with a bottle, face to face and alone. [*With a bitter smile*] Do you know what we shall be, witness for Mankind? A couple like any other couple. [*She pours herself some champagne and raises her glass.*] I drink to us. [*She drains the glass and throws it at the portrait of Hitler. The glass breaks as it hits the portrait. She takes an armchair from the heap of broken furniture, sets it up and sits in it.*] Well?

FRANZ [*disconcerted*]: Johanna . . . do you mean . . .?

JOHANNA: I'm asking the questions. Well? What have you to say?

FRANZ: You haven't understood me. If it were only us two, I swear . . .

JOHANNA: Who else is there?

FRANZ [*with an effort*]: My sister Leni. If I decide to speak, it's to save us from her. I shall say . . . what there is to say, without sparing myself, and in my own way, little by little. It will take months, years, it doesn't matter. I only ask you to trust me, and I shall trust you, if you promise you'll believe no one but me.

[*She looks at him for a time, and speaks more gently.*]

JOHANNA: Right, I'll only believe you.

FRANZ [*with a touch of solemnity, but sincerely*]: So long as you keep that promise, Leni will have no power over us. [*He sits down.*] I was afraid. You were in my arms, I desired you, I was about to live . . . and all of a sudden I saw my sister, and I said to myself: she'll smash us. [*He takes a handkerchief from his pocket and mops his brow.*] Whew! [*In a low voice*] It's summer, isn't it? It must be hot. [*Pause. He looks into space.*] Do you know that he has made me into a rather formidable machine?

JOHANNA: Your father?

FRANZ: Yes. A machine to give orders. [*A short laugh. Pause.*] Another summer, and the machine is still turning. Empty as usual. [*He stands up.*] I'll tell you my life, but don't expect any great villainies. Oh no, not even that. Do you know why I reproach myself? I've done nothing. [*The light fades slowly.*] Nothing! Nothing! Never!

A WOMAN'S VOICE [*softly*]: Soldier!

JOHANNA [*not hearing the woman*]: You were in the war.

FRANZ: I was in it, all right. [*The lights fade.*]

WOMAN'S VOICE [*louder*]: Soldier!

FRANZ: [*He is standing downstage, and only he is visible.* JOHANNA, *seated in the armchair, is now in darkness.*] It's not a matter of being in the war; it's what war does to us. While the fighting was on, I had a good laugh. I was a civilian in uniform. One night I became a soldier for good. [*He takes an officer's hat from the table behind him and places it on his head with a sharp movement.*] A poor tramp, defeated, useless. I was crossing Germany on the way back from Russia, hiding, and I came to a ruined village.

WOMAN'S VOICE [*louder, from the darkness*]: Soldier!

FRANZ: What's that? [*He turns sharply. He has an electric torch in his left hand, and with his right hand he draws his revolver from his holster. The torch is not alight.*] Who's calling me?

WOMAN: Take a look around.

FRANZ: How many are you?

WOMAN: There's nobody left up where you are. There's just me, on the ground. [FRANZ *quickly lights the torch and shines it on the floor. A woman in black is huddled against the wall, half-lying on the floor.*] Put that out! You're blinding me. [FRANZ *puts out the torch. They can be seen in the diffused light which surrounds them.*] Ha! Ha! Shoot, then! Shoot! Finish your war by murdering a German woman!

[FRANZ *becomes aware that, without noticing it, he has trained his revolver on the woman. Horrified, he puts it back in its holster.*]

FRANZ: What are you doing there?

WOMAN: You can see, I'm up against the wall. [*Proudly*] It's my wall. The strongest one in the village. The only one left standing.

FRANZ: Come with me.

WOMAN: Light your torch. [*He lights it, the pool of light showing on the floor. It reveals a blanket which covers the woman from head to foot.*] Look! [*She raises the blanket a little, and he shines the torch on what she is showing him, but it is unseen by the audience. Then, with a grunt, he quickly switches off the torch.*] Yes, those were my legs.

FRANZ: What can I do for you?

WOMAN: Sit down a minute. [*He sits down near her.*] I've got one of our soldiers up against the wall. [*Pause.*] That's all I wanted. [*Pause.*] I was hoping that it would be my brother, but he was killed in Normandy. Never mind. You'll do. I would have said to him: 'Look!' [*Pointing to the ruins of the village*] 'That's your doing!'

FRANZ: His doing?

WOMAN [*speaking directly to Franz*]: And yours, son.

FRANZ: Why?

WOMAN [*as though stating an obvious fact*]: You let yourself be beaten.

FRANZ: Don't talk rubbish. [*He gets up quickly, facing the woman. He sees a poster, previously invisible, but now lighted by a spotlight. It is posted on the wall to the right of the woman, about six feet from the ground, and reads:* YOU ARE GUILTY!] Again! They've put them everywhere. [*He goes to tear it down.*]

WOMAN [*looking at him with her head thrown back*]: Leave it! Leave it, I tell you! It's *my* wall. [FRANZ *draws back.*] You are guilty. [*She reads it and points to him.*] You, my brother, all of you.

FRANZ: You agree with what they say?

WOMAN: As night follows day. They're telling God that we're cannibals and God listens to them because they have won. But I'll always believe that the real cannibal is the victor. Admit it, soldier, you didn't want to eat human flesh.

FRANZ [*wearily*]: We've destroyed. Destroyed! Towns and villages! Capital cities!

WOMAN: They've destroyed more; that's why they've beaten you. [FRANZ *shrugs his shoulders.*] Have you eaten human flesh?

FRANZ: What about your brother? Has he?

WOMAN: Not likely. He kept his good manners. Like you.

FRANZ [*after a pause*]: Have they told you about the camps?

WOMAN: What camps?

FRANZ: You know very well – the extermination camps.

WOMAN: I've heard about them.

FRANZ: If you were told that your brother, when he was killed, was a guard in one of those camps, would you be proud?

WOMAN [*fiercely*]: Yes. You listen to me, my boy; if my brother had thousands of dead on his conscience, if among those dead there were women like me, children like those who are rotting under those stones there, I should be proud of him. I would know that he is in Heaven, and that he has the right to think: 'I did what I could.' But I know him. He loved us less than his honour, less than his virtues. That's it! [*Violently, with a sweeping gesture*] What we needed was a Terror – you should have wiped out everything.

FRANZ: We did.

WOMAN: Never enough. Not enough camps. Not enough executioners. You betrayed us by giving away what didn't belong to you. Every time you spared an enemy life, even in the cradle, you took one of ours. You wanted to fight without hatred, and you have infected me with the hatred which is eating out my heart. Where is your virtue, you poor soldier, you routed soldier, where is your honour? You are guilty. God won't judge you by your deeds, but by what you haven't dared to do, by the crimes which should have been committed, and which you didn't commit. [*The lights have faded gradually, leaving only the poster visible. The voice continues, slowly dying away*] You are guilty! You're guilty! You! You! [*The light fades from the poster, leaving the stage in complete darkness.*]

FRANZ [*in darkness*]: Johanna!

[*The lights come on.* FRANZ *is standing bare-headed near the table.* JOHANNA *is seated in the armchair. The woman has disappeared.*]

JOHANNA [*with a start*]: What?

[FRANZ *goes towards her. He looks at her steadily.*]

FRANZ: Johanna! [*He looks at her, trying to banish his memories.*]

JOHANNA [*drawing back rather coldly*]: What happened to her?

FRANZ: The woman? That depends.

JOHANNA [*surprised*]: On what?

FRANZ: My dreams.

JOHANNA: Wasn't it a memory?

FRANZ: It was also a dream. Sometimes I take her with me, sometimes I leave her there, and sometimes . . . In any case, she dies. It's a nightmare. [*He looks at her fixedly, and talks to himself.*] I wonder whether I killed her.

JOHANNA [*not surprised, but with fear and disgust*]: Ah! [*He laughs.*]

FRANZ [*with a gesture, as though pulling a trigger*]: Like that. [*Smiling defiantly*] Would you have left her to suffer? There are crimes along all the roads. Prefabricated crimes which are only awaiting their criminals. The real soldier comes along and does the job. [*Sharply*] Don't you like history? I don't like your eyes. Ah! Finish her off any way you like. [*He strides away, and turns near the table.*] 'You are guilty!' What do you say? Was she right?

JOHANNA [*shrugging her shoulders*]: She was mad.

FRANZ: Yes. What does that prove?

JOHANNA [*strong and clear*]: We lost because we were short of men and planes.

FRANZ [*interrupting her*]: I know. I know. That was Hitler's fault. [*Pause.*] I'm talking about myself. War was my lot. To what point should I have loved it? [*She wants to speak.*] Think! Think carefully! Your answer will be decisive.

JOHANNA [*ill at ease, annoyed and hard*]: I have thought.

FRANZ [*after a pause*]: If indeed I had committed all the crimes that were condemned at Nuremberg. . . .

JOHANNA: What crimes?

FRANZ: How should I know! Genocide and the whole works.

JOHANNA [*shrugging her shoulders*]: Why should you have committed them?

FRANZ: Because war was my lot. When our fathers put our mothers in the family way, they made soldiers. I don't know why.

JOHANNA: A soldier is a man.

FRANZ: He's a soldier first and foremost. Well? Would you still love me? [*She wants to speak.*] But take your time, for God's sake! [*She remains silent.*] Well?

JOHANNA: No.

FRANZ: You would no longer love me? [*She signifies no.*] Would I horrify you?

JOHANNA: Yes.

FRANZ [*bursting into laughter*]: Good, good, good. Rest assured, Johanna, you're dealing with a virgin. Guaranteed innocent. [*She remains hard and challenging.*] You can have a good laugh at me. I killed Germany through being sentimental.

[*The door of the bathroom opens.* KLAGES *enters, closes the door and goes slowly over to sit in Franz's chair. Neither* FRANZ *nor* JOHANNA *pays any attention to him.*]

FRANZ: There were five hundred of us near Smolensk. Holding on to a village. Major killed, captains killed, two of us left, two lieutenants and a sergeant-major. A hell of a triumvirate. Lieutenant Klages was a pastor's son, an idealist, up in the clouds . . . Heinrich, the sergeant-major, had his feet on the ground, but he was a hundred-per-cent Nazi. The partisans had cut us off from the rear, and they had the road under fire. Three days' rations left. We had found two Russian peasants, locked them in a barn, and given the prisoners a baptism.

KLAGES: What a brute!

FRANZ [*without turning round*]: What?

KLAGES: Heinrich! What a brute, I said.

FRANZ [*vaguely, still without turning round*]: Ah, ye —

KLAGES [*piteously, but with ominous undertones*]: I'm in a hell of a mess, Franz. [FRANZ *turns quickly towards him.*] The two peasants; he's determined to make them talk.

FRANZ: Ah! [*Pause.*] And you don't want him to give them the once-over?

KLAGES: Am I wrong?

FRANZ: That's not the question.

KLAGES: What is it, then?

FRANZ: Have you forbidden him to go into the barn? [KLAGES *nods.*] Then he mustn't go in.

KLAGES: You know very well he'll take no notice of me.

FRANZ [*pretending indignation and astonishment*]: What?

KLAGES: I can't find the words.

FRANZ: What words?

KLAGES: The words to convince him.

FRANZ [*astounded*]: You want him to be convinced as well? [*Brutally*] Treat him like a dog. Make him crawl!

KLAGES: I can't. If I despise a man, only one, even a butcher, I'll never again have any respect for anyone.

FRANZ: If any subordinate, just one, refuses to obey you, you'll never again be obeyed by anyone. I don't care tuppence about respect for man, but if you throw discipline to the winds, we'll be routed or massacred, or both.

KLAGES [*he goes to the door, half opens it and peeps through*]: He's outside the barn. He's on the look-out. [*He closes the door and turns towards Franz.*] Let's spare them!

FRANZ: You will save them if you save your authority.

KLAGES: I thought. . . .

FRANZ: What?

KLAGES: Heinrich listens to you as though you were God.

FRANZ: Because I treat him like dirt. It's understandable.

KLAGES [*embarrassed*]: If the order came from you . . . [*Appealing*] Franz!

FRANZ: No. The prisoners come under you. If I gave an order instead of you, I would undermine you. And if I were to be killed in an hour's time, after having knocked the props from under you, Heinrich would take sole command. That would be a catastrophe: for my men because he's stupid, and for your prisoners because he's vicious. [*He crosses the room and goes over to Johanna.*] Especially for Klages. Even though he was a lieutenant, Heinrich would have bumped him off.

JOHANNA: Why?

FRANZ: Klages hoped for our defeat.

KLAGES: I don't hope for it; I want it.

FRANZ: You have no right.

KLAGES: It'll be the end of Hitler.

FRANZ: And of Germany. [*Laughing*] Kaput! Kaput! [*Turning back to Johanna*] He was the champion of mental reservation. He condemned the Nazis in spirit, to hide the fact that he was serving them in the flesh.

JOHANNA: He wasn't serving them.

FRANZ [*to Johanna*]: Go on! You're just the same. His hands served them, his voice served them. He said to God: 'I don't like what I'm doing,' but he did it. [*Turning back to Klages*] You don't want anything to do with the war, and by refusing to take part, you condemn yourself to impotence. You've sold your soul for nothing, you moralist. I'll sell mine to some purpose. [*Pause.*] Win the war first, then we'll take care of Hitler.

KLAGES: It'll be too late then.

FRANZ: We'll see. [*Turning threateningly to Johanna*] I had been deceived, madam, and I had decided that I wouldn't be deceived again.

JOHANNA: Who deceived you?

FRANZ: You're asking me? Luther. [*Laughing*] See! Understand! I sent Luther to the Devil, and I went off. War was my destiny, and I desired it with all my soul. I acted, at last. I interpreted the orders. I was at one with myself.

JOHANNA: To act means to kill?

FRANZ [*to Johanna*]: That's acting. Writing one's name.

KLAGES: On what?

FRANZ [*to Klages*]: On what's there. I write mine on those fields there. I'll take responsibility for the war as though I were carrying it on alone, and then, when I've won, I'll sign on again.

JOHANNA [*very abruptly*]: What about the prisoners, Franz?

FRANZ [*turning to her*]: Eh?

JOHANNA: You who take responsibility for everything; did you take responsibility for them?

FRANZ [*after a pause*]: I got them out of it. [*To Klages*] How can I give him the order without undermining your authority? Wait a bit! [*He thinks.*] I know. [*He goes to the door, opens it, and calls out*] Heinrich! [*He goes back to the table.* HEINRICH *runs in.*]

HEINRICH [*standing to attention and giving a military salute*]: Here, lieutenant!

   [*When he addresses Franz, his face breaks into a happy, confident, almost tender smile.* FRANZ *goes over to him slowly, and inspects him from head to foot.*]

FRANZ: You're becoming careless, sergeant-major. [*Pointing to a button which is hanging by a thread through a buttonhole.*] What's this?

HEINRICH: It's . . . er . . . it's a button, lieutenant.

FRANZ [*good-naturedly*]: You'll lose it, my friend. [*He pulls it off with a sudden jerk and holds it in his left hand.*] You'll sew it on.

HEINRICH [*disconsolate*]: No one has any cotton left, lieutenant.

FRANZ: You dare to answer back, you pig's offal! [*He slaps him hard on the face with his right hand.*] Pick it up! [*He drops the button. The sergeant-major stoops down to pick it up.*] Attention! [*The sergeant-major picks up the button and springs to attention.*] Lieutenant Klages and I have decided to change duties every week as from today. In a moment you will escort him to the outposts. I'll take over his duties till Monday. Dismiss!

[HEINRICH *gives a military salute.*] Wait! [*To Klages*] I believe there are some prisoners.

KLAGES: Two.

FRANZ: Very well. I'll take charge of them.

HEINRICH [*his eyes sparkling, believing that Franz will accept his suggestions*]: Lieutenant.

FRANZ [*brutally, with an air of astonishment*]: What?

HEINRICH: They're partisans.

FRANZ: Possibly. Well?

HEINRICH: If you would allow me . . .

KLAGES: I have already forbidden you to touch them.

FRANZ: You hear, Heinrich? That's an order. Get out!

KLAGES: Wait! Do you know what he said to me?

HEINRICH: I . . . I was joking, lieutenant.

FRANZ [*raising his eyebrows*]: With a superior officer? [*To Klages*] What did he say to you?

KLAGES: 'What will you do if I don't obey you?'

FRANZ [*coldly*]: Oh! [*He turns to Heinrich.*] I'll answer you now, sergeant-major. If you don't obey . . . [*Tapping his revolver-holster*] I'll put a bullet through you. [*Pause.*]

KLAGES [*to Heinrich*]: Escort me to the outposts.

[*He exchanges a wink with* FRANZ, *and goes out behind* HEINRICH.]

FRANZ: Was it right to kill my soldiers?

JOHANNA: You didn't kill them.

FRANZ: I didn't do *everything* to stop them being killed.

JOHANNA: The prisoners wouldn't have talked.

FRANZ: How do you know?

JOHANNA: Peasants? They had nothing to tell.

FRANZ: Does that prove that they weren't partisans?

JOHANNA: Partisans don't usually talk.

FRANZ: Usually they didn't. [*Insistently, with an air of madness*] Germany is worth a crime, isn't she? [*Cynical, with an almost clownish offhandedness*] I don't know if I'm making myself

understood. You are already another generation. [*Pause.
Hard, violent, earnest, without looking at her, his eyes staring,
standing almost at attention.*] A short life, with a first-class
death. March! March! Plunge into the ultimate horrors. To
Hell and beyond! A powder magazine! I would have blown
it up in the darkness. Everything would have gone up except
my country. For a moment I would have been the cluster
spinning above a mighty firework display, and then nothing
more. The night and my name alone on the brass. [*Pause.*]
Let's admit that I shirked it. Principles, my dear, principles.
You can guess that I preferred my own soldiers to those two
unknown prisoners. Nevertheless, I had to say no. Would
that make me a cannibal? Pardon me. A vegetarian, rather.
[*Pause. Pompously and in a legal manner*] He who does not do
all does nothing – I did nothing. He who has done nothing is
nobody. Nobody? [*Pointing to himself, as though answering a
roll-call*] Present! [*Pause. To Johanna*] That's the first point
of the case for the prosecution.

JOHANNA: I acquit you.

FRANZ: I tell you, it must be debated.

JOHANNA: I love you.

FRANZ: Johanna! [*There is a knock at the landing door: five, four,
then twice three. They look at each other.*] Well, it was a little late.

JOHANNA: Franz . . .

FRANZ: A little late to acquit me. [*Pause.*] Father has talked.
[*Pause.*] Johanna, you're going to witness an execution.

JOHANNA [*looking at him*]: Yours? [*The knocking begins again.*]
And will you allow yourself to be throttled? [*Pause.*] Don't
you love me then?

FRANZ [*laughing silently*]: I'll talk to you about our love in a
moment . . . [*Pointing to the door*] . . . in front of her. It won't
be nice. And remember this; I'll ask for your help and you
won't give it to me. [*Pause.*] If there's any chance left . . . Go
in there!

[*He pulls her to the bathroom, and she goes in. He closes the bathroom door, and then goes to open the landing door to* LENI. *He quickly takes off his wrist-watch and puts it into his pocket.* LENI *comes in, carrying a plate with a small iced Savoy cake on it. There are four candles on the cake. She is carrying a newspaper under her left arm.*]

FRANZ: Why are you disturbing me at this time of day?

LENI: Do you know what time it is?

FRANZ: I know that you've only just left me.

LENI: Did it seem such a short time to you?

FRANZ: Yes. [*Pointing to the cake*] What's that?

LENI: A little cake. I would have given it to you tomorrow for your dessert.

FRANZ: Well?

LENI: You see, I'm bringing it to you this evening. With candles.

FRANZ: Why candles?

LENI: Count them.

FRANZ: One, two, three, four. Well?

LENI: You're thirty-four.

FRANZ: I was – on February the fifteenth.

LENI: The fifteenth of February was a birthday.

FRANZ: And what's today?

LENI: A date.

FRANZ: Good. [*He takes the cake and carries it to the table.*] 'Franz.' Was it you who wrote my name?

LENI: Who else?

FRANZ: Fame! [*He looks at his name.*] 'Franz' in pink icing. Prettier and more flattering than brass. [*He lights the candles.*] Burn slowly, candles. As you burn out, so will I. [*Casually*] Have you seen father?

LENI: He came to see me.

FRANZ: In your room?

LENI: Yes.

FRANZ: Did he stay long?

LENI: Long enough.

FRANZ: In your room. That's a special favour.

LENI: I'll pay for it.

FRANZ: So will I.

LENI: You will.

FRANZ [*cutting the cake in two*]: This is my body. [*Pouring champagne into two glasses*] This is my blood. [*Handing the cake to Leni*] Help yourself. [*She smiles and shakes her head.*] Poisoned?

LENI: Why should it be?

FRANZ: You're right. Why? [*He offers her a glass.*] Will you drink a toast? [LENI *takes the glass, and looks at it suspiciously.*] A crab?

LENI: Lipstick. [*He takes the glass from her and smashes it against the table.*]

FRANZ: It's yours. You can't wash up properly. [*He offers her the filled glass. She takes it. He pours champagne into a third glass for himself.*] Drink to me!

LENI: To you! [*She raises her glass.*]

FRANZ: To me! [*He clinks his glass against hers.*] What do you wish me?

LENI: That nothing should happen.

FRANZ: Nothing? Oh! Anything else? An excellent idea. [*Raising his glass*] I drink to nothing. [*He drinks and puts down his glass.* LENI *sways, and he catches her in his arms and leads her to the armchair.*] Sit down, little sister.

LENI [*sitting down*]: Excuse me, I'm tired. [*Pause.*] And the hardest part is still to come.

FRANZ: You're right. [*He mops his brow.*]

LENI [*as though to herself*]: I'm freezing. Another rotten summer.

FRANZ [*amazed*]: It's stifling.

LENI [*agreeably*]: Is it? Perhaps it is. [*She looks at him.*]

FRANZ: Why are you looking at me like that?

LENI [*after a pause*]: You've changed. It should show.

FRANZ: Doesn't it, then?

LENI: No, I see *you*. It's deceptive. [*Pause.*] It's no one's fault, my dear. You should have loved me, but I suppose you couldn't.

FRANZ: I loved you a lot.

LENI [*violently angry*]: Be quiet! [*She masters herself, but to the end her voice remains very hard.*] Father tells me that you've met our sister-in-law.

FRANZ: She comes to see me occasionally. A very nice girl. I'm pleased for Werner's sake. What was it you told me? She isn't a hunchback.

LENI: She is.

FRANZ: She isn't. [*Drawing a line down with his hand*] She's . . .

LENI: Yes, her back is straight enough. But that doesn't stop her from being a hunchback. [*Pause.*] Do you think she's beautiful?

FRANZ: Do you?

LENI: Beautiful as death.

FRANZ: It's funny you should say that. I thought the same myself.

LENI: I drink to her! [*She empties her glass and throws it away.*]

FRANZ [*casually*]: Are you jealous?

LENI: I feel nothing.

FRANZ: No, it's too soon.

LENI: Much too soon. [*Pause.* FRANZ *takes a piece of cake and eats it. He points to the cake and laughs.*]

FRANZ: A gag for the rascal, eh? [*He holds his piece of cake in his left hand, while he opens the drawer with his right hand, takes out the revolver, and still eating the cake, hands it to* LENI.] Here!

LENI: What should I do with it?

FRANZ [*showing her*]: Shoot. And leave her alone.

LENI [*laughing*]: Put it back in the drawer. I don't even know how to use it.

FRANZ [*still holding the revolver on the palm of his outstretched hand*]: You won't harm her?

LENI: Have I looked after her for thirteen years? Have I begged for her caresses? Swallowed her insults? Have I fed her, washed her, clothed her, defended her against everyone? She owes me nothing, and I shan't touch her. I want her to suffer a little, but only because of my love for you.

FRANZ [*a statement rather than a question*]: Do I owe everything to you?

LENI [*fiercely*]: Everything!

FRANZ [*pointing to the revolver*]: Take it, then.

LENI: You'd love me to. What a memory you would leave her! And wouldn't she make a fine widow! She's cut out for it. [*Pause.*] I'm not thinking of killing you, my love, and there's nothing in the world I fear more than your death. Only I'm obliged to hurt you deeply. I intend to tell Johanna everything.

FRANZ: Everything?

LENI: Everything. I'll shatter her love for you. [FRANZ's *hand tightens on the revolver.*] Go on, shoot your poor sister. I've written a letter in case of accidents. Johanna will get it this evening. [*Pause.*] Do you think I'm getting my revenge?

FRANZ: Aren't you?

LENI: I'm doing what's right. Dead or alive, it's right that you should belong to me, for I'm the only one who loves you as you are.

FRANZ: The only one? [*Pause.*] Yesterday, I would have committed murder. Today I see a gleam of hope. One chance in a hundred that she'll accept me. [*Replacing the revolver in the drawer*] If you're still alive, Leni, it's because I've decided to play this chance to the end.

LENI: Very well, let her know what I know, and we'll see who wins. [*She stands up and goes to the bathroom door. In passing behind him, she throws the newspaper on the table.* FRANZ *starts.*]

FRANZ: What's that?

LENI: The *Frankfurter Zeitung*. There's an article about us.

FRANZ: You and me?

LENI: The family. They're doing a series: 'The giants who have rebuilt Germany.' Honour where it's due. They start with the Gerlachs.

FRANZ [*undecided whether or not to take the newspaper*]: Is father a giant?

LENI [*pointing to the article*]: That's what they say. You've only to read it. They say he's the greatest of the lot.

[FRANZ *picks up the paper with a kind of hoarse growl and opens it. He is seated facing the audience with his back to the bathroom, his head hidden by the opened paper.* LENI *knocks on the bathroom door.*]

LENI: Open up! I know you're there.

JOHANNA [*opening the door*]: All right. I don't like hiding. [*In a friendly tone*] Hallo!

LENI [*likewise*]: Hallo!

[JOHANNA, *worried, pushes past Leni and goes straight over to Franz and looks at him as he is reading.*]

JOHANNA: Newspapers? [FRANZ *does not even turn round. She turns to Leni.*] You're moving fast.

LENI: I'm in a hurry.

JOHANNA: In a hurry to kill him?

LENI [*shrugging her shoulders*]: Of course not.

JOHANNA: Run! We've beaten you to it. From today I'm sure he'll be able to bear the truth.

LENI: That's funny. He's also sure that you'll be able to bear the truth.

JOHANNA [*smiling*]: I'll bear anything. Did your father tell you?

LENI: Yes, he did.

JOHANNA: He threatened me he would. It was he who told me how to get in here.

LENI: Oh!

JOHANNA: Didn't he tell you that?

LENI: No.

JOHANNA: He's using us.

LENI: So it seems.

JOHANNA: And you don't mind?

LENI: No.

JOHANNA: What do you want?

LENI [pointing to Franz]: I want you to get out of his life.

JOHANNA: I never will.

LENI: I'll make you.

JOHANNA: Try! [Pause.]

FRANZ [puts down the paper, gets up and goes right up to Johanna]: You promised to believe only me, Johanna. This is the time to remind you of your promise. Today our love depends completely on that.

JOHANNA: I shall only believe you. [They look at each other. She smiles at him tenderly and confidently, but FRANZ's face is pale and twitching. He forces a smile, turns, goes back to his seat and picks up his paper again.] Well, Leni?

LENI: There are two of us. One too many. We'll see which one it is.

JOHANNA: How?

LENI: We need a real test. If you win, you'll take my place.

JOHANNA: You'll cheat.

LENI: I don't need to.

JOHANNA: Why?

LENI: You're sure to lose.

JOHANNA: Let's have the test.

LENI: Right! [Pause.] Has he told you about Sergeant-Major Heinrich and some Russian prisoners? Did he accuse himself of condemning his comrades to death by saving the life of two partisans?

JOHANNA: Yes.

LENI: And did you tell him he was right?

JOHANNA [*sarcastically*]: You know everything.

LENI: Don't be surprised. He tried it on me.

JOHANNA: Well? Are you suggesting that he lied?

LENI: Nothing he told you was untrue.

JOHANNA: But . . .

LENI: But that's not the end of the story. That's the test, Johanna.

FRANZ: Terrific! [*He throws the paper on the table and gets up, his face pale, madness in his eyes.*] A hundred and twenty slipways! The total distance covered by our ships every year would reach from here to the moon. Germany is on her feet. Long live Germany! [*He goes towards Leni with mechanical strides.*] Thank you, sister. Now leave us alone.

LENI: No.

FRANZ [*shouting, commandingly*]: I said leave us alone. [*He tries to pull her towards the door.*]

JOHANNA: Franz!

FRANZ: What?

JOHANNA: I want to know the end of the story.

FRANZ: It has no end. Everybody was killed except me.

LENI: Look at him. One day in '49 he admitted everything to me.

JOHANNA: Admitted? What?

FRANZ: All made up. Can one talk seriously to her? I was joking. [*Pause.*] Johanna, you promised to believe no one but me.

JOHANNA: Yes.

FRANZ: Believe me. Good God, believe me, then!

JOHANNA: I. . . . You're not the same when she's here. [*LENI laughs.*] Make me want to believe you. Tell me she's lying. Speak! You didn't do anything, did you?

FRANZ [*almost a groan*]: Nothing.

JOHANNA [*urgently*]: But say it. I must hear you. Say: I didn't do anything.

FRANZ [*in a distraught voice*]: I didn't do anything.

JOHANNA [*looking at him in a kind of terror, cries out*]: Ha! [*She stifles her cry.*] I no longer recognize you.

FRANZ [*stubbornly*]: I didn't do anything.

LENI: But you let someone else do it.

JOHANNA: Who?

LENI: Heinrich.

JOHANNA: The two prisoners . . .?

LENI: Those two to begin with.

JOHANNA: Were there others?

LENI: After the first time you lose your scruples.

FRANZ: I'll explain. I lose my head when I see the two of you. You're killing me . . . Johanna, when we're alone . . . Everything has happened so quickly. . . . But I'll be able to explain. It'll all come back. I'll tell you the whole truth, Johanna, I love you more than my life. . . . [*He takes her by the arm, but she tears herself free, shouting at him.*]

JOHANNA: Let me go! [*She stands alongside Leni.* FRANZ *stands bewildered in front of her.*]

LENI [*to Johanna*]: The test came off badly.

JOHANNA: I lost it. Keep him.

FRANZ [*distracted*]: Listen to me, both of you. . . .

JOHANNA [*with hatred*]: You were a torturer! You!

FRANZ: Johanna! [*She looks at him.*] Not with those eyes! No. Not with those eyes! [*Pause.*] I knew it. [*He bursts out laughing and goes down on his hands and knees.*] Back we go! Back we go! [LENI *cries out. He stands up.*] You've never seen me as a crab, little sister? [*Pause.*] Get out, both of you! [LENI *goes to the table, intending to open the drawer.*] Ten past five. Tell father I'll meet him at six o'clock in the conference room. Get out! [*A long silence. The lights begin to fade.* JOHANNA *goes out first, without looking back.* LENI *hesitates a little, then follows her.* FRANZ *sits down and picks up the paper.*] A hundred and twenty slipways! An empire!

CURTAIN

The same decor as Act One. It is six o'clock. Daylight is fading, but this is not at first apparent because the shutters of the french windows are closed, and the room is in semi-darkness.

> [*The clock strikes six. On the third stroke, the shutter of the left-hand french window is opened from the outside, and the light streams in. The* FATHER *pushes the french window open, and enters. At the same time,* FRANZ'*s door opens, and* FRANZ *appears on the landing. The two men look at each other for a moment.* FRANZ *is carrying in his hand a small square black case: his tape-recorder.*]

FRANZ [*without moving*]: Hallo, father.

FATHER [*in a natural and familiar voice*]: Hallo, son.

> [*He sways for a moment, and steadies himself against the back of a chair.*]

FATHER: Wait! I'll let some light in.

> [*He opens the other french window and pushes back the other shutter. A green light, as at the end of Act One, streams into the room.*]

FRANZ [*descending one step*]: I'm listening.

FATHER: I've nothing to say to you.

FRANZ: What? You importune Leni with requests . . .

FATHER: My boy, I've come to this lodge because you asked me to come.

FRANZ [*looking at his Father in amazement, then breaking into a laugh*]: That's true, I'll admit. [*He comes down one more step, then stops.*] A fine game. You played off Johanna against Leni, then Leni against Johanna. Mate in three.

FATHER: Who is checkmate?

FRANZ: Me – the black king. Aren't you tired of winning?

FATHER: I'm tired of everything, my son, except that. One never wins. I'm trying to hedge my bet.

FRANZ [*shrugging his shoulders.*]: You always end up by doing what you want.

FATHER: That's the surest way of losing.

FRANZ [*bitterly*]: Perhaps so. [*Sharply*] What *do* you want?

FATHER: Now? To see you.

FRANZ: Well, here I am! Take a good look at me while you still can. I've reserved some very choice news for you. [*The* FATHER *coughs.*] Don't cough.

FATHER [*with a touch of humility*]: I'll try. [*He coughs again.*] It's not very easy . . . [*Regaining control of himself*] There!

FRANZ [*slowly, looking at his Father*]: How sad you look. [*Pause.*] Come on, smile! It's a celebration. Father and son reunited. Kill the fatted calf. [*Suddenly*] You shan't judge me.

FATHER: Who's talking of that?

FRANZ: It's in your eyes. [*Pause.*] Two criminals. One condemns the other in the name of principles they have both violated. What do you call that farce?

FATHER [*calmly and without expression*]: Justice. [*A short pause.*] Are you a criminal?

FRANZ: Yes. So are you. [*Pause.*] I don't accept your competence to judge me.

FATHER: Then why did you want to speak to me?

FRANZ: To tell you I've lost everything, and you'll lose everything. [*Pause.*] Swear on the Bible that you will not judge me! Swear, or I'll go straight back into my room.

FATHER [*going to the Bible and placing his hand on it*]: I swear!

FRANZ: All right! [*He comes right down and places his tape-recorder on the table. He turns, and father and son are face to face on a level.*] Where are the years? You're still the same.

FATHER: No.

FRANZ [*approaching him as though fascinated, with a marked but defensive insolence*]: I feel nothing at seeing you again. [*Pause.*

With an almost involuntary movement, he places his hand on his Father's arm.] Old Hindenburg, eh? [*He draws back, speaking harshly.*] I'm a torturer. [*Silence. He shouts*] Do you hear?

FATHER [*with no change of expression*]: Yes; go on.

FRANZ: That's all. We were being harassed by partisans, and the village was in league with them. I tried to make two villagers talk. [*Pause. Abruptly and nervously*] The same old story.

FATHER [*heavily and slowly, but with no expression*]: The same.

[*Pause.* FRANZ *looks at him disdainfully.*]

FRANZ: I think you're judging me, aren't you?

FATHER: No.

FRANZ: You'd better not. My dear father, let's be clear on this: it's because you're an informer that I'm a torturer.

FATHER: I didn't inform on anyone.

FRANZ: What about the Polish rabbi?

FATHER: Not even him. I took some . . . unpleasant risks.

FRANZ: I'll say no more. [*Thinking of the past*] Unpleasant risks? So did I. [*Laughing.*] Oh, very unpleasant. [*He laughs. The* FATHER *takes advantage of this to cough.*] What's the matter?

FATHER: I'm laughing with you.

FRANZ: You're coughing. Stop, for God's sake. You're rasping my throat.

FATHER: Forgive me.

FRANZ: Are you going to die?

FATHER: You know I am.

FRANZ [*he starts forward, then quickly jumps back*]: Good riddance! [*His hands tremble.*] That must hurt like hell.

FATHER: What?

FRANZ: That damned cough.

FATHER [*annoyed*]: No, it doesn't. [*He has another fit of coughing, then calms down.*]

FRANZ: I feel your pain. [*Staring at him*] I lacked imagination.

FATHER: When?

FRANZ: Out there. [*A long silence. He turns from his Father and looks towards the door upstage. When he speaks, he sees his past, except when he speaks directly to his Father.*] The superior officers wiped out. The sergeant-major and Klages at my beck and call. The soldiers at my mercy. Only one order: hold on! I hold on. I choose the living and the dead. You, go and get yourself killed! You, stay here! [*Pause. He comes downstage, proud and sinister.*] I have supreme power. [*Pause.*] What? [*He seems to be listening to an invisible questioner, then he turns to his Father.*] Someone kept asking me: 'What will you do with it?'

FATHER: Who?

FRANZ: It was in the night air. Every night. [*Imitating the whispering of unknown questioners*] What will you do with it? What will you do with it? [*Shouting*] Idiots! I'll go right through with it. Right to the limits of my power. [*Quickly, to his Father*] Do you know why?

FATHER: Yes.

FRANZ [*rather disconcerted*]: Oh?

FATHER: For once in your life you were powerless.

FRANZ [*loudly, laughing*]: Old Hindenburg has his head screwed on. Good old Hindenburg! Yes, I was. [*Stops laughing.*] Here, and because of you. You handed over the rabbi to them. Four of them held me down while the others beat him to death. What could I do? [*Lifting the little finger of his left hand and looking at his Father*] Not even raise my little finger. [*Pause.*] A curious experience, but I wouldn't recommend it for future leaders. You never get over it. You made me a prince, father. And do you know who made me a king?

FATHER: Hitler.

FRANZ: Yes; through shame. After that . . . incident, power became my vocation. Do you know that I admired him too?

FATHER: Hitler?

FRANZ: Didn't you know? Oh, I hated him, before and after. But that day he possessed me. Two leaders: either they have to kill each other, or one becomes the other's wife. I was Hitler's wife. The rabbi was bleeding, and I discovered at the heart of my powerlessness, some strange kind of approval. [*He is back again in the past.*] I have supreme power. Hitler has changed me, made me, made me implacable and sacred, made me himself. I am Hitler, and I shall surpass myself. [*Pause. To the Father*] No rations left. My soldiers were prowling around the barn. [*Back in the past*] Four good Germans will crush me to the earth, and my own men will bleed the prisoners to death. No! I shall never again fall into abject powerlessness. I swear it. It's dark. Horror has not yet been let loose. . . . I'll grab them quickly. If anyone lets it loose, it will be me. I'll assume the evil; I'll display my power by the singularity of an unforgettable act; change *living* men into vermin. I alone will deal with the prisoners. I'll debase them into abject wretches. They'll talk. Power is an abyss, and I see its depths. It is not enough to choose who shall live and who shall die. I shall decide life or death with a penknife and a cigarette lighter. [*Distractedly*] Fascinating! It is the glory of kings to go to Hell. I shall go there. [*He stands as though in a trance, front stage.*]

FATHER [*in a matter-of-fact voice*]: Did they talk?

FRANZ [*rudely awakened from his memories*]: What's that? [*Pause.*] No. [*Pause.*] They died without talking.

FATHER: Loser wins.

FRANZ: Eh! Everything has to be learnt. I hadn't the knack . . . then.

FATHER [*with a sad smile*]: Nevertheless, it was they who decided life or death.

FRANZ [*shouting*]: I'd have done the same. I would have died under the blows without saying a word. [*He calms down.*] So, what the hell! I kept my authority.

FATHER: How long?

FRANZ: Ten days. Ten days later enemy tanks attacked, and we were all dead – including the prisoners. [*Laughing*] I beg your pardon. Except me! I wasn't killed. Not in the least. [*Pause.*] I'm not sure about anything I've told you – except that I tortured them.

FATHER: And then what? [FRANZ *shrugs his shoulders.*] You kept on walking? You hid? Then you came home?

FRANZ: Yes. [*Pause.*] The ruins gave me my justification. I loved our looted houses and our mutilated children. I pretended that I was locking myself up so that I shouldn't witness Germany's agony. It's a lie. I wanted my country to die, and I shut myself up so that I shouldn't be a witness to its resurrection. [*Pause.*] Judge me!

FATHER: You made me swear on the Bible . . .

FRANZ: I've changed my mind. Let's get it over with.

FATHER: No.

FRANZ: I tell you, I release you from your oath.

FATHER: Would the torturer accept the verdict of the informer?

FRANZ: There isn't a God, is there?

FATHER: I'm afraid there isn't. It's rather a nuisance at times.

FRANZ: Then, informer or no informer, you're my natural judge. [*Pause. The* FATHER *shakes his head.*] Won't you judge me? Not at all? Then you've something else in mind. Something worse. [*Sharply*] You're waiting. What for?

FATHER: Nothing. You're here.

FRANZ: You're waiting. I know your long, long waits. I've seen you facing real hard cases, real scoundrels. They'd insult you, and you'd say nothing; you would wait. And in the end, they'd dissolve. [*Pause.*] Speak! Speak! Say anything! I can't stand it. [*Pause.*]

FATHER: What are you going to do?

FRANZ: I'm going back up there.

FATHER: When will you come down again?

FRANZ: Never.

FATHER: Won't you see anyone?

FRANZ: I'll see Leni – for what I need.

FATHER: And Johanna?

FRANZ [*curtly*]: Finished. [*Pause.*] She had no guts, that girl ...

FATHER: Were you in love with her?

FRANZ: The loneliness was getting me down. [*Pause.*] If she had accepted me as I am. ...

FATHER: And do you accept yourself?

FRANZ: What about you? Do you accept me?

FATHER: No.

FRANZ [*deeply hurt*]: Not even a father.

FATHER: Not even a father.

FRANZ [*in a changed voice*]: Well? What the hell are we doing together? [*The* FATHER *does not reply, and* FRANZ *continues in a voice of deep anguish.*] Ah, I should never have agreed to see you again. I knew it. I knew it.

FATHER: Knew what?

FRANZ: What would happen to me.

FATHER: Nothing is happening to you.

FRANZ: Not yet; but you're there and I'm here, as in my dreams. And you're waiting, as in my dreams. [*Pause.*] Very well; I can wait too. [*Pointing to the door of his room*] I'll put that door between us. Six months' patience. [*He points to his* FATHER'*s head.*] In six months that skull will be empty, those eyes will no longer see, and the worms will be eating those lips, and the contempt written on them.

FATHER: I have no contempt for you.

FRANZ [*sarcastically*]: Really? After what I've told you?

FATHER: You've told me nothing.

FRANZ [*stunned*]: What do you mean?

FATHER: I've known about your Smolensk business for three years.

FRANZ [*violently*]: Impossible! Dead! No witnesses! Dead and buried! All of them!

FATHER: Except two, whom the Russians released. They came to see me. It was in March '56. Ferist and Scheidemann. You remember them?

FRANZ [*taken aback*]: No. [*Pause.*] What did they want?

FATHER: Money, to keep their mouths shut.

FRANZ: Well?

FATHER: I don't fall for blackmail.

FRANZ: And they?

FATHER: Not a word. You had forgotten them. Go on.

FRANZ [*looking into space*]: Three years ago?

FATHER: Three years. I announced your death almost immediately, and the following year I sent for Werner. It was the wisest thing.

FRANZ [*who has not been listening*]: Three years! I was making speeches to the Crabs. I was lying to them. And down here I had been found out for three years. [*Suddenly*] It was from that time that you wanted to see me, wasn't it?

FATHER: Yes.

FRANZ: Why?

FATHER [*shrugging his shoulders*]: I wanted to.

FRANZ: They were sitting in your office, and you were listening to them because they had known me, and then, at a certain point, one of them said: 'Franz von Gerlach is a butcher.' Sensation! [*Trying to joke*] I hope you were very surprised.

FATHER: No. Not very.

FRANZ [*crying out*]: I was clean when I left you. I was pure. I wanted to save the Pole. . . . You weren't surprised? [*Pause.*] What did you think? You knew nothing till then, and suddenly you knew everything! [*Shouting louder*] For God's sake, what did you think?

FATHER [*with deep tenderness*]: My poor boy!

FRANZ: What?

FATHER: You ask me what I thought, and I'm telling you. [*Pause.* FRANZ *stands up straight, then he collapses, sobbing, on his Father's shoulder.*] My poor boy! [*He awkwardly caresses the back of Franz's neck.*] My poor boy! [*Pause.*]

FRANZ [*suddenly jumping up*]: Stop! [*Pause.*] It's the effect of the shock. I haven't cried for sixteen years, and I won't do it again for another sixteen. Don't pity me; it makes me want to bite. [*Pause.*] I don't love myself very much.

FATHER: Why should you love yourself?

FRANZ: You're right there.

FATHER: That's my concern.

FRANZ: You love me! You? You love the butcher of Smolensk?

FATHER: The butcher of Smolensk is still you, son.

FRANZ: All right, all right, don't bother. [*With a deliberately coarse laugh*] It takes all kinds to make a world. [*Suddenly*] You're using me. When you show your feelings, it's because it suits your plans. I say you're using me. A few hard knocks, and then one goes soft. When you think you've got me where you want me . . . Come on! You've had plenty of time to think about this affair, and you're too domineering not to want to settle it your own way.

FATHER [*deeply ironical*]: Domineering! I've got over that. [*Pause. He laughs to himself, grimly amused, then turns to Franz, speaking softly, but firmly.*] As for that business, I'll settle it.

FRANZ [*jumping back*]: I'll stop you. Is it any concern of yours?

FATHER: I don't want you to suffer any more.

FRANZ [*hard and brutal, as though accusing someone other than himself*]: I'm not suffering; I made others suffer. Perhaps you see the distinction.

FATHER: I do.

FRANZ: I've forgotten everything. Even their cries. I'm empty.

FATHER: I expect so. But it's even harder, isn't it?

FRANZ: Why should you care?

FATHER: For fourteen years you have been a prey to suffering which you created, and which you don't feel.

FRANZ: Who's asking you to talk about me? Yes, it's even harder. I am its horse, and it bestrides me. I wouldn't wish you to carry such a rider. [*Suddenly*] Well? What's the solution? [*He looks at his Father; his eyes staring.*] Go to the Devil!

[*He turns his back to him and climbs the stairs slowly and painfully. The Father makes no attempt to stop him until he has reached the landing.*]

FATHER [*in a loud voice*]: Germany is in your room! [FRANZ *turns slowly.*] She's alive, Franz! You'll never forget her again.

FRANZ: She's struggling along, I know, in spite of her defeat. I'll put up with it.

FATHER: As a result of her defeat, she's the greatest power in Europe. Will you put up with that? [*Pause.*] We're the apple of discord and the prize at stake. They pander to us. All markets are open to us, and our machines are going full blast. We're a foundry. A lucky defeat, Franz. We have guns and butter. And soldiers, son. Tomorrow, the bomb. Then we shall toss our mane, and you'll see our patrons jump like fleas.

FRANZ [*in a last defence*]: We're beaten, and we dominate Europe! What should we have done if we had won?

FATHER: We couldn't have won.

FRANZ: Did we have to lose the war, then?

FATHER: We had to play loser wins – as always.

FRANZ: Is that what you did?

FATHER: Yes; from the opening of hostilities.

FRANZ: And those who loved their country enough to sacrifice their military honour for victory . . .

FATHER [*in a hard, level voice*]: Risked prolonging the massacre and hindering reconstruction. [*Pause.*] The truth is that they did nothing at all except commit individual murders.

FRANZ: A fine subject for meditation. Something for me to think about in my room.

FATHER: You won't stay there a minute longer.

FRANZ: That's where you're wrong. I'll deny this country which rejects me.

FATHER: You have tried for thirteen years without much success. How could you go back to that game you've been playing?

FRANZ: How could I drop it? Either Germany must die, or I shall become a common criminal.

FATHER: Precisely.

FRANZ [*quickly, looking at his Father*]: Well, I don't want to die.

FATHER [*calmly*]: Why not?

FRANZ: You may well ask. You've made your name.

FATHER: If you knew how little I care.

FRANZ: You're lying, Father. You wanted to build ships, and you built them.

FATHER: I built them for you.

FRANZ: What! I thought you made me for them. At any rate, they are there. When you're dead, you'll be a fleet. What about me? What will I leave behind?

FATHER: Nothing.

FRANZ [*wildly*]: That's why I shall live to a hundred. I have only my life. [*Overwrought*] That's all I have. They shan't take it from me. Believe me, I hate it, but I prefer it to *nothing*.

FATHER: Both your life and your death are merely *nothing*. You are nothing, you do nothing, you have done nothing and you can do nothing. [*A long pause. The* FATHER *goes slowly over to the stairs, leans against the banisters and looks up at Franz.*] Forgive me.

FRANZ [*stiffening in fear*]: Me forgive you? It's a trick! [*The* FATHER *waits. Suddenly*] Forgive you for what?

FATHER: For you. [*Pause. He smiles.*] Parents are a load of idiots. They stop the sun. I thought the world would never change. It has changed. Do you remember that future I had mapped óut for you?

FRANZ: Yes.

FATHER: I was always talking to you about it, and you could see it. [FRANZ *nods assent*.] Well, it was my own past.

FRANZ: Yes.

FATHER: You knew?

FRANZ: I always knew. At first I liked it.

FATHER: My poor boy. I wanted you to run the firm after me. But it does the running. It chooses its own men. It has got rid of me. I own it, but I no longer run it. And you, little prince, it rejected you from the start. What does it need with a prince? It trains and recruits its own managers. [FRANZ *comes slowly downstairs while his* FATHER *is speaking*.] I had given you all the talents, and my bitter taste for power, but it was no use. What a pity! In order to act, you took the greatest risks, and, you see, the firm turned all your acts into gestures. In the end, your torment drove you to crime, and because of that very crime it casts you out. It fattens on your defeat. I don't like regrets, Franz. They serve no purpose. If I could believe that you might be useful somewhere else, and in some other sphere . . . but I made you a monarch, and today that means: good for nothing.

FRANZ [*with a smile*]: Was I destined . . .?

FATHER: Yes.

FRANZ: To impotence?

FATHER: Yes.

FRANZ: To crime?

FATHER: Yes.

FRANZ: By you?

FATHER: By my passions, which I implanted in you. Tell your Court of Crabs that I alone am guilty – of everything.

FRANZ [*smiling again*]: That's what I wanted to hear you say. [*He comes right down the stairs, level with his Father*.] Well, I accept.

FATHER: What?

FRANZ: What you expect of me. [*Pause.*] On one condition only; that it is both of us, and at once.

FATHER [*taken aback*]: At once?

FRANZ: Yes.

FATHER [*huskily*]: Do you mean today?

FRANZ: I mean this very moment. [*Pause.*] Isn't that what you wanted?

FATHER [*he coughs*]: Not . . . so soon.

FRANZ: Why not?

FATHER: I have just found you again.

FRANZ: You have found *no one*. Not even yourself. [*He is calm and straightforward for the first time, but completely desperate.*] I shall only have been one of your images. The others have remained in your head. As luck would have it, this is the one that became incarnate. In Smolensk one night it had . . . what? A moment of independence. So you are guilty of everything except that. [*Pause.*] I lived for thirteen years with a loaded revolver in my drawer. Do you know why I didn't kill myself? I said to myself: what's done is done. [*Pause. With deep sincerity*] Dying won't settle anything. That won't settle anything for me. I wished – you will laugh – I wished I had never been born. I didn't always lie to myself up there. In the evenings, I used to walk up and down the room and think of you.

FATHER: I was here, in this armchair. You walked: I listened.

FRANZ [*indifferent and unmoved*]: Oh? [*Continuing*] I used to think: if only he could find a way of recapturing that rebel image, of putting it back into me so that it again becomes incorporate with me, then there would never have been anything but him.

FATHER: Franz, there never has been anything but me.

FRANZ: That's easily said. Prove it. [*Pause.*] While we live, we shall be two. [*Pause.*] The Mercedes was a six-seater, but you only used to take me in it. You would say: 'Franz, we must make a soldier of you. We will go really fast.' I was eight. We took the road along the Elbe. . . . Is the Teufelsbrücke still there?

FATHER: Yes.

FRANZ: A dangerous road. There were deaths there every year.

FATHER: There are even more every year now.

FRANZ: You would say: 'Here we go!' as you stepped on the accelerator. I was wild with fear and joy.

FATHER [*smiling lightly*]: We almost capsized once.

FRANZ: Twice. Cars go much faster these days, don't they?

FATHER: Your sister's Porsche does 112 miles an hour.

FRANZ: Let's take it.

FATHER: So soon. . . .

FRANZ: What are you hoping for?

FATHER: A respite.

FRANZ: You're having it. [*Pause.*] You know very well that it will not last. [*Pause.*] Within an hour I would hate you.

FATHER: Don't you, now?

FRANZ: At this moment, no. [*Pause.*] Your image will be shattered together with all those which never left your head. You will be my cause and my fate, right to the end. [*Pause.*]

FATHER: Very well. [*Pause.*] I made you. I will unmake you. My death will enshroud yours, and in the end I shall be the only one to die. [*Pause.*] Wait. I did not think it would go so fast for me either. [*With a smile that barely hides his anguish*] It's funny, a life that goes up in smoke. That . . . that means nothing. [*Pause.*] I shall not be judged. [*Pause.*] You know, I didn't like myself either.

FRANZ [*placing his hand on his Father's arm*]: That was my concern.

FATHER [*with the same anguished smile*]: Well, there you are. I am the shadow of a cloud. There will be a shower of rain, and then the sun will shine on where I lived. To hell with it.

Winner loses. I built the firm which is destroying us. There is nothing to regret. [*Pause.*] Franz, would you like to go for a fast drive? It will make a soldier of you.

FRANZ: Shall we take the Porsche?

FATHER: Certainly. I'll go and bring it from the garage. Wait for me.

FRANZ: Will you give me the signal?

FATHER: The headlights? Yes. [*Pause.*] Leni and Johanna are on the terrace. Say good-bye to them.

FRANZ: I. . . . All right. Call them.

FATHER: See you in a moment, my boy.

[*He goes out, and he can be heard offstage as he calls Leni and Johanna.*]

FATHER [*offstage*]: Johanna! Leni!

[FRANZ *approaches the mantelpiece and looks at his photo. Suddenly he snatches off the crepe and throws it on to the floor.*]

LENI [*appearing on the threshold*]: What are you doing?

FRANZ [*laughing*]: I'm alive, aren't I?

[JOHANNA *enters. He comes downstage.*]

LENI: You're in civilians, lieutenant?

FRANZ: Father is driving me to Hamburg, and I shall take the boat tomorrow. You will never see me again. You have won, Johanna. Werner is free. Free as air. Good luck. [*He is near the table. He places his forefinger on the tape-recorder.*] I make you a gift of my tape-recorder. With my best recording – 17 December 1953. I was inspired. You will listen to it later. Some day when you want to know the case for the defence, or when you merely want to recall my voice. Do you accept it?

JOHANNA: I accept it.

FRANZ: Good-bye.

JOHANNA: Good-bye.

FRANZ: Good-bye, Leni. [*He caresses her hair in the same way as the Father did.*] Your hair is soft.

LENI: Which car are you taking?

FRANZ: Yours.

LENI: Which road are you taking?

FRANZ: The Elbe Embankment.

[*Two car headlamps shine outside, lighting up the room through the french windows.*]

LENI: I see. Father is signalling you. Good-bye.

[FRANZ *goes out. There is the sound of a car engine, which grows louder then fades away. The headlights sweep the french windows as the car goes past.*]

LENI: What time is it?

JOHANNA [*who is nearer the clock*]: Six thirty-two.

LENI: At six thirty-nine my Porsche will be in the water. Good-bye!

JOHANNA [*taken aback*]: Why?

LENI: Because the Teufelsbrücke is seven minutes from here.

JOHANNA: They are going to ...

LENI: Yes.

JOHANNA [*hard and tense*]: You have killed him!

LENI [*just as hard*]: And you? [*Pause.*] What does it matter? He didn't want to live.

JOHANNA [*still in control of herself, but on the verge of breaking down*]: Seven minutes.

LENI [*going up to the clock*]: Six now. No; five and a half.

JOHANNA: Can't we do anything?

LENI [*still hard*]: Bring them back? Try. [*Pause.*] What are you going to do now?

JOHANNA [*trying to control herself*]: Werner will decide that. And you?

LENI [*pointing to Franz's room*]: Someone must occupy that room. It shall be me. I shall not see you any more, Johanna. [*Pause.*] Be good enough to tell Hilda to knock on that door tomorrow morning. I will give her my orders. [*Pause.*] Still two minutes. [*Pause.*] I did not hate you. [*She walks over to the tape-recorder.*] The case for the defence. [*She opens the tape-recorder.*]

JOHANNA: I don't want to . . .

LENI: Seven minutes! Leave it! They are dead.

[*She presses the button of the tape-recorder immediately after her last words. Franz's voice is heard almost at once.* LENI *crosses the room while Franz is speaking. She climbs the stairs and enters the room.*]

VOICE OF FRANZ [*from the tape-recorder*]: Centuries of the future, here is my century, solitary and deformed – the accused. My client is tearing himself open with his own hands. What you take for white lymph is blood. There are no red corpuscles for the accused is dying of hunger. But I will tell you the secret of these multiple incisions. The century might have been a good one had not man been watched from time immemorial by the cruel enemy who had sworn to destroy him, that hairless, evil, flesh-eating beast – man himself. One and one make one, there's our mystery. The beast was hiding, and suddenly we surprised his look deep in the eyes of our neighbours. So we struck. Legitimate self-defence. I surprised the beast. I struck. A man fell, and in his dying eyes I saw the beast still living – myself. One and one make one – what a misunderstanding! Where does it come from, this rancid, dead taste in my mouth? From man? From the beast? From myself? It is the taste of the century. Happy centuries, you who do not know our hatreds, how could you understand the atrocious power of our fatal loves? Love. Hatred. One and one . . . Acquit us! My client was the first to know shame. He knows he is naked. Beautiful children, you are born of us, our pain has brought you forth. This century is a woman in labour. Will you condemn your mother? Eh? Answer! [*Pause.*] The thirtieth century no longer replies. Perhaps there will be no more centuries after ours. Perhaps a bomb will blow out all the lights. Everything will be dead: eyes, judges, time. Night. Oh, Tribunal of the Night, you who were, who will be and who are; I have been! I have been! I, Franz von Gerlach, here in this room, have taken the century upon my shoulders and have said: I will answer for it. This day and for ever. What do you say?

[LENI *has entered Franz's room.* WERNER *appears at the door of the lodge.* JOHANNA *sees him and goes towards him. Their faces are expressionless. They go out without speaking. From Franz's words: 'Eh? Answer!' the stage is empty.*]

CURTAIN

MEN WITHOUT SHADOWS

CHARACTERS

FRANÇOIS

SORBIER

CANORIS

LUCIE

HENRI

JEAN

LANDRIEU

PELLERIN

CLOCHET

Militiamen

ACT ONE

SCENE ONE

An attic with a dormer window set high in the wall. Miscellaneous objects scattered pell-mell; trunks, an old stove, a dressmaker's stand.
    [CANORIS *the Greek and* SORBIER *are sitting, one on a trunk, the other on an old stool.* LUCIE *sits on the stove.* FRANÇOIS *is walking up and down restlessly.* HENRI *is lying on the ground asleep. They all wear handcuffs.*]

FRANÇOIS: Why doesn't somebody say something?

SORBIER [*raising his head*]: What do you want us to say?

FRANÇOIS: Anything – provided it makes a noise.
    [*Suddenly there is a burst of loud, vulgar music. It is the radio from the floor below.*]

SORBIER: There you are.

FRANÇOIS: Not that – that's *their* noise. [*He goes back to his restless pacing. Suddenly he stops dead.*] Ah!

SORBIER: What now?

FRANÇOIS: They can hear me; they are saying: the first's beginning to crack.

CANORIS: All right, don't crack. Sit down. Put your hands on your knees, your wrists will hurt less. And then shut up. Go to sleep. Do some thinking.

FRANÇOIS: What's the use?
    [CANORIS *shrugs his shoulders.* FRANÇOIS *goes back to his pacing.*]

SORBIER: François!

FRANÇOIS: What?

SORBIER: Your shoes squeak.

FRANÇOIS: I know. I'm doing it on purpose. [*Pause. Then he stops in front of Sorbier.*] What are you thinking?

SORBIER [*lifting his head*]: Do you really want to know?

FRANÇOIS [*meets his gaze and falls back a step*]: No. Don't tell me.

SORBIER: I'm thinking about the kid who screamed.

LUCIE [*coming out of her dream abruptly*]: Which kid?

SORBIER: The little girl at the farm. I heard her screaming as they took us away. The stairs were on fire.

LUCIE: The little girl at the farm! Oh, God! I didn't know.

SORBIER: Lots of people died in that fire. Women and children. I didn't hear them. But that kid . . . I can still hear her screaming.

LUCIE: She was only fourteen. It's our fault she's dead.

SORBIER: It's our fault they are all dead.

CANORIS [*to François*]: You see, it's much better not to talk.

FRANÇOIS: What of it? We can't last much longer either. Perhaps they're the lucky ones.

SORBIER: They weren't ready to die.

FRANÇOIS: Am I? It wasn't our fault we failed.

SORBIER: Yes, it was.

FRANÇOIS: We were only obeying orders.

SORBIER: Maybe.

FRANÇOIS: They told us: go up and take the village. We told them: it's ridiculous – the Huns will be warned in twenty-four hours. They said: attack all the same. So we said: okay. And we attacked. Was it our fault?

SORBIER: We should have succeeded.

FRANÇOIS: We couldn't possibly.

SORBIER: I know. We should have succeeded all the same. [*Pause.*] Three hundred. Three hundred people who weren't ready to die, and who died for nothing. They are lying between the stones, rotting slowly in the sun. It's our fault. It's our fault that there is nothing left in this village but soldiers, dead bodies, and stones. It's terrible to die with those cries still ringing in my ears.

FRANÇOIS [*shouting*]: Shut up! We don't want to hear about your dead bodies. I'm the youngest – I was only carrying out orders. I don't want to die – I don't want to die!

LUCIE [*gently – from beginning to end of the preceding scene she has maintained her control*]: François!

FRANÇOIS [*disconcerted – in a softened voice*]: What?

LUCIE: Come and sit here, little brother. [*He hesitates. She repeats even more gently*] Come! [*He sits down. She passes her chained hands awkwardly over his face.*] How hot you are! Where's your handkerchief?

FRANÇOIS: In my pocket. I can't get at it.

LUCIE: This one?

FRANÇOIS: Yes.

[LUCIE *puts a hand into the pocket of his jacket, draws out a handkerchief with some difficulty and wipes his face.*]

LUCIE: You're soaking wet, and you're shaking all over. You shouldn't walk so much.

FRANÇOIS: If only I could get my coat off . . .

LUCIE: It's impossible, so don't think about it. [*He pulls on his handcuffs.*] Keep still – breathe deeply. You see: I am quiet, I'm saving myself.

FRANÇOIS: Saving yourself? What for? To scream later on? There's so little time left. I want to be everywhere at once. [*He tries to get up.*]

LUCIE: Sit still.

FRANÇOIS: I must keep moving. As soon as I stop, my thoughts go round and round. I don't want to think.

LUCIE: Poor darling.

FRANÇOIS [*he lets himself slip down against her knees*]: Lucie – it's awful. I can't look at your faces, they frighten me.

LUCIE: Put you head on my knees. Yes, it's very hard, and you are so young. If only someone could still smile and say, poor little François. I used to be able to look after you. My little François – my poor little François. [*She straightens herself abruptly.*] I can't. Grief has dried me up inside. I can't cry any more.

FRANÇOIS: Don't leave me. I'm ashamed of my own thoughts.

LUCIE: Listen. There's someone who can help you. . . . I'm not really alone. . . . [*Pause.*] Jean is with me.

FRANÇOIS: Jean?

LUCIE: They didn't catch him. He's on the road to Grenoble by now. Tomorrow, he'll be the only one of us left.

FRANÇOIS: And then?

LUCIE: He'll find the others – they'll begin again somewhere else. And then the war will be over. They will live quietly in Paris, with real pictures on real identity cards, and people will call them by their real names.

FRANÇOIS: All right. He's lucky. What's that got to do with me?

LUCIE: He's walking through the forest now. There are poplars on both sides of the road. He is thinking of me. He is the only person left in the world who thinks of me. He's thinking of you, too. He's sorry for you. Try to see yourself with his eyes. He can even cry. [*She cries.*]

FRANÇOIS: So can you.

LUCIE: I'm crying with his tears.

[*Pause.* FRANÇOIS *gets up abruptly.*]

FRANÇOIS: That's enough – you'll make me hate him.

LUCIE: You used to love him.

FRANÇOIS: Not the way you loved him.

LUCIE: No. Not the way I loved him.

[*Footsteps in the corridor. The door opens.* LUCIE *gets up quickly. The* MILITIAMAN *looks in at them, then he shuts the door again.*]

SORBIER [*shrugging his shoulders*]: They're having a wonderful time. Why did you get up?

LUCIE [*sitting down again*]: I thought they had come for us.

CANORIS: They won't come so soon.

LUCIE: Why not?

CANORIS: They believe waiting demoralizes. What a mistake!

SORBIER: Mistake? It's not funny to wait and imagine things.

CANORIS: Of course not. But it gives you time to get a grip on yourself. The first time it happened to me was in Greece, under Metaxas. They arrested me at four o'clock in the morning. If they'd pressed me a little, I'd have talked. Out of sheer surprise. They didn't ask me a thing. Ten days later, they tried everything, but it was too late; the surprise had worn off.

SORBIER: Did they beat you up?

CANORIS: Uh-huh.

SORBIER: Fists?

CANORIS: Fists, and feet.

SORBIER: Did you . . . did you want to talk?

CANORIS: No. As long as they hit you, it's all right.

SORBIER: Oh? . . . Oh, it's all right? . . . [*Pause.*] But if they hit you on the shins, or the elbows?

CANORIS: No, no. It's all right. [*Gently*] Sorbier.

SORBIER: What?

CANORIS: You mustn't be afraid of them. They have no imagination.

SORBIER: I'm afraid of myself.

CANORIS: Why? We've nothing to tell them. Everything we know they know. Listen. [*Pause.*] It's not in the least like you think.

FRANÇOIS: What's it like?

CANORIS: I can't really say. For instance, the time went very quickly. [*He laughs.*] My teeth were so tightly clenched I couldn't open my mouth for three hours. One bastard wore old-fashioned boots. With pointed toes. He kicked me in the face. It was at Nauplia. Some women were singing under the window. I've always remembered that song.

SORBIER: Nauplia? What year?

CANORIS: '36.

SORBIER: I was there then. I came to Greece in the *Théophile Gautier*. On a camping tour. I saw the prison. There are fig trees growing against the wall. So you were inside and I was outside? [*He laughs.*] What a coincidence!

CANORIS: Yes!

SORBIER [*abruptly*]: Suppose they mess you up?

CANORIS: What?

SORBIER: Mess you up with their instruments? [CANORIS *shrugs his shoulders.*] I think I'd be able to force myself to hold out. Each minute, I'd say to myself: I'll hold out for another minute. Is that a good method?

CANORIS: There are no methods.

SORBIER: What did you do?

LUCIE: Can't you keep quiet? Look at the kid. Do you think you're being any help to him? Just wait and see, they'll soon show you what to do.

SORBIER: Leave us alone! He can stuff up his ears, if he doesn't want to listen.

LUCIE: What about me? Must I stuff my ears too? I don't want to listen to you because I don't want to despise you. Do you need words to give you courage? I've seen animals die, and I want to die like them – in silence.

SORBIER: Who's talking of dying? We're talking about what they'll do to us *first*. We must be ready for them.

LUCIE: I don't want to be ready. Why should I go through the whole thing twice? Look at Henri; he's asleep. Why not go to sleep too?

SORBIER: Sleep? And have them wake me up? I won't. I've no time to lose.

LUCIE: Then think about something you like. I'm thinking about Jean, and my life, and François. That time he was ill at the hotel in Arcachon, and I looked after him. From my window I could see pine trees, and great green waves on the sea.

SORBIER [*ironically*]: Waves on the sea, really? I tell you I've no time to lose.

LUCIE: Sorbier, I don't know you any more.

SORBIER: I'm all right! It's my nerves. I'm as nervous as a schoolgirl. [*He rises and goes to her.*] Everyone must defend himself as best he can. I'm no good when I'm caught off my guard. If I could only feel the pain a little in advance, just to be able to recognize it – I'd feel more sure of myself. It's not my fault. I've always been very methodical. [*Pause.*] I like you. But I feel very much alone. [*Pause.*] If you'd like me to keep quiet...

FRANÇOIS: Let them talk. It makes a noise.

LUCIE: Do as you please. [*A silence.*]

SORBIER [*more softly*]: Hey, Canoris! [CANORIS *lifts his head.*] Have you met any of them? I mean, anyone who has squealed?

CANORIS: Yes, I have met them.

SORBIER: Well?

CANORIS: What's it got to do with you? We've nothing to squeal about.

SORBIER: I want to know. Could they stand it?

CANORIS: Depends. One tried to shoot himself with a shot-gun. It went off in his face and all he did was blind himself. I used to meet him in the streets of the Piraeus, being led about by a fat Armenian woman. He thought he had paid the penalty. We shot another during a fair, just as he was buying some Turkish Delight. Ever since he got out of prison he'd developed a passion for Turkish Delight.

SORBIER: Lucky bastard.

CANORIS: Hm!

SORBIER: If I broke down and squealed, I don't think I could console myself with sweets.

CANORIS: No one can tell until they've been through it.

SORBIER: I think I'd choose the shot-gun.

FRANÇOIS: I'd take the Turkish Delight.

SORBIER: François!

FRANÇOIS: How do you mean, François! Did you warn me when I came to you in the first place? You told me, the Resistance has need of men, you didn't tell me it needed heroes. I'm no hero – I tell you! I did as I was told, that's all. I distributed pamphlets and guns, and you said I was always good-tempered. But no one told me what to expect in the end. I swear I had no idea what I was letting myself in for.

SORBIER: Of course you knew. You knew René was tortured.

FRANÇOIS: I never thought about it. [*Pause.*] That kid who died up at the farm, you're sorry for her. You say, it's our fault she's dead. But if I talk, when they burn me with their cigars, you'll say – he was a coward, and you'll offer me a shot-gun. Or you'll shoot me in the back. But I'm only two years older than she was.

SORBIER: I was speaking for myself.

CANORIS [*going up to François*]: You have no duty to anyone, François. No duty, no responsibilities. We know nothing, it's nothing to do with us. Each man must do what he can and suffer as little as possible. The method doesn't matter.

[FRANÇOIS *grows gradually calmer, but he remains lying down.* LUCIE *hugs him to her.*]

SORBIER: The method doesn't matter. . . . Obviously. Scream, cry, ask their pardon, search your memory to find something to confess, someone to betray. What does it matter, nothing is any good. You won't find anything to say. All our little squalors will remain strictly confidential. Perhaps it's better like that. [*Pause.*] I'm not sure.

CANORIS: What do you want? To know a name, or a date, so that you can refuse to tell them?

SORBIER: I don't know. I don't even know if I could keep silent.

CANORIS: So?

SORBIER: I want to know myself. I knew they'd end by catching me, and one day I'd be up against a wall, face to face with myself, absolutely helpless. I used to say, will you be able to stand it? It's my body that worries me, you see. I've a miserable body, badly made, with nerves like a woman. Well, the moment has come. They're going to use their instruments on me. But I've been cheated. I'm going to suffer for nothing, and I shall die without finding out what I'm worth.

[*The music stops. They all start, and then listen intently.*]

HENRI [*waking abruptly*]: What is it? [*Pause.*] The polka is over, it's our turn to dance.

[*The music starts again.*]

HENRI: False alarm. Funny how they seem to like music. [*He gets up.*] I dreamt I was dancing. At Schéhérazade. You know, the night-club in Paris. I've never been there. [*He wakes up slowly.*] Ah! . . . there you are . . . there you all are. . . . Want to dance, Lucie?

LUCIE: No.

HENRI: Are your wrists sore, too? The flesh must have swollen while I was asleep. What time is it?

CANORIS: Three o'clock.

LUCIE: Five o'clock.

SORBIER: Six o'clock.

[*They laugh.*]

CANORIS: We don't know.

HENRI: Where's your watch.

CANORIS: They broke it on my wrist. We know one thing. You slept for a long time.

HENRI: Time stolen from me. [*To Canoris.*] Give us a hand. [CANORIS *bends down*, HENRI *climbs on his back and lifts himself up to the dormer window.*] It's five o'clock by the sun. Lucie was right. [*He drops down again.*] The Town Hall is still burning. Sure you don't want to dance? [*Pause.*] I loathe that music.

CANORIS [*indifferently*]: Bah!

HENRI: They must be able to hear it up at the farm.

CANORIS: No one there to hear it.

HENRI: I know. The music slips through the window, and slides over the corpses. Music, sunshine, curtain. And the bodies are all black. Ah! We made a nice mess of things. [*Pause.*] What's the matter with the kid?

LUCIE: He's not well. He hasn't slept for eight days. How did you manage to sleep?

HENRI: It just happened. I felt so lonely I fell asleep. [*He laughs.*] We're forgotten. Forgotten by the whole world. [*Going to* FRANÇOIS.] Poor kid . . . [*He caresses his hair, then stops abruptly. To Canoris.*] What have we done?

CANORIS: I don't know. What does it matter?

HENRI: Someone committed a crime. I feel guilty.

SORBIER: You, too? I'm glad. I thought I was the only one.

CANORIS: Fine – I feel guilty too. What difference does it make?

HENRI: I don't want to die in the wrong.

CANORIS: Don't worry. I'm sure the boys don't hold anything against you. They'll just think we had bad luck.

HENRI: I don't give a damn for the boys.

CANORIS [*shocked, dryly*]: Then what do you want? A confessor?

HENRI: To hell with all confessors. I don't have to account to anyone but myself now. [*Pause, as if to himself.*] Things shouldn't have turned out like this. If I could discover my crime . . .

CANORIS: It'd help you a lot.

HENRI: I could at least face up to it and say: that's why I'm dying. Good God! A man can't die like a rat, for nothing, without a protest.

CANORIS [*shrugging his shoulders*]: Bah!

SORBIER: Why shrug your shoulders? He has the right to save his death – it's all he's got.

CANORIS: Of course. Let him save it, if he can.

HENRI: Thanks for the permission. [*Pause.*] You'd better get on with saving your own: we haven't much time.

CANORIS: Mine? Why? Who would it help? It's a strictly personal affair.

HENRI: Yes. Strictly personal. So?

CANORIS: I've never been able to interest myself in personal affairs. Neither mine nor anyone else's.

HENRI [*without listening to him.*]: If only I could say to myself, I did what I could. But it's probably too much to ask. We've done something. I feel guilty. For thirty years, I've felt guilty of something. Guilty of being alive. Just now, houses are burning because of me, innocent people are dead, and I am going guilty to my grave. My whole life has been one long mistake.

CANORIS[*getting up and going to him.*]: You're not very modest, Henri.

HENRI: What do you mean?

CANORIS: You're torturing yourself because you aren't being modest. I think we've been dead for a long time, from the moment we stopped being useful. All that's left to us is a little posthumous existence, a few hours to kill. There's nothing for you to do but kill time and gossip with your neighbours. Let yourself go, Henri, relax. You can let yourself go because there's nothing more we can do. We don't matter any more. We are completely useless. [*Pause.*] For the first time in my life I realize I've earned the right to rest.

HENRI: For the first time in three years I've been able to face up to myself. They gave me their orders. I obeyed them, and I felt justified. Now, no one can give me orders, and nothing can justify me any more. A little bit of superfluous life; yes. Just time to think about myself. [*Pause.*] Canoris, why are we dying?

CANORIS: Because we were given a difficult job and we had bad luck.

HENRI: Yes. That's what the boys will say. That's what they'll say in the official reports. But what do you think?

CANORIS: I don't think. I lived for the cause, and I always knew I'd die like this.

HENRI: You lived for the cause, fine. But don't tell me you're dying for it. Maybe, if we'd been successful and died on the job then, maybe . . . [*Pause.*] We're dying because we were given stupid orders, because we carried them out badly, and our death isn't helping anyone. The cause didn't want us to attack this village. It didn't want it, because it was an impossible job. The cause never gives orders, never says anything; we have to decide what it wants. Don't talk about the cause. Not here. While we could still work for the cause, it's all right. Afterwards, we must keep our mouths shut, and above all, not use the cause as a personal consolation. The cause has rejected us because we are no longer useful. Others will be found to serve it. In Tours, in Lille, in Carcassonne, women are having babies who will replace us. We tried to justify our existence and we have failed. So now we are going to die, and we cannot justify our deaths.

CANORIS [*indifferently*]: If you like. Nothing that happens between these four walls has any importance. Hope or despair, nothing can come of it. [*Pause.*]

HENRI: If only there were something we could do. Or if we had something to hide! [*Pause. To Canoris*] Got a wife?

CANORIS: Yes. In Greece.

HENRI: Think of her much?

CANORIS: I try. It's very far away.

HENRI [*to Sorbier*]: What about you?

SORBIER: Only my parents. They think I'm in England. Just now, they'll be having supper. They always have it early. If only I could believe that they will feel something, in their hearts, some kind of presentiment. But I'm sure they're perfectly happy. They'll wait for me for years, more and more peacefully, and I shall die in their hearts without their noticing. My father will be talking about his garden. He always talks about the garden at supper-time. Later on, he'll go out and water the cabbages. [*He sighs.*] Poor old man. Why did I think of him? It doesn't help.

HENRI: No. It doesn't help. [*Pause.*] All the same, I wish my people were still alive. I've got nobody.

SORBIER: No one at all?

HENRI: No one.

LUCIE [*with conviction*]: You're being unfair. You've got Jean. We've all got Jean. He is our leader, and he is thinking of us.

HENRI: He's thinking of you because he loves you.

LUCIE: All of us.

HENRI [*gently*]: Lucie! How often did we talk about our dead? We had no time to bury them, even in our hearts. [*Pause.*] No. I shan't be missed anywhere, I leave no gap. The underground is crammed, the restaurants crowded. I shall slip out of this world and still leave it full. Like an egg. I've got to realize that I'm not indispensable. [*Pause.*] I wish I could be indispensable. To something, or to someone. [*Pause.*] Incidentally, Lucie, I love you. I can tell you now because it doesn't matter any more.

LUCIE: No, it doesn't matter.

HENRI: That's that. [*He laughs.*] There was really no point in my being born.

   [*The door opens. Several* MILITIAMEN *come in.*]

SORBIER: Good evening. [*To Henri.*] They did that three times while you were asleep.

MILITIAMAN: Are you the one called Sorbier? [*Pause.*]

SORBIER: That's right.

MILITIAMAN: Come with me.

   [*Fresh silence.*]

SORBIER: Oh well, I'm just as glad they're beginning with me. [*Pause. He walks to the door.*] I wonder if I'm going to know myself. [*As he goes out.*] It's time for my father to water his garden.

[*He goes out, the* MILITIAMEN *following. The key turns in the lock. Another long silence.*]

HENRI [*to Canoris*]: Give us a cigarette.

CANORIS: That was my last one.

HENRI: Hell. [*The gramophone plays a rhumba.*] They want us to dance. How about it, Lucie?

LUCIE: I told you no.

HENRI: Just as you like. Plenty of partners. [*He goes to the dressmaker's stand, raises his chained hands, and slides them over the shoulders and hips of the stand. Then he begins to dance, holding it against him. The music comes to an end.* HENRI *stops, puts the stand down, and slowly raises his arms to free himself.*] They've begun.

[*They all listen.*]

CANORIS: Hear anything?

HENRI: No.

FRANÇOIS: What do you think they're doing to him?

CANORIS: I don't know. [*Pause.*] I hope he holds out. If not, he'll suffer far more.

HENRI: Of course he'll hold out.

CANORIS: I hope so, it's much more difficult when you've nothing to hide. [*Pause.*]

HENRI: He hasn't screamed yet. That's something.

FRANÇOIS: Perhaps they're just questioning him.

CANORIS: You think so?

[SORBIER *screams. They all jump.*]

LUCIE [*talking very fast, in an unnatural voice*]: Jean must have arrived at Grenoble by now. I'd be very surprised if it took him more than fifteen hours. He must feel very strange; the town is quiet, there are people on the terraces of the cafés, and the Vercors must seem like a dream. [SORBIER's *cries intensify* – LUCIE's *voice grows louder*.] He's thinking of us. He hears the radio through an open window, the sun is shining down on the mountains. It's a lovely summer afternoon. [*Louder cries*] Ha! [*She slips down on to a trunk and sobs, as she repeats*.] A lovely summer afternoon.

HENRI [*to Canoris*]: I shan't scream.

CANORIS: You're wrong. It helps.

HENRI: I can't bear the idea of your hearing me, and of her weeping overhead.

    [FRANÇOIS *begins to tremble*.]

FRANÇOIS [*on the verge of a breakdown*]: I can't bear it, I can't bear it another minute, I tell you.

    [*Footsteps in the corridor*.]

CANORIS: Shut up. Someone's coming.

HENRI: Whose turn?

CANORIS: Yours or mine. They'll keep the girl and the kid to the last. [*The key turns in the lock*.] I hope it's me. I don't like other people's screams.

    [*The door opens, and* JEAN *is pushed into the room. He has no handcuffs. He half-closes his eyes as he comes in to get used to the darkness. They all turn towards him. The* MILITIA-MAN *goes out, closing the door behind him*.]

LUCIE: Jean!

JEAN: Be quiet. Don't say my name. Come here, against the wall, they may be watching us. [*He looks at her*.] It's you! It's really you! I thought I would never see you again. Who else is here?

CANORIS: Canoris.

HENRI: Henri.

JEAN: I can hardly see you. Pierre and Jacques are . . . ?

HENRI: Yes.

JEAN: The kid is here too? Poor little devil. [*Rapidly, in a low voice*.] I hoped you were all dead.

HENRI [*laughing*]: We did our best.

JEAN: I'm sure you did. [*To Lucie*] What's the matter?

LUCIE: Oh! Jean, it's all over. I was thinking . . . he has reached Grenoble, he is walking down the streets, he can see the mountains. . . . And . . . And . . . now everything is over.

JEAN: Don't cry. I've every chance of getting away.

HENRI: How did they catch you?

JEAN: They haven't yet. I stumbled on one of their patrols down there, on the road to Verdone. I said I had come from Cimiéro.

HENRI: From Cimiéro?

JEAN: It's a little town, farther down the valley. They brought me back, while they sent to see if I was telling the truth.

LUCIE: But at Cimiéro, they'll find out.

JEAN: It's all right; I've got friends there who'll know what to say. I'll get clear. [*Pause.*]

FRANÇOIS: You can't possibly get away.

JEAN: I must get away; the boys haven't been warned that the attack failed.

HENRI [*whistles*]: Exactly. [*Pause.*] Well, what do you say? Did we make a big enough mess of things?

JEAN: We can start again somewhere else.

HENRI: You mean, you can start again.

[*Footsteps in the corridor.*]

CANORIS: Come away from him. They mustn't see us talking to him.

JEAN: What is it?

HENRI: They're bringing Sorbier back.

JEAN: Oh, so they . . .

HENRI: Yes. They began with him.

[*The* MILITIAMEN *come in, supporting* SORBIER, *who collapses against a trunk. The* MILITIAMEN *go out again.*]

SORBIER [*without noticing Jean*]: Did they keep me long?

HENRI: Quite a while.

SORBIER: You're right, Canoris. The time does go quickly. Did you hear me scream. [*They do not reply.*] Of course you heard.

FRANÇOIS: What did they do to you?

SORBIER: You'll see. You'll soon see. No need to be in such a hurry.

FRANÇOIS: Is it . . . is it very bad?

SORBIER: I don't know. But I can tell you this. They asked me where Jean was, and if I'd known, I'd have told them. [*He laughs.*] You see: I know myself now. [*They are silent.*] What's the matter? [*He follows their gaze. He sees Jean, standing against the wall, his arms outstretched.*] Who is it? Is it Jean?

HENRI [*quickly*]: Shut up. They think he's just someone from Cimiéro.

SORBIER: From Cimiéro. [*He sighs.*] Just my luck.

HENRI [*surprised*]: What did you say?

SORBIER: I said: just my luck. Now I have got something to hide from them.

HENRI [*almost happily*]: That's true. Now we've all got something to hide.

SORBIER: I wish to God they'd killed me.

CANORIS: Sorbier! I swear to you that you won't tell them. You *couldn't* tell them.

SORBIER: I tell you I'd have betrayed my own mother. [*Pause.*] It's all wrong that one moment can destroy your whole life.

CANORIS [*gently*]: It takes much more than a moment. Do you think a moment's weakness can destroy the hour when you decided to give up everything and come with us? What about these three years of courage and patience? And the day you carried the kid's rifle and equipment, although you were half-dead yourself?

SORBIER: Stop making excuses. At last I know. At last I know what I really am.

CANORIS: What you really are? Why should you be more yourself today when they beat you, than yesterday when you wouldn't drink so that Lucie could have your share? We aren't meant to live always at the limit of our strength. Even in the valleys there are pathways.

SORBIER: If I had squealed just now, would you have been able to look me in the face?

CANORIS: You won't squeal.

SORBIER: But if I had? [CANORIS *is silent.*] You see. [*Pause. He laughs.*] Lots of people die in their beds, with a clear conscience. Good sons, good husbands, good citizens, good fathers. . . . Ha! They are cowards like me and they'll never know it. They're just lucky. [*Pause.*] Make me shut up! Why don't you make me shut up?

HENRI: Sorbier, you are the best of us.

SORBIER: Liar!

[*Footsteps in the corridor. They are all quiet. The door opens.*]

MILITIAMAN: Which one is the Greek?

CANORIS: I am.

MILITIAMAN: Come on.

[CANORIS *goes out with the* MILITIAMAN.]

JEAN: He's going to suffer for me.

HENRI: Just as well it's for you, otherwise it would be for nothing.

JEAN: When he comes back, how can I bear to look at him? [*To Lucie*] Do you hate me?

LUCIE: Do I look as though I hate you?

JEAN [*she gives him her manacled hands*]: I'm ashamed not to have handcuffs too. So here you are! And I thought everything was over. No more fear, no more hunger, no more pain. And here you are! They'll come for you soon, and when they bring you back, they'll be half-carrying you.

LUCIE: There will be nothing in my eyes but love for you.

JEAN: I will have to hear your cries.

LUCIE: I'll try not to scream.

JEAN: But the kid will scream. I'm sure he'll scream.

FRANÇOIS: Shut up! Shut up! Shut up! Do you want to make me mad? I'm not a hero, and I don't want to be martyred because of you.

LUCIE: François!

FRANÇOIS: Go to hell. I don't sleep with him. [*To Jean*] I hate you, if you want to know.

· [*Pause.*]

JEAN: You're quite right. [*He goes towards the door.*]

LUCIE: Jean!

HENRI: Hey! What are you doing?

JEAN: I'm not in the habit of sending my people to die in my place.

HENRI: Who's going to tell the boys the attack failed?
    [JEAN *stops.*]

FRANÇOIS: Let him alone! If he wants to give himself up …

HENRI [*to Jean, without paying any attention to François*]: It'll be a pretty thing when they get here, thinking that we still hold the village. [JEAN *turns back, his head lowered.*] Much better give me a cigarette. [JEAN *gives him a cigarette.*] Give one to the kid too.

FRANÇOIS: Leave me alone. [*He withdraws to the farthest part of the room.*]

HENRI: Give us a light. [JEAN *lights the cigarette.* HENRI *draws two puffs, then sobs nervously once or twice.*] It's all right. I like smoking, but I didn't realize it could give so much pleasure. How many have you got left?

JEAN: One.

HENRI [*to Sorbier*]: Here.
    [SORBIER *takes the cigarette without a word, and takes a few puffs, then passes it back.* HENRI *turns to Jean.*]

HENRI: I'm glad you're here. First, because you've given me a cigarette, and second because you will be a witness. To die without witnesses is real annihilation. You can go and see Sorbier's parents, and you can write to Canoris's wife.

LUCIE: Tomorrow, you'll go back to the town. You'll take with you the last living sight of me, you will be the only person in the world to know how I looked. You mustn't forget me. I am you. If you live. I live.

JEAN: Forget you . . . [*He goes towards her. Footsteps outside.*]

HENRI: Stay where you are and shut up. They're coming. It's my turn. I must be quick, or I won't have time to finish. Listen; if you hadn't come, we'd have suffered like animals, without knowing why. But you have come, and now everything has got a meaning. We can fight. Not for you alone, but for all the boys. [*Pause.*] I thought I was finished, but I see I might still be useful. With a bit of luck, I might even feel I'm not dying for nothing.

[*The door opens.* CANORIS *appears, supported by two militiamen.*]

SORBIER: He didn't make a sound, did he?

CURTAIN

SCENE TWO

A school-room. Desks and benches. Whitewashed walls. On the back wall, a map of Africa and a photograph of Pétain. The scene is very dark. Window on the left. Door up-stage. A radio on the table, under the window.

[CLOCHET, PELLERIN, *and* LANDRIEU *are discovered.*]

CLOCHET: Shall we go on to the next?

LANDRIEU: Just a minute. Give us time for some grub.

CLOCHET: Eat if you like. I could be questioning one of them meantime.

LANDRIEU: No. You enjoy it too much. Aren't you hungry?

CLOCHET: No.

LANDRIEU [*to Pellerin*]: Fancy. Clochet isn't hungry! [*To Clochet*] Are you ill?

CLOCHET: I'm never hungry when I'm working. [*He goes to the radio and turns the switch.*]

PELLERIN: Stop that bloody noise.

CLOCHET [*muttering. One hears*]: . . . don't like music.

PELLERIN: What's that?

CLOCHET: I said I'm always surprised when I find people don't like music.

PELLERIN: Maybe I do like music, but I don't like that kind, and I don't like it here.

CLOCHET: Really? I know the kind you like. . . . [*Regretfully*] We should have gone at him more gently. . . .

PELLERIN: Shut up!

CLOCHET: You're just animals. [*Pause.*] Can't we send for one of them?

LANDRIEU: For God's sake let us alone! We've got three of them to see, it'll take until ten o'clock. I get all nervous when I have to work on an empty stomach.

CLOCHET: But there're only two of them, since we decided to keep the kid for tomorrow. With a little organization we could be through in a couple of hours. [*Pause.*] Radio Toulouse is broadcasting *Tosca* tonight.

LANDRIEU: Oh, shut up. Go down and see what they've found for supper.

CLOCHET: I know: chicken.

LANDRIEU: Again! I couldn't face it. Go down and get us some bully.

CLOCHET [*to Pellerin*]: What about you?

PELLERIN: Bully.

LANDRIEU: And send someone to clean up this mess.

CLOCHET: What mess?

LANDRIEU: There, where the Greek bled on the floor. It's disgusting.

CLOCHET: You shouldn't clean up the blood. It might impress the others.

LANDRIEU: I shan't eat while that filth is on the floor. [*Pause.*] What are you waiting for?

CLOCHET: You shouldn't clean up that blood.

LANDRIEU: Who gives the orders here?

[CLOCHET *shrugs his shoulders and goes out.*]

PELLERIN: Go easy with Clochet.

LANDRIEU: I'll do as I please.

PELLERIN: I'm just warning you. . . . He has a cousin on Darnand's staff. He sends in reports. I think he was the one who got Daubin sacked.

LANDRIEU: The filthy swine! If he wants to get rid of me, he'll have to get a move on. I've an idea Darnand might be liquidated before me.

PELLERIN: Quite possible. [*He sighs and goes mechanically to the radio.*]

LANDRIEU: Oh, no – not you too.

PELLERIN: Just for the news.

LANDRIEU [*sneering*]: I think I know what it is.

[PELLERIN *turns the dials on the radio.*]

LOUDSPEAKER: At the third stroke it will be eight o'clock. Pip, Pip. Pip. [*They adjust their watches.*] Ladies and gentlemen, in a few seconds you will hear our usual Sunday concert. [*First bars of 'Lilli Marlene'.*]

LANDRIEU [*sighing*]: Sunday. Wring its neck.

PELLERIN: Sundays. I used to take the car. I'd pick up a skirt in Montmartre, and run down to Le Touquet.

LANDRIEU: When was that?

PELLERIN: Oh! Before the war.

[PELLERIN *has been twisting the dial of the radio. The 'V' sign is heard.*]

LANDRIEU: Filthy saboteurs. . . . [*He picks up an empty tin and throws it at the radio.*]

PELLERIN: Are you mad? You'll break the damn thing.

LANDRIEU: To hell with it. I don't want to listen to the bloody spies.

    [PELLERIN *turns the dials again.*]

LOUDSPEAKER: German troops are holding out at Cherbourg and at Caen. In the Saint-Lô sector, they have not been able to prevent a slight advance by the enemy.

LANDRIEU: Are you deaf? Shut it off.

LOUDSPEAKER: However, this is a purely strategic withdrawal and the high command is doubtless aiming at creating a fluid front. [PELLERIN *turns it off.*]

LANDRIEU: What'll you do? Where'll you go?

PELLERIN: What do you expect? It's all over.

LANDRIEU: Yes. The swine.

PELLERIN: Who do you mean?

LANDRIEU: All of them. The Germans too. They're all alike. [*Pause.*] If we could start again....

PELLERIN: I don't regret a thing. I've had a lot of fun, until quite recently.

    [CLOCHET *comes back, carrying the tins of food.*]

LANDRIEU: I say, Clochet. The English have landed at Nice.

CLOCHET: Nice?

LANDRIEU: They met with no resistance. They're marching on Puget-Théniers.

    [CLOCHET *slips on to a bench.*]

CLOCHET: Holy Virgin! [LANDRIEU *and* PELLERIN *laugh.*] Is it a joke? You shouldn't joke about such things.

LANDRIEU: It's all right. You can put it in your report tonight. [*A* MILITIAMAN *enters.*] Clean up that filth. [*To Pellerin*] Ready to eat? [PELLERIN *joins him, picks up his tin of bully, looks at it, then puts it down again.* LANDRIEU *yawns.*] I always feel odd before we start. [*He yawns again.*] I'm not tough enough; I only get angry when they get stubborn. What's he like, the next one?

CLOCHET: Tall, broad, about thirty. We should see some sport.

LANDRIEU: Provided he doesn't play us the same dirty trick as the Greek.

PELLERIN: Bah! The Greek! An animal!

LANDRIEU: Doesn't matter. It hurts me when they won't talk. [*He yawns.*] You're making me yawn. [*Pause.* LANDRIEU *looks at the bottom of his tin without a word, then suddenly, to the militiaman.*] Well? Go and fetch him.

> [*The* MILITIAMAN *goes out. Silence.* CLOCHET *whistles.* PELLERIN *goes to the window and opens it wide.*]

CLOCHET: Don't open the window. It's getting cold.

PELLERIN: Window? Oh, yes.... [*He laughs.*] I opened it without thinking. [*He starts to shut it.*]

LANDRIEU: Leave it. There's a terrible stink in here.

CLOCHET: As you like.

> [HENRI *comes in with three* MILITIAMEN.]

LANDRIEU: Put him in that chair. Take off his handcuffs. Tie his wrists to the arms. [*The* MILITIAMEN *tie him up.*] What's your name?

HENRI: Henri.

LANDRIEU: Henri what?

HENRI: Henri.

> [LANDRIEU *makes a sign. The* MILITIAMEN *beat Henri.*]

LANDRIEU: Now. What's your name?

HENRI: My name is Henri, that's all.

> [*They beat him again.*]

LANDRIEU: That's enough, you'll make him muzzy. Age?

HENRI: Twenty-nine.

LANDRIEU: Profession?

HENRI: Before the war, I was a medical student.

PELLERIN: An educated bastard, eh? [*To the militiamen*] Hit him.

LANDRIEU: Don't let's waste time.

PELLERIN: Medical student! I told you to hit him!

LANDRIEU: Pellerin! [*To Henri*] Where is your captain?

HENRI: I don't know.

LANDRIEU: Naturally. No, don't hit him. Do you smoke? Wait. [*He puts a cigarette in his own mouth, lights it and holds it out. One of the militiamen puts it into Henri's mouth.*] Smoke. What do you expect? You won't impress us. Come, Henri, don't be stupid. No one can see you. You're only wasting your time and mine. You haven't many more hours to live.

HENRI: Neither have you.

LANDRIEU: Perhaps not. But you smoke. And think a little. You've got education, be a realist. If you don't talk, your girl-friend or the boy will.

HENRI: That's their business.

LANDRIEU: Where is your captain?

HENRI: Make me tell you!

LANDRIEU: All right. Take away that cigarette. Clochet, fix him up.

CLOCHET: Put the sticks under the ropes. [*The* MILITIAMEN *slip two sticks under the ropes that fasten Henri's wrists.*] Right. They'll be twisted until you talk.

HENRI: I shan't.

CLOCHET: Not immediately. You'll scream first.

HENRI: Try to make me scream.

CLOCHET: You're not humble, Henri. You must be very humble. Pride goes before a fall, you know. If you fall from too high, you might break your neck. Turn. Slowly? Well? Nothing? Good. Turn. Turn. Wait. He's beginning to feel it. Well? Of course, I understand. Pain means nothing to a man of your intelligence. Or does it? I think it does. [*Gently*] You're sweating. I can feel for you. [*He wipes Henri's face with his handkerchief.*] Turn. He'll scream. He won't scream? You're moving. You can stop yourself screaming, but you can't help moving your head. How it hurts. [*He passes a finger over Henri's cheek.*] Your jaws are like iron; you must be in such agony. Are you afraid? What are you thinking? 'If I can only hold out for one moment, one little moment...' But after that moment, another will come, and another and another, until the pain is too much and you won't be able to think of anything. We shall never let you go. [*He takes Henri's head in his hands.*] Already, your eyes are beginning to fail. You can't see clearly any more. What do you see? [*Gently*] Handsome boy. Turn. [*Pause. Triumphantly*] You're going to scream, Henri, you're going to scream. I can see the cry swelling in your throat; it's reached your lips. One little effort. Turn. [HENRI *cries out.*] Ha! [*Pause.*] How ashamed you must be. Turn. Don't stop. [HENRI *cries again.*] You see; it's only the first scream that matters. And now, quite gently, quite naturally, you're going to talk.

HENRI: You'll get nothing from me but screams.

CLOCHET: No, Henri, no. You've no right to be proud now. 'Try to make me scream!' Well, you see, it didn't take long. Where is your captain? Be humble, Henri, quite, quite humble. Tell us where he is. Well, what are you waiting for? Scream or speak. Turn. Turn again; good God, break his wrists. Stop! He's fainted. [*He fetches a bottle of spirits and a glass. He makes* HENRI *drink. Very gently.*] Drink, poor martyr. Feel better? Well, we can start again. Fetch the instruments.

LANDRIEU: No!

CLOCHET: What?

LANDRIEU [*passes his hand over his forehead*]: Take him out. You can work on him downstairs.

CLOCHET: We won't have much room.

LANDRIEU: I give the orders here, Clochet. That's the second time I've had to remind you.

CLOCHET: But ...

LANDRIEU [*shouting*]: Do you want me to smash your face?

CLOCHET: Okay, okay. Bring him along. [*He goes out. The* MILITIAMEN *untie Henri and take him out.*]

PELLERIN: Are you coming?

LANDRIEU: No. Clochet makes me feel sick.

PELLERIN: He talks too much. [*Pause.*] Medical student! The bastard. I left school when I was thirteen – I had to earn my own living. I wasn't lucky. I had no rich parents to pay for my education.

LANDRIEU: I hope he talks.

PELLERIN: God in heaven, of course he'll talk.
[HENRI *screams.* LANDRIEU *goes to the door and shuts it. Fresh screams that can be clearly heard through the door.* LANDRIEU *goes to the radio and turns it on.*]

PELLERIN [*amazed*]: You're at it, too?

LANDRIEU: It's those screams. You need strong nerves.

PELLERIN: Let him scream. He's a bastard, a bloody intellectual. [*Piercing music*] Turn it down. I can't hear him.

LANDRIEU: Go and join them. [PELLERIN *hesitates, then goes out.*] He must talk. He's a coward. He must be a coward. [*Music and screams. The screams stop. Pause.* PELLERIN *comes back, pale.*]

PELLERIN: Stop that music.

LANDRIEU [*turning it off*]: Well?

PELLERIN [*goes to the door*]: Stop. Bring him back in here. [CLOCHET *and the* MILITIAMEN *return, bringing* HENRI. *Going to Henri*] It isn't over. We'll pay you back, don't worry. Don't look at me. I told you not to look at me. [*He hits him.*] Bastard. [*The* MILITIAMEN *untie Henri.*]

CLOCHET: One moment. [*Going to Henri*] Hold out your wrists, I want to put the bracelets on again. [*He puts the handcuffs on, very gently.*] That hurts, doesn't it? That hurts like hell? Poor chap. [*He strokes his hair.*] You mustn't be so proud. You screamed, you know, you did scream. To-morrow, you'll talk.

[*The* MILITIAMEN *take Henri away at a gesture from* LANDRIEU.]

PELLERIN: The bastard!

LANDRIEU: I don't like it.

CLOCHET: What?

LANDRIEU: I don't like it when they won't talk.

CLOCHET: He screamed, though. He did scream. . . . [*Shrugs his shoulders.*]

PELLERIN: Fetch the girl.

LANDRIEU: The girl . . . And if she doesn't talk?

PELLERIN: Well?

LANDRIEU: Nothing. [*With sudden violence*] Surely one of them will talk!

CLOCHET: We ought to fetch the blonde back. He's just ready.

LANDRIEU: The blonde?

CLOCHET: Sorbier. He's a coward.

LANDRIEU: A coward? Get him.

[CLOCHET *goes out.*]

PELLERIN: They're all cowards. Only some of them are stubborn.

LANDRIEU: Pellerin! What would you do if someone tore off your nails?

PELLERIN: The English don't tear off your nails.

LANDRIEU: What about the maquis?

PELLERIN: They won't tear off our nails.

LANDRIEU: Why not?

PELLERIN: Things like that couldn't happen to us.

[CLOCHET *re-enters, preceding* SORBIER.]

CLOCHET: Let me question him. Take off his handcuffs. Tie his arms to the chair. Good. [*He goes to Sorbier*] Well, well, here you are again. Here you are again in this nice chair. And here we are. Do you know why we brought you back?

SORBIER: No.

CLOCHET: Because you're a coward and you're going to squeal. Aren't you a coward?

SORBIER: Yes.

CLOCHET: You see, of course you are. I read it in your eyes. Show me your eyes – your big staring eyes. . . .

SORBIER: Yours will be like mine when you're hanged.

CLOCHET: Don't get fresh, or you'll be sorry.

SORBIER: Like mine; we're brothers. I attract you, don't I? It's not me you're torturing. It's yourself.

CLOCHET [abruptly]: Are you a Jew?

SORBIER [astonished]: Me? No.

CLOCHET: I swear you are a Jew. [He makes a sign to the militiamen who strike Sorbier.] Are you a Jew?

SORBIER: Yes. I am a Jew.

CLOCHET: Good. Now, listen. The nails first. That will give you time to think; we're in no hurry, we've got the whole night. Will you talk?

SORBIER: Bastard!

CLOCHET: What did you say?

SORBIER: I said: bastard. You and I, we're both bastards.

CLOCHET [to the militiamen]: Take the pincers and begin.

SORBIER: Leave me alone! Leave me alone! I'll talk. I'll tell you everything you want to know.

CLOCHET [to the militiamen]: Pull the nail a little all the same, to show him we're serious.

[SORBIER groans.]

CLOCHET: Good. Where is your captain?

SORBIER: Let me go. I can't bear this chair any more! I can't bear it! I can't bear it!

LANDRIEU: That's enough: let him go.

[The MILITIAMEN set him free. He rises and staggers to the table.]

SORBIER: Cigarette.

LANDRIEU: Afterwards.

SORBIER: What do you want to know? Where is our captain? I know. The others don't, but I do. I know everything. He is ... [*Abruptly pointing behind them*] ... there! [*Everyone turns round. He springs to the window and jumps on to the window-sill.*] I've won. Don't come near me, or I'll jump. I've won! I've won!

CLOCHET: Don't play the fool. If you speak, we'll let you go.

SORBIER [*spits. Shouting*]: Hey, up there! Henri, Canoris, I didn't squeal.

[*The* MILITIAMEN *rush towards him. He jumps into the void.*]

PELLERIN: The bastard! The cowardly bastard! Get hold of him.

[*They lean out of the window.*]

LANDRIEU [*to the militiamen*]: Go down after him. If he's still alive, bring him back. We'll go over him until he breaks between our hands.

[*The* MILITIAMEN *go out. Pause.*]

CLOCHET: I told you to shut the window.

[LANDRIEU *goes to him and hits him in the face.*]

LANDRIEU: Put that in your report.

[*Pause.* CLOCHET *takes his handkerchief and wipes his mouth. A* MILITIAMAN *comes back.*]

MILITIAMAN: Dead!

LANDRIEU [*after a pause*]: Get the girl. [*The* MILITIAMAN *goes out.*] They'll squeal, by God! They'll squeal!

CURTAIN

ACT TWO

The attic.

> [FRANÇOIS, CANORIS, *and* HENRI *are sitting on the ground, huddled against each other. They are talking softly.* JEAN *is pacing up and down, unhappily. From time to time he makes as if to join in the conversation, but stops himself, and goes back to his restless pacing.*]

CANORIS: While they were tying my arms, I watched them. One bastard came and hit me. I looked at him, and I thought, I've seen you somewhere before. After that, some of them came and started to kick me, and I tried to remember.

HENRI: Which one was it?

CANORIS: The little bastard who talks so much. I used to see him in Grenoble. You know Chasières, the cake-shop in the main street? He used to sell cream cakes in the back-room. Every Sunday morning, this bastard used to come out of there, carrying a box of cakes tied up with pink string. I remembered him because of his ugly mug. I thought he was probably working for the police.

HENRI: You should have told me.

CANORIS: What, that he was working for the police?

HENRI: That Chasières sold cream cakes. Did he have his little jokes with you too?

CANORIS: I'll say he did. He bent down and breathed in my face.

JEAN [*abruptly*]: What did he say?

> [*They all turn towards him and look at him in surprise.*]

HENRI: Nothing. Bloody nonsense.

JEAN: I couldn't have stood it.

HENRI: Why not? Gives you something to think about.

JEAN: Oh, really? Of course I wouldn't know.
[*Pause.* HENRI *turns back to Canoris.*]

HENRI: What do you think they were in civvy street?

CANORIS: The fat one who takes notes all the times might be a dentist.

HENRI [*laughs*]: I say! Lucky for us he didn't bring his drill.
[*They laugh.*]

JEAN [*violently*]: Stop laughing. [*They stop and look at Jean.*]
I know, you can laugh. You have the right to laugh. And I
have no more orders to give you. [*Pause.*] If anyone had told
me that one day you would frighten me . . . [*Pause.*] How can
you laugh?

HENRI: It's possible.

JEAN: Of course. And you can bear your own sufferings. That
gives you a clear conscience. I was married once; I never
told you. In this kind of life, marriage is one of those things
one hides. My wife died in childbirth. It was a summer's
day, just like today. I walked up and down in the corridor
of the hospital, and I knew she was going to die. It's just the
same, just the same! I wanted to help her, and I couldn't. I
walked up and down, and I tried to hear her cries. She didn't
cry. It was much easier for her. For you too.

HENRI: It's not our fault.

JEAN: It wasn't hers either. I wish I could help you.

CANORIS: There's nothing you can do.

JEAN: I know. [*Pause.*] They took her away two hours ago. They
didn't keep any of you so long.

HENRI: She's a girl. They amuse themselves with girls.

JEAN [*exploding*]: I'll come back in a week, in a month. I'll
come back, and make them pay for this.

HENRI: You're lucky to be able to hate them still.

JEAN: Am I? It gives me something to think about.
[*He paces up and down a moment longer, then has an idea and
drags an old stove under the window.*]

CANORIS: What are you doing now? You make me tired.

JEAN: I want to see him again before it gets dark.

HENRI: See who?

JEAN: Sorbier.

HENRI [*indifferently*]: Oh!

[JEAN *climbs on the stove and looks out of the window.*]

JEAN: He's still lying there. They'll leave him until he rots. Do you want to see? I'll help you.

CANORIS: What for?

JEAN: Yes. What for? You can leave the dead to me.

FRANÇOIS: I want to see.

HENRI: I wouldn't advise you to.

FRANÇOIS [*to Jean*]: Help me. [JEAN *helps him to climb on the stove. He looks out of the window.*] He . . . his head's all battered in.

[*He climbs down, and crouches in a corner, trembling.*]

HENRI [*to Jean*]: That was clever.

JEAN: Well, why not? I thought you were all so tough you could stand the sight of a corpse.

HENRI: Me perhaps, but not that kid. [*To François*] Leave the funeral service to Jean, it's his business. You don't have to worry about Sorbier. He's finished, forget it. You've still got a lot of ground to cover. Worry about yourself.

FRANÇOIS: My head will be crushed like that . . . my eyes . . .

HENRI: That's got nothing to do with you. You won't be there to see.

[*Pause.* JEAN *paces up and down, then comes back and stands in front of Canoris and Henri.*]

JEAN: Henri, must I have my nails torn off before I can become one of you?

CANORIS: You have always been one of us.

JEAN: You know I haven't. [*Pause.*] Who told you I wouldn't have held out? [*To Henri*] Maybe I wouldn't have screamed either?

203

HENRI: So what?

JEAN: I'm sorry. I've no right to say anything.

HENRI: Jean! Come and sit here with us. [JEAN *hesitates, then sits down.*] You would be like us if you were in our place. And besides, we haven't the same responsibilities. [JEAN *gets up abruptly.*] What's up?

JEAN: Until they bring her back, I can't keep still.

HENRI: You're only making things worse for yourself.

JEAN: For six months I didn't tell her I loved her, and at night, when I took her in my arms, I put out the light. Now she is in the midst of them, and they are pawing her with their filthy hands.

HENRI: What does it matter? The important thing is to win.

JEAN: Win what?

HENRI: Win. There are two teams, one trying to make the other talk. [*He laughs.*] It's a bit idiotic. But it's all we've got. If we talk, we've lost everything. They've marked up a few points because I screamed, but on the whole, we aren't so badly off.

JEAN: Win or lose, I don't give a damn! Those are just words. But she is suffering real shame, real agony.

HENRI: So what? I was ashamed myself, when they forced me to scream. But it doesn't last. And if she keeps quiet, their hands can't leave any marks. They are miserable bastards, you know.

JEAN: They are men.

HENRI: If you want to know, I love her too.

JEAN: You?

HENRI: Why not? And I didn't think it so funny when you went up the ladder, the pair of you. I often wondered if you put out the light.

JEAN: You love her? And you can sit there like that?

HENRI: Her suffering is bringing us together. The pleasure you gave her kept us apart. Today I am nearer to her than you are.

JEAN: That's not true! She's thinking of me, only of me. It's to protect me that she is enduring the suffering and the shame.

HENRI: No. It's to win.

JEAN: Liar! [*Pause.*] She said herself: when I come back, there will be nothing in my eyes but love for you.
  [*Footsteps in the corridor.*]

HENRI: Here she comes. See for yourself.
  [*The door opens.* HENRI *rises.*]

JEAN: Oh, God! I can never look at her again.
  [LUCIE *enters.* JEAN *and* HENRI *look at her in silence. She comes in quite steadily, without looking at them, and sits downstage. Pause.*]

LUCIE: François. [FRANÇOIS *comes to her and sits down at her knee.*] Don't touch me. Give me Sorbier's coat. [FRANÇOIS *picks up the jacket.*] Put it round my shoulders. [*She clutches it to her tightly.*]

FRANÇOIS: Are you cold?

LUCIE: No. [*Pause.*] What are they all doing? Why are they looking at me? Why don't they say something?

JEAN [*coming up behind her*]: Lucie!

CANORIS: Leave her alone.

JEAN: Lucie!

LUCIE [*gently*]: What do you want?

JEAN: You promised me there would be nothing in your eyes but love.

LUCIE: Love? [*She shrugs her shoulders sadly.*]

CANORIS [*who has risen*]: Leave her alone! You can talk to her later on.

JEAN [*violently*]: Leave her alone! She's mine. You have deserted me, you others, and I say nothing. But you don't take her from me. [*To Lucie*] Speak to me, Lucie. You aren't like the others? You can't be! Why don't you answer? Are you angry with me?

LUCIE: I'm not angry with you.

JEAN: My sweet Lucie.

LUCIE: I shall never be your sweet Lucie again, Jean.

JEAN: Don't you love me?

LUCIE: I don't know. [*He takes a step towards her.*] Please – don't touch me. [*With an effort*] I think I ought to love you. But I can't feel my love any more. [*Very tired*] I can't feel anything.

CANORIS [*to Jean*]: Come away. [*He drags him away and makes* JEAN *sit down beside him.*]

LUCIE [*as if to herself*]: None of this matters very much. [*To François.*] What are they doing?

FRANÇOIS: They're sitting with their back to you.

LUCIE: I see. [*Pause.*] Tell them I didn't talk.

CANORIS: We know, Lucie.

LUCIE: Good.

[*Long pause, then sound of steps in the corridor.* FRANÇOIS *starts upright and cries out.*]

LUCIE: What's the matter? Oh yes, it's your turn. You must be very brave; you must make them feel ashamed.

[*The steps come nearer, then fade away again.*]

FRANÇOIS [*collapses against Lucie*]: I can't bear it! I can't bear it!

LUCIE: Look at me. [*She lifts his head.*] How frightened you are! You won't talk, will you? Answer me!

FRANÇOIS: I don't know any more. I had a little bit of courage left, but I shouldn't have seen you. Look at you, with your hair in a mess, and your blouse torn! I know they took you in their arms.

LUCIE [*violently*]: They didn't touch me. No one touched me. I was made of stone, and I didn't even feel their hands. I looked at them, and I thought, nothing is going to happen. [*Passionately*] And nothing did happen. They were frightened of me. [*Pause.*] François, if you talk, they will have really raped me. They will say: 'We got them at last!' They will

smile when they remember. They will say: 'We had lots of
fun with the boy.' You must make them feel ashamed; if I
didn't think I'd see them again, and make them feel ashamed
again, I'd hang myself now from the bars of the window.
Will you keep silent?

[FRANÇOIS *shrugs his shoulders without replying. Silence.*]

HENRI [*softly*]: Well, Jean, who was right? She wants to win;
that's all.

JEAN: Shut up! Why are you trying to take her from me? You
have everything; you will die proudly and joyfully. I have
nothing left but her, and I have got to live.

HENRI: I want nothing, and I haven't taken her.

JEAN: Go on! Go on! You have all the rights, even the right
to torture me; you have paid in advance. [*He gets up.*] How
sure you all are of yourselves. A little bodily pain and your
conscience is clear. [HENRI *doesn't reply.*] Don't you see that
I am suffering more than any of you?

FRANÇOIS [*who has straightened up abruptly*]: Ha! Ha! Ha!

JEAN [*crying*]: More than any of you! Any of you!

FRANÇOIS [*springing at him*]: Look at him! Just look at him!
He's suffering more than any of us! He can sleep and eat.
His hands are free, he will see the sun again, he will live.
But he's suffering more than we are. What do you want us
to do? Feel sorry for you? Swine!

JEAN [*who has folded his arms*]: Quite right.

FRANÇOIS: I jump every time I hear a noise. I can't swallow. I
feel I'm dying. But he's suffering more than any of us. Of
course he is! I am going to die happy. [*Exploding*] I'll make
you happy, see if I don't!

LUCIE [*who has risen abruptly*]: François!

FRANÇOIS: I'll denounce you! I'll denounce you! I'll help you
to share our happiness.

JEAN [*softly and quickly*]: Go ahead. You don't know how much
I want you to go ahead.

LUCIE [*taking François by the scruff of the neck, and twisting his head round to face her*]: Look at me! Will you dare to betray him?

FRANÇOIS: Dare! That's a fine word! I'll denounce him, that's all. It will be so easy; they'll come up to me, my lips will open of their own accord, the name will come out, and I will be glad. What's so difficult about that? When I look at you, pale and haggard, like a bunch of maniacs, I'm not frightened of your scorn any more. [*Pause.*] I'm going to save you, Lucie. They will let us live.

LUCIE: I don't want that kind of life.

FRANÇOIS: I do. I don't care what kind of life it is.

CANORIS: They won't let you live, François. Even if you do speak.

FRANÇOIS [*meaning Jean*]: At least I'll see him suffer.

HENRI [*rising and going to Lucie*]: Think he'll speak?

LUCIE [*turning to François and looking at him*]: Yes.

HENRI: Sure? [*They look at each other.*]

LUCIE [*after a long hesitation*]: Yes.

> [HENRI goes to François. CANORIS rises and comes to stand beside Henri. Both of them look at François.]

HENRI: François, I'm not your judge. You're only a kid still, and all this was too tough for you. I expect at your age I'd have done the same.

CANORIS: It's our fault. We shouldn't have brought you with us. Some risks should only be taken by men. Forgive us.

FRANÇOIS [*retreating*]: What do you mean? What are you going to do to me?

HENRI: We can't allow you to speak, François. They'll kill you all the same, you know. And you will die in despair.

FRANÇOIS [*frightened*]: All right, I won't speak. I tell you, I won't speak. Leave me alone.

HENRI: We can't trust you. They know you are our weak point. They'll work on you until you squeal. And we can't let that happen.

JEAN: Do you really think I'm going to let you do this? Don't be afraid, François. My hands are free, and I am with you.

LUCIE [*standing in his way*]: Why are you interfering?

JEAN: He is your brother.

LUCIE [*shrugs*]: He will die tomorrow.

JEAN: Is this really you?

LUCIE: He must be silenced. The method doesn't matter.

FRANÇOIS: You aren't going to . . . [*They do not answer.*] I swear to you I won't say anything. [*They do not answer.*] Lucie, help, help. Stop them from hurting me! I won't talk! I swear to you, I won't talk!

JEAN [*standing beside François*]: You shan't touch him.

HENRI: Do you want the militiamen to make mincemeat of our boys when they march into the village? Take care, Jean; if you prevent us from handling this affair, you'll be responsible for their deaths.

JEAN: Let him take his chance; maybe he won't talk.

CANORIS: We have no right to give him a chance.

[*They look at each other for a long moment, then* JEAN *moves away.*]

FRANÇOIS [*looks at him, then begins to shout*]: Lucie! Help! I don't want to die here, not in this darkness. Henri, I am only sixteen, let me live. Don't kill me in the dark.

[HENRI *grips him by the throat.*]

FRANÇOIS: Lucie!

[LUCIE *turns away her head.*]

LUCIE: My darling, my poor darling, my only love, forgive me. [*She turns away. Pause.*] Do it quickly.

HENRI: I can't; my wrists are half-broken.

[*Pause.*]

LUCIE: Is it over?

HENRI: He is dead.

[LUCIE *turns round, and takes the body of François in her arms. His head rests on her knees. A very long silence; then* JEAN *begins to speak softly. All the following dialogue is spoken in an undertone.*]

JEAN: What has become of you all? Why didn't you die with the others? You horrify me.

HENRI: Do you think I like myself?

JEAN: It doesn't matter. In twenty-four hours you'll be rid of yourself. But for the rest of my days I shall see that child begging for mercy, and the look on your face as you strangled him. [*He goes up to François and looks down at him.*] Sixteen! He died in anger and in fear. [*He goes back to Henri.*] He loved you; he used to sleep with his head on your shoulder; he used to say, 'I sleep better when you are with me.' [*Pause.*] Damn you!

HENRI [*to Canoris and Lucie*]: Why don't you say something? Don't leave me alone. Lucie! Canoris! You killed him with my hands. [*No answer. He turns to Jean.*] And what about you? You curse me, but what did you do to defend him?

JEAN [*violently*]: What could I do? What would you have let me do?

HENRI: Your hands were free, you should have hit me. [*Passionately*] If you had hit me . . . if you had knocked me down . . .

JEAN: My hands were free? You had cut my throat. If I say a word, if I make a movement: 'What about the others?' You had shut me out. You had decided I must live, and he must die. Coldly. Don't tell me now that I am your accomplice; that's too easy. I am your witness, that is all. And I say you are murderers. [*Pause.*] You killed him out of vanity.

HENRI: It's not true! Lucie, tell him it isn't true! [LUCIE *doesn't answer. He takes a step towards her.*] Answer me! Do you think I killed him out of vanity?

LUCIE: I don't know. [*A pause, then painfully*] We had to be sure he wouldn't talk.

HENRI: He was your brother. You are the only one who has the right to judge me. Do you hate me for it?

LUCIE: I don't hate you. [*He takes a step towards the body she still holds in her arms. Tensely*] Don't touch him.

[HENRI *turns slowly, and goes back to Canoris.*]

HENRI: Don't desert me. You have no right to desert me. When my hands were round his neck, I felt as though they were our hands, and that we were all choking him, otherwise I would never have been able ...

CANORIS: He had to die; if he had been beside me, I would have strangled him. As for what goes on inside your head ...

HENRI: Well?

CANORIS: That doesn't matter. Nothing matters between these four walls. He had to die; that's all.

HENRI: All right. [*He goes up to the body. To Lucie*] Don't worry, I won't touch him. [*He bends over François and looks at him for a long time, then he straightens up.*] Jean, when we threw our first grenade, how many hostages were shot? [JEAN *does not reply.*] Twelve. There was a boy amongst them; he was called Destrechez. Remember? We saw the placards in the rue des Minimes. Charbonnel wanted to give himself up, and you prevented him.

JEAN: Well?

HENRI: Do you ever wonder why you stopped him?

JEAN: It's not the same thing.

HENRI: Perhaps. So much the better for you if your motives were clearer. You have kept a clean conscience. But Destrechez died all the same. I shall never have a clear conscience again, until they stick me up against a wall with a bandage over my eyes. But why do I want a clear conscience? The kid had to die.

JEAN: I wouldn't like to be in your place.

HENRI [*gently*]: This doesn't concern you, Jean, you cannot understand, or judge us.

[*A long silence, then* LUCIE's *voice. She strokes François's hair without looking at him. For the first time since the beginning of the scene she speaks aloud.*]

LUCIE: You are dead, my darling, and my eyes are dry; forgive me. I have no more tears, and death doesn't matter any more. Outside three hundred bodies are lying on the grass, and tomorrow I shall be cold and naked too, with no one to smooth my hair. There's nothing to regret, you know; life has no real importance any more. Good-bye, my darling brother, you did what you could. If you fell short, it was only because you weren't strong enough. No one has the right to blame you.

JEAN [*a long silence. He comes to sit beside Lucie*]: Lucie! [*She makes a movement.*] Don't drive me away. I want to help you.

LUCIE [*astonished*]: Help me? I don't need help.

JEAN: Yes, you do. I think I'm afraid you'll break down.

LUCIE: I'll be all right until tomorrow evening.

JEAN: You've been through too much, you won't be able to hold out. Your courage will snap all of a sudden.

LUCIE: Why do you worry about me? [*She looks at him.*] You are very unhappy. All right, I'll reassure you, and then you can go. Everything has become very clear since the boy died; I've only myself to think about. And I don't need courage to die. In any case, I wouldn't have been able to survive him for long. Go away now. I shall say good-bye to you later when they come for me.

JEAN: Let me stay here with you. I won't talk, if you don't want me to, but I'll be there, and you won't feel so alone.

LUCIE: Not alone? With you? Oh, Jean, you haven't understood. We have nothing more in common.

JEAN: Have you forgotten I love you?

LUCIE: You loved someone else.

JEAN: It's you I love.

LUCIE: I've become another person. I don't know myself. Something has got blocked in my head.

JEAN: Maybe. Maybe you have become another person. All right, it's this new person I love, and tomorrow, when you die, it will be a dead Lucie that I love. It's you I love, Lucie, *you*, it's always you.

LUCIE: All right. You love me. And then?

JEAN: You used to love me.

LUCIE: Yes. And I loved my brother, and allowed Henri to kill him. Our love is so far away, why talk to me about it? It really doesn't matter at all.

JEAN: That's not true! You know it's not true! It was our life, our whole life. Everything we have lived through, we have lived through together.

LUCIE: Our life, yes. Our future. I lived in an eternal expectation. I loved you in expectation. I was waiting for the end of the war. Waiting for the day when we could be married in the eyes of the world. Each night I waited for you. Now I have no future. I expect nothing but my death, and I shall die alone. [*Pause.*] Leave me alone. We have nothing to say to each other. I am not in pain and I have no need of consolation.

JEAN: Do you think I'd try to console you? I can see your dry eyes, and I know that your heart is a hell. Not a trace of suffering, not even the moisture of a tear, everything burnt to ashes. Lucie, I wish I could help you to pity yourself a little. If you could only relax, put your head on my shoulder . . . Speak to me, look at me.

LUCIE: Don't touch me.

JEAN: Lucie, whatever you do, we are still together. The harm they did you, they did to me, and if you come into my arms, it will become our suffering. If you could only shed one tear . . .

LUCIE [*violently*]: A tear? All I want is for them to come for me again, and beat me, so that I can keep silent again, and fool them and frighten them.

JEAN [*overcome*]: Then it's nothing but pride.

LUCIE: Is it my fault? It was my pride they attacked. I hate them, but they still hold me; and I hold them. I feel nearer to them than I do to you. [*She laughs*]. Are your wrists crushed like Henri? Are your legs cut like Canoris? It's only a game for you; you have felt nothing, you only imagine things.

JEAN: . . . Ah! If that's all you need to make me one of you . . .

[*He looks around him, sees a heavy log, and picks it up.*]

LUCIE: What are you doing?

JEAN [*laying his left hand on the floor, he strikes it with the log*]: I've had enough of your boastings. What they did to you, I can do to myself; anyone can do it.

[LUCIE *bursts out laughing.*]

LUCIE [*laughing*]: No good, no good. You can break your bones, you can tear out your eyes. It's you, you who have chosen to inflict the pain. Each of our wounds is a violation because they were inflicted by other people. You can't catch up with us.

[*A pause.* JEAN *throws down the log and looks at her. Then he gets up.*]

JEAN: You are right. You are together and I am alone. I won't speak to you, I'll hide in the shadows and you can forget my existence. I suppose it's my part in this story and I must accept it as you have accepted your own. [*Pause.*] Just now I had an idea. Pierre was killed outside the grotto at Servaz where we used to hide the guns. If they let me go, I'll go back there; I'll put some papers in his pockets and drag his body into the grotto. Allow four hours after I've gone, and when they start questioning you again, tell them about the hiding-place. They'll find Pierre and they'll think it's me. So then they'll have nothing to torture you for, and they'll finish with you. That's all. Good-bye.

[*He withdraws into the shadows. Long silence. Then footsteps in the corridor. A* MILITIAMAN *appears carrying a lantern. He throws the light all round the room.*]

MILITIAMAN [*seeing François*]: What's the matter with him?

LUCIE: He's asleep.

MILITIAMAN [*to Jean*]: Here, you. They want you.

[JEAN *hesitates, looks at each of them in turn with a sort of despair, and follows the militiaman. The door closes again.*]

LUCIE: He'll be all right, won't he?

CANORIS: I think so.

LUCIE: Good. That's one worry less. He'll go back to his friends, and everything will be for the best. Come here to me. [HENRI *and* CANORIS *go to her.*] Nearer. Henri, what's stopping you? We're all friends here. Come, come. [*She looks at them and understands.*] Ah! [*Pause.*] It's the ones downstairs who killed him with our hands. I am his sister, and I tell you you are not guilty of his death. Lay your hands on him. Since he died he has become one of us again. See how stern he looks; he has closed his lips on a secret. Touch him.

HENRI [*stroking François's hair*]: Poor boy! Poor little boy!

LUCIE: They made you cry out, Henri, I heard you. You must feel very ashamed.

HENRI: Yes.

LUCIE: I feel your shame with the warmth of your body. It is my shame too. I told him I was alone, and I lied to him. With you two, I don't feel alone. [*To Canoris*] You didn't cry out, did you; it's a pity.

CANORIS: I am ashamed too.

LUCIE: Why?

CANORIS: When Henri cried out, I was ashamed for him.

LUCIE: I see. Come close to me. I feel your arms and your shoulders; my brother's weight is heavy on my knees. Tomorrow I must be brave again. Oh, how brave I shall be. For him, for myself, for Sorbier, for you two. We are all one.

CURTAIN

ACT THREE

[*Before the curtain rises, a deafening and vulgar voice is heard singing: 'If every cuckold wore a bell.' The curtain rises on the school-room. It is the following morning.* PELLERIN *is sitting on a bench, drinking. He looks exhausted.* LANDRIEU *is at the desk drinking; he is half-drunk.* CLOCHET *is standing near the window. He yawns from time to time.* LANDRIEU *bursts out laughing.*]

PELLERIN: What's the matter?

LANDRIEU [*putting his hand to his ear*]: What?

PELLERIN: What's the joke?

LANDRIEU [*pointing to the radio*]: That.

PELLERIN: Eh?

LANDRIEU: I think that's a bloody funny idea.

PELLERIN: What is?

LANDRIEU: To hang bells on cuckolds.

PELLERIN: Oh, hell! I can't hear what you're saying. [*He goes to the radio.*]

LANDRIEU [*shouting*]: Don't turn it off. [PELLERIN *turns the knob. Silence.*] You see!

PELLERIN [*taken aback*]: See what?

LANDRIEU: It's cold.

PELLERIN: You're cold? In July?

LANDRIEU: I tell you it's cold: you don't understand anything.

PELLERIN: What were you saying just now?

LANDRIEU: When?

PELLERIN: About cuckolds.

LANDRIEU: Who the hell's talking about cuckolds? Cuckold yourself. [*Pause.*] I'm going to get the news. [*He rises and goes to the radio.*]

CLOCHET: There isn't any.

LANDRIEU: No news?

CLOCHET: It's not time.

LANDRIEU: Let's see. [*He turns the knob. Music, static.*]

PELLERIN: You're deafening us.

LANDRIEU [*speaking to the radio*]: Bastard. [*Pause.*] What the hell, I'm going to get the B.B.C. What's the wave-length?

PELLERIN: Twenty-one metres.

[LANDRIEU *turns the dial. A speech in Czech.* LANDRIEU *begins to laugh.*]

LANDRIEU [*laughing*]: It's Czech. D'you get it? There's a Czech talking from London. What a small world. [*He shakes the radio.*] Talk French, can't you? [*He turns it off.*] Give us a drink. [PELLERIN *pours out a glass of wine.* LANDRIEU *goes to him and drinks.*] What the hell are we doing here?

PELLERIN: Here or anywhere . . .

LANDRIEU: I'd much rather be with the fighting.

PELLERIN: Hum!

LANDRIEU: That's right – I wish I were. [*He seizes him by the sleeve of his coat.*] Don't you tell me I'm afraid to die.

PELLERIN: I didn't say a word.

LANDRIEU: What's death, anyway? What's it all about? . . . All got to die, tomorrow, day after tomorrow, three months time. . . .

CLOCHET [*quickly*]: It's not true! It's not true! We'll push the English back into the sea.

LANDRIEU: Into the sea! You'll feel them in your backside, make no mistake about that. Here in this village. Then there'll be fireworks. Bang-bang. Bang! on the church! Bang! on the town hall! What'll you do, Clochet? You'll be in the cellar. Ha! Ha! in the cellar! Won't we have fun! [*To Pellerin*] Once we're dead . . . I'd forgotten what I was thinking about. Listen, those clever little chaps, upstairs, we'll knock them off, and I don't give a damn. Turn and

218

turn about, that's what I say to myself. Today it's their turn, tomorrow it'll be mine. That's fair enough, isn't it? I'm always fair, aren't I? [*He drinks.*] We aren't animals. [*To Clochet*] Why are you yawning?

CLOCHET: I'm bored.

LANDRIEU: All you've got to do is drink. Am I bored? You like spying on us, don't you? You're thinking what you'll put in your report. [*He pours out a glass of wine and holds it out to Clochet.*] Drink, damn you, drink!

CLOCHET: I can't. It's bad for my liver.

LANDRIEU: You'll drink this, or you'll get it in your face. [*Pause.* CLOCHET *puts out his hand, takes the glass and drinks.*] Ha! Ha! Animals, all animals, and everything's fine. [*Steps can be heard, someone is walking up and down in the attic. All three look up. They listen in silence, then abruptly* LANDRIEU *turns away, runs to the door and calls.*] Corbier! Corbier! [*A* MILITIAMAN *appears.*] Go and make them shut up. Hit them. [*The* MILITIAMAN *goes out.* LANDRIEU *shuts the door again and goes back to the others. All three are still looking up, listening. Pause.*] I suppose we've got to see them again. What a filthy day.

PELLERIN: Will you need me when you question them?

LANDRIEU: Why?

PELLERIN: I've been thinking. Their leader is probably hiding in the forest. I could take twenty men and organize a beat.

LANDRIEU [*looking at him.*]: Ah? [*Pause. Footsteps still sound from upstairs.*] You'll stay here.

PELLERIN: Okay. [*Shrugging his shoulders*] We're wasting time.

LANDRIEU: Maybe, but we'll waste it together. [*They look at the ceiling despite themselves, and speak the following lines in the same way, until the noise stops.*]

CLOCHET: It's time to bring the kid down.

LANDRIEU: I don't give a damn for the kid. I want to make the other bastard talk.

PELLERIN: They won't talk.

LANDRIEU: I tell you they will. They're just animals. You've got to know how to handle them. We didn't go at them hard enough. [*Scuffle in the attic, then silence. Satisfied*] What did I tell you? They're quiet now. Just got to take a firm hand. [*They are visibly relieved.*]

CLOCHET: All the same, you ought to begin with the kid.

LANDRIEU: Okay. [*He goes to the door.*] Corbier. [*No answer.*] Corbier! [*Hurried footsteps in the corridor.* CORBIER *appears.*] Go and fetch the kid.

CORBIER: The kid? They've knocked him off.

LANDRIEU: What?

CORBIER: They knocked him off during the night. I found him with his head on his sister's lap. She said he was asleep; he's cold already, with finger-marks on his throat.

LANDRIEU: Ah? [*Pause.*] Who was walking about?

CORBIER: The Greek.

LANDRIEU: Good. You can go. [CORBIER *goes. Pause. In spite of himself,* CLOCHET *looks at the ceiling.*]

PELLERIN: Let's get this over. A firing-squad, straightaway. Never see them again.

LANDRIEU: Shut up. [*He goes to the radio and turns the knob. A slow waltz. Then he goes back to the desk, and pours out a drink. As he puts his glass down, he sees the portrait of Pétain.*] You see this, you see this, but you wash your hands of it. . . . You sacrifice yourself, you dedicate yourself to France, and you don't give a damn for the details. You belong to history, and we can wallow in the slime. Bastard! [*He hurls his glass at his face.*]

CLOCHET: Landrieu!

LANDRIEU: Put that in your report. [*Pause. He controls himself with an effort, and goes back to Pellerin.*] A firing-squad ... that's too easy. That's what they want, don't you see?

PELLERIN: All right – it's what they want. But let's get this over and never see them again.

LANDRIEU: I don't want them to die without talking.

PELLERIN: They can't tell us anything. They've been up there for twenty-four hours – their leader has had plenty of time to make his getaway.

LANDRIEU: I don't give a damn for their leader. I want them to squeal.

PELLERIN: And if they don't?

LANDRIEU: You don't have to worry.

PELLERIN: But supposing they don't talk?

LANDRIEU: I told you to shut up. [*Pause.*]

PELLERIN: Well, why not send for them?

LANDRIEU: Of course I'm going to send for them. [*He doesn't move.* CLOCHET *begins to laugh.*]

CLOCHET: Supposing they're bloody martyrs, eh?
    [LANDRIEU *goes abruptly to the door.*]

LANDRIEU: Bring them down.

CORBIER [*appearing*]: All three?

LANDRIEU: Yes. All three. [CORBIER *goes out.*]

PELLERIN: You should have left the girl up there.
    [*Sound of footsteps overhead.*]

LANDRIEU: They're coming down. [*He goes to the radio and stops it.*] If they'll give their leader away, I'll let them live.

CLOCHET: Landrieu! Are you mad?

LANDRIEU: Shut up.

CLOCHET: They deserve to die ten times over.

LANDRIEU: I don't give a damn for what they deserve. I want them to crack. They can't play the martyr with me.

PELLERIN: I ... Listen, I couldn't bear it. If I had to think they were going to live, that they'd even live longer than us and for the rest of their lives they'd remember us ...

LANDRIEU: You don't have to worry. If they squeal to save their skins, they won't care to remember us very often. Here they are.

[PELLERIN *rises abruptly, and pushes the bottles and glasses under a chair. They wait, standing motionless.*]

LUCIE, HENRI, CANORIS *and the three* MILITIAMEN *come in. They look at each other in silence.*

LANDRIEU: What have you done to the boy?

[*No answer.*]

PELLERIN: Murderers!

LANDRIEU: Shut up. [*To the others*] He wanted to talk, eh? And you wanted to stop him.

LUCIE [*violently*]: It's a lie. He didn't want to talk. None of us wants to talk.

LANDRIEU: So?

HENRI: He was too young. There was no point in letting him suffer.

LANDRIEU: Which of you strangled him?

CANORIS: We decided together, and we are all responsible.

LANDRIEU: I see. [*Pause.*] If you give the information we require, your lives will be spared.

CLOCHET: Landrieu!

LANDRIEU: I told you to shut up. [*To the others*] Do you accept? [*Pause.*] Well? Yes or no? [*They keep silent.* LANDRIEU *is embarrassed.*] You refuse? You would sacrifice three lives to save one? You're mad! [*Pause.*] It's life I am offering you! Life! Life! Are you all deaf?

[*Pause, then* LUCIE *takes a step towards them.*]

LUCIE: We've won! We've won! This moment makes everything worthwhile. Everything that happened last night, everything I was trying to forget, I'm proud to remember. I can say it now, I can shout it now. You raped me and you are ashamed. I am clean again. Where are your pincers and your thumbscrews? Where are your whips? This morning you beg us to live. The answer is no. No! You must finish what you've begun.

PELLERIN: Enough! Enough! Hit them!

LANDRIEU: Stop! Pellerin, I may not be your commanding officer much longer, but while I am here, no one else gives orders.

CLOCHET: Can't we just work on them a little? That was only words. Words. Wind. [*Pointing to Henri*] That bastard came to us swelling like a turkey-cock, and we made him scream like a woman.

HENRI: See if you can make me scream today.

LANDRIEU: Work them if you want to.

CLOCHET: Oh, you know, even if they are martyrs, I don't care. I enjoy the work for its own sake. [*To the militiamen*] Take them down to the tables.

CANORIS: One moment. If we agree, what proof have we that you'll let us live?

LANDRIEU: You have my word.

CANORIS: I see. I suppose that should be enough. It's heads or tails, anyway. What will you do with us?

LANDRIEU: Surrender you to the German authorities.

CANORIS: Who'll shoot us at sight.

LANDRIEU: No. I'll explain your case to them.

CANORIS: Good. [*Pause.*] I'm ready to speak if my friends allow me.

HENRI: Canoris!

CANORIS: May I be alone with them? I think I can persuade them.

LANDRIEU [*surveying him*]: Why do you want to talk? Are you afraid to die?

[*A long pause, then* CANORIS *drops his head.*]

CANORIS: Yes.

LUCIE: Coward!

LANDRIEU: Good. [*To the militiamen*] Stand below the window. Guard the door. Come on. You've got fifteen minutes in which to convince them.

[LANDRIEU, PELLERIN, *and* CLOCHET *go out.*
During the first part of the scene LUCIE *is silent, and appears not to be listening to the discussion.*]

CANORIS: Are you mad? You're looking at me as if I really meant it. All I'm going to do is send them to the grotto at Servaz, as Jean told us to. [*Pause. He smiles.*] They have chipped us a little, but we're still quite usable. [*Pause.*] Come now; we must talk; why throw away three lives? [*Pause. Gently*] Why do you want to die? What good will it do? Answer me! What good will it do?

HENRI: None.

CANORIS: Well?

HENRI: I'm tired.

CANORIS: I'm more tired than you are. I'm fifteen years older, and they treated me much more roughly. The life they are giving me isn't particularly enjoyable.

HENRI [*gently*]: Are you so afraid of death?

CANORIS: Of course not. But we have no right to die for nothing.

HENRI: Why not? Why not? They broke my wrist, they cut my flesh; haven't I done enough? Look: Jean is out of danger, and in their eyes we have caught a look of shame. We have won all along the line; now it's all over, there's nothing to do but pull the trigger. Why do you want me to start life over again when I can die at peace with myself?

CANORIS: We've got friends to help.

HENRI: What friends? Where?

CANORIS: Everywhere.

HENRI: What are you talking about? If they do spare our lives, they'll send us to the salt mines.

CANORIS: All right. Then we'll escape.

HENRI: You! Escape? You're only a rag.

CANORIS: If I don't, you will.

HENRI: A hundred to one chance.

CANORIS: But worth taking. And even if we don't escape, there are other people in the mines; old men who are sick, women who can't stand the work. They need us.

HENRI: Listen, when I saw him lying there, white and lifeless, I thought: it's done. I've done what I've done, and I regret nothing. Only, I was assuming that I should die at dawn. If I thought that six hours later we'd still be on this filthy earth . . . [*Shouting*] I don't want to live without him. I don't want to live another thirty years without that boy. Canoris, it will be so easy; we shan't even have time to see the muzzles of their guns.

CANORIS: Why do you want to die for nothing?

HENRI: Do you still feel alive while men beat you until they break your bones? [*He looks out of the window.*] It's very dark – it's going to rain.

CANORIS: The sky is clouded over. We're in for a storm.

HENRI [*suddenly*]: It was vanity.

CANORIS: What?

HENRI: The boy. I did kill him out of vanity.

CANORIS: What does it matter? He had to die.

HENRI: I shall always have this horrible uncertainty – all my life I'll be questioning myself. I can't go on living.

CANORIS: Listen, Henri. If you die today, you've made your choice. You killed him out of vanity. But if you live . . .

HENRI: Well?

CANORIS: Then nothing is settled. Each one of your actions will be judged in the light of your whole life. If you let yourself be killed now when you could still go on living, then nothing could be more stupid than your death. [*Pause.*]

HENRI [*to Lucie*]: Let her decide.

CANORIS: Do you hear, Lucie?

LUCIE: Decide what? What does my consent matter? It's your lives you're saving, not mine. I have decided to die.

CANORIS: What about our friends, Lucie?

LUCIE: That doesn't count. All my life I've helped others. So I am quits, and I say I can go. You'll allow me to look after myself?

CANORIS: No.

LUCIE: Fool! Idiot! Oh yes, you can live! Your conscience is clear! They've knocked you about a bit, that's all. But they have destroyed me – there isn't a piece of my own skin that doesn't sicken me. You take on airs because you strangled a boy! Remember that boy was my brother, and I said nothing. I took all the blame on myself. I must die and all my shame with me. Get out! Get out – live, since that's what you want. But I cannot bear myself, and after my death I pray that everything on earth may be as though I had never lived.

CANORIS [gently]: You do take yourself seriously, don't you?

LUCIE [disconcerted]: What?

CANORIS: You do take your body seriously. And your life, and your death, and the boy's death. Come now, Lucie: none of that matters.

LUCIE: My hate and my shame and my remorse – does none of that matter?

CANORIS: Bah! Buzzing in your ears.

LUCIE: What about the men who tortured us? Their eyes gleamed when they realized you were going to squeal. You've given them back their self-respect.

CANORIS: They are men of straw. In six months they'll be skulking in a cellar, and the first grenade tossed in through a ventilator will write *finis* to this whole story.

LUCIE: What does matter?

CANORIS: Everything else. The world and what you do in the world; our friends and what you do for them.

LUCIE: I am dried up. I feel so alone. I don't want to think of anyone but myself.

HENRI: It's your pride that isolates you. You're clinging to yourself, and you're afraid to open your hands. I was afraid. You must let go – you must relax.

LUCIE: If I relaxed, I'd become stupid. I would cry.

HENRI: Why keep back your tears? Be humble. Oh, I know, heroes don't cry. But the orders have changed. No one wants us to be heroes any more. We must live. Won't you regret anything on the earth?

LUCIE: Nothing. Everything has been poisoned.

HENRI: Even the pale sky over the Tigne? Even the snow around the lake? You'll see it again, if you live. You'll see it again. Remember the children we used to meet, in the spring, sitting on the fallen trees, outside the sawmill. They smiled at us as we passed, and we could smell the freshly sawn wood.

LUCIE: Poor kids.

HENRI: Won't you miss them?

LUCIE: They ran away when the Germans arrived. I wouldn't be able to find them again.

HENRI: There'll be other kids in the concentration camps. Even there, we'll be able to see the sky.

[*It starts to rain outside, beginning slowly, but the wind blows it gustily against the roof, and soon it is raining heavily.*]

LUCIE: What's that – rain? I haven't heard the rain for three months. Oh God! All this time the sun has been shining – it was horrible. I didn't remember. I thought we always had to live in the sun. It's raining hard. We are going to smell the wet earth. I can't! I can't!

HENRI: Lucie! Lucie!

LUCIE: I don't want to cry. I don't want to be so stupid. . . . Let me go. . . . I want to live. I want to live.

[HENRI *puts his arms round her*.]

LUCIE: Is it really true we are going to live? I was nearly on

227

the other side. Look at me. Smile at me. It's so long since I saw a smile. [HENRI *looks at her, and they smile.*] Are we doing right, Henri, are we doing right?

CANORIS: Of course we are doing right. We've got to live! [*He goes to the militiaman.*] Go and tell them we're ready to talk.

   [*The* MILITIAMAN *goes out.* LANDRIEU, PELLERIN, *and* CLOCHET *return.*]

LANDRIEU: Well?

CANORIS: On the road to Grenoble, at the forty-second milestone, take the right-hand path. Fifty metres inside the forest you'll find a copse. Behind the copse there is a grotto. Our captain is hidden there with our guns.

LANDRIEU [*to the militiaman*]: Ten men. Leave at once. Try and bring him back alive. [*Pause.*] Take the prisoners back upstairs.

   [*The* MILITIAMAN *take the prisoners out.* CLOCHET *hesitates for a moment, then slips out after them.*]

PELLERIN: Think they were telling the truth?

LANDRIEU: Of course. They're just animals. [*He sits down at the desk.*] Well! We got them in the end. Did you see them go out? They were not so proud as when they came in. [CLOCHET *returns. Amiably*] Well, Clochet? We got them, didn't we?

CLOCHET [*rubbing his hands absent-mindedly*]: Yes, yes. We got them in the end.

PELLERIN: Are you really going to let them live?

LANDRIEU: Oh, for the time being anyway. . . . [*A salvo rings out from under the window.*] What the hell . . . ? [CLOCHET *sniggers in a slightly embarrassed way.*] Clochet, you haven't . . . [CLOCHET *nods, still laughing.*] Bastard!

   [*Second salvo. He runs to the window.*]

PELLERIN: Wait for it – third time lucky.

LANDRIEU: I won't allow . . .

PELLERIN: What would the survivor think of us?

CLOCHET: In a moment, no one will think of this any more. No one but us.

[*Third salvo.* LANDRIEU *sinks into a chair.*]

LANDRIEU: Ouf!

[CLOCHET *goes to the radio and turns the knob. Music.*]

CURTAIN

THE FLIES

CHARACTERS

ZEUS	CLYTEMNESTRA
ORESTES	FIRST FURY
ELECTRA	SECOND FURY
THE TUTOR	A YOUNG WOMAN
FIRST SOLDIER	AN OLD WOMAN
SECOND SOLDIER	THE HIGH PRIEST

Men and Women, Townsfolk of Argos

Furies

Servants

Palace Guards

ACT ONE

*A public square in Argos, dominated by a statue of Zeus, god of
flies and death. The image has white eyes and blood-smeared cheeks.*

> [*A procession of* OLD WOMEN *in black, carrying urns, ad-
> vances; they make libations to the statue. An* IDIOT BOY *is
> squatting in the background.* ORESTES *enters, accompanied by
> the* TUTOR.]

ORESTES: Listen, my good women.

> [*The* OLD WOMEN *swing round, emitting little squeals.*]

THE TUTOR: Would you kindly tell us ... [*The* OLD WOMEN
spit on the ground, and move back a pace.] Steady on, good
ladies, steady on. I only want a piece of simple information.
We are travellers, and we have lost our way. [*Dropping their
urns, the* WOMEN *take to their heels.*] Stupid old hags! You'd
think I had intentions on their virtue ... ! [*Ironically.*]
Ah, young master, truly this has been a pleasant journey!
And how well inspired you were to come to this city of
Argos, when there are hundreds of towns in Greece and
Italy where the drink is good, the inns are hospitable and
the streets full of friendly, smiling people! But these un-
couth hillmen – one would suppose they'd never seen a
foreigner before. A hundred times and more I've had to
ask our way, and never once did I get a straight answer. And
then the grilling heat! This Argos is a nightmare city. Squeals
of terror everywhere, people who panic the moment they
set eyes on you, and scurry to cover, like black beetles, down
the glaring streets. Pfoo! I can't think how you bear it –
this emptiness, the shimmering air, that fierce sun overhead.
What's deadlier than the sun?

ORESTES: I was born here.

THE TUTOR: So the story goes. But, if I were you, I wouldn't brag about it.

ORESTES: I was born here – and yet I have to ask my way, like any stranger. Knock at that door.

THE TUTOR: What do you expect? That someone will open it? Only look at those houses and tell me how they strike you. You will observe there's not a window anywhere. They open on closed courtyards, I suppose, and turn their backsides to the street. [ORESTES *makes a fretful gesture.*] Very good, sir. I'll knock – but nothing will come of it.
[*He knocks. Nothing happens. He knocks again, and the door opens a cautious inch.*]

A VOICE: What do you want?

THE TUTOR: Just a word of information. Can you tell me where . . . ? [*The door is slammed in his face.*] Oh, the devil take you! Well, my lord Orestes, is that enough, or must I try elsewhere? If you wish, I'll knock at every door.

ORESTES: No, that's enough.

THE TUTOR: Well I never! There's someone here. [*He goes up to the idiot boy.*] Excuse me, sir . . .

THE IDIOT: Hoo! Hoo! Hoo!

THE TUTOR [*bowing again*]: My noble lord . . .

THE IDIOT: Hoo!

THE TUTOR: Will Your Highness deign to show us where Aegistheus lives?

THE IDIOT: Hoo!

THE TUTOR: Aegistheus, King of Argos.

THE IDIOT: Hoo! Hoo! Hoo!
[ZEUS *passes by, back stage.*]

THE TUTOR: We're out of luck. The only one who doesn't run away is a half-wit. [ZEUS *retraces his steps.*] Ah, that's odd! He's followed us here.

ORESTES: Who?

THE TUTOR: That bearded fellow.

236

ORESTES: You're dreaming.

THE TUTOR: I tell you, I saw him go by.

ORESTES: You must be mistaken.

THE TUTOR: Impossible. Never in my life have I seen such a beard – or, rather, only one: the bronze beard on the chin of Zeus Ahenobarbos at Palermo. Look, there he is again. What can he want of us?

ORESTES: He is only a traveller like ourselves.

THE TUTOR: Only that? We met him on the road to Delphi. And when we took the boat at Itéa, there he was, fanning that great beard in the bows. At Nauplia we couldn't move a step without having him at our heels, and now – here he is again! Do you think that chance explains it? [*He brushes the flies off his face.*] These flies in Argos are much more sociable than its townfolk. Just look at them! [*Points to the idiot boy.*] There must be a round dozen pumping away at each of his eyes, and yet he's smiling quite contentedly; probably he likes having his eyes sucked. That's not surprising; look at that yellow muck oozing out of them. [*He flaps his hand at the flies.*] Move on, my little friends. Ha! They're on you now. Allow me! [*He drives them away.*] Well, this should please you – you who are always complaining of being a stranger in your native land. These charming insects, anyhow, are making you welcome; one would think they know who you are. [*He whisks them away.*] Now leave us in peace, you buzzers. We know you like us, but we've had enough of you. . . . Where can they come from? They're as big as bumble-bees and noisy as a swarm of locusts.

[*Meanwhile* ZEUS *has approached them.*]

ZEUS: They are only bluebottles, a trifle larger than usual. Fifteen years ago a mighty stench of carrion drew them to this city, and since then they've been getting fatter and fatter. Give them another fifteen years, and they'll be as big as toads.

[*A short silence.*]

THE TUTOR: Pray, whom have I the honour of addressing?

ZEUS: Demetrios is my name, and I hail from Athens.

ORESTES: Did I not see you on the boat, a fortnight ago?

ZEUS: Yes, and I saw you, too.

[*Hideous shrieks come from the Palace.*]

THE TUTOR: Listen to that! I don't know if you will agree with me, young master, but I think we'd do better to leave this place.

ORESTES: Keep quiet!

ZEUS: You have nothing to fear. It's what they call Dead Men's Day, today. Those cries announce the beginning of the ceremony.

ORESTES: You seem well posted on the local customs.

ZEUS: Yes, I often visit Argos. As it so happened, I was here on the great day of Agamemnon's homecoming, when the Greek fleet, flushed with victory, anchored in the Nauplia roads. From the top of the rampart one saw the bay dappled with their white sails. [*He drives the flies away.*] There were no flies, then. Argos was only a small country town, basking in the sun, yawning the years away. Like everyone else I went up to the sentry-path to see the royal procession, and I watched it for many an hour wending across the plain. At sundown, on the second day, Queen Clytemnestra came to the ramparts, and with her was Aegistheus, the present King. The people of Argos saw their faces dyed red by the sunset, and they saw them leaning over the battlements, gazing for a long while seawards. And the people thought: 'There's evil brewing.' But they kept silence. Aegistheus, you should know, was the Queen's lover. A hard, brutal man, and even in those days he had the cast of melancholy. . . . But you're looking pale, young sir.

ORESTES: It's the long journey I have made, and this accursed heat. But pray go on; you interest me.

ZEUS: Agamemnon was a worthy man, you know, but he
made one great mistake. He put a ban on public executions.
That was a pity. A good hanging now and then – that
entertains folk in the provinces and robs death of its glamour.
... So the people here held their tongues; they looked
forward to seeing, for once, a violent death. They still kept
silent when they saw their King entering by the city gates.
And when Clytemnestra stretched forth her graceful arms,
fragrant and white as lilies, they still said nothing. Yet at
that moment a word, a single word, might have sufficed.
But no one said it; each was gloating in imagination over
the picture of a huge corpse with a shattered face.

ORESTES: And you, too, said nothing?

ZEUS: Does that rouse your indignation? Well, my young
friend, I like you all the better for it; it proves your heart's
in the right place. No, I admit I, too, held my peace. I'm a
stranger here, and it was no concern of mine. And next
day when it started, when the folk of Argos heard their
King screaming his life out in the Palace, they still kept
silence, but they rolled their eyes in a sort of ecstasy, and
the whole town was like a woman on heat.

ORESTES: So now the murderer is on the throne. For fifteen
years he has enjoyed the fruits of crime. And I thought the
gods were just!

ZEUS: Steady, my friend. Don't blame the gods too hastily.
Must they always punish? Wouldn't it be better to use such
breaches of the law to point a moral?

ORESTES: And is this what they did?

ZEUS: They sent the flies.

THE TUTOR: The flies? How do the flies come in?

ZEUS: They are a symbol. But if you want to know what the
gods did, look around you. See that old creature over there,
creeping away like a beetle on her little black feet, and
hugging the walls. Well, she's a good specimen of the squat

black vermin that teems in every cranny of this town. Now watch me catch our specimen, it's well worth inspection. Here it is. A loathsome object, you'll agree. . . . Hah! You're blinking now. Still, you're an Argive and you should be used to the white-hot rapiers of the sun. . . . Watch her wriggling, like a hooked fish! . . . Now, old lady, let's hear your tale of woe. I see you're in black from head to foot. In mourning for a whole regiment of sons, is that it? Tell us, and I'll release you—perhaps. For whom are you in mourning?

OLD WOMAN: Sir, I am not in mourning. Everyone wears black at Argos.

ZEUS: Everyone wears black? Ah, I see. You're in mourning for your murdered King.

OLD WOMAN: Whisht! For God's sake, don't talk of that.

ZEUS: Yes, you're quite old enough to have heard those huge cries that echoed and re-echoed for a whole morning in the city streets. What did you do about it?

OLD WOMAN: My good man was in the fields, at work. What could I do, a woman alone? I bolted my door.

ZEUS: Yes, but you left your window not quite closed, so as to hear the better, and, while you peeped behind the curtains and held your breath, you felt a little tingling itch between your loins, and didn't you enjoy it!

OLD WOMAN: Oh, please stop, sir!

ZEUS: And when you went to bed that night, you had a grand time with your man. A real gala night.

OLD WOMAN: A what? . . . No, my lord, that was a dreadful, dreadful night.

ZEUS: A red gala, I tell you, and you've never been able to blot out its memory.

OLD WOMAN: Mercy on us! Are you . . . are you one of the Dead?

ZEUS: I, dead? You're crazy, woman. . . . Anyhow, don't trouble your head who I am; you'd do better to think of yourself, and try to earn forgiveness by repenting of your sins.

OLD WOMAN: Oh sir, I do repent, most heartily I repent. If you only knew how I repent, and my daughter too, and my son-in-law offers up a heifer every year, and my little grandson has been brought up in a spirit of repentance. He's a pretty lad, with flaxen hair, and he always behaves as good as gold. Though he's only seven, he never plays or laughs, for thinking of his original sin.

ZEUS: Good, you old bitch, that's as it should be – and be sure you die in a nice bitchy odour of repentance. It's your one hope of salvation. [*The* OLD WOMAN *runs away.*] Unless I'm much mistaken, my masters, we have there the real thing, the good old piety of yore, rooted in terror.

ORESTES: What man are you?

ZEUS: Who cares what I am? We were talking of the gods. Well now, should they have struck Aegistheus down?

ORESTES: They should. . . . They should. . . . Oh, how would I know what they should have done? What do I care, anyhow? I'm a stranger here. . . . Does Aegistheus feel contrition?

ZEUS: Aegistheus? I'd be much surprised. But what matter? A whole city's repenting on his account. And it's measured by the bushel, is repentance. [*Eerie screams in the Palace.*] Listen! Lest they forget the screams of the late king in his last agony, they keep this festival of death, each year, when the day of the king's murder comes round. A herdsman from the hills – he's chosen for his lung-power – is set to bellow in the Great Hall of the Palace. [ORESTES *makes a gesture of disgust.*] Bah! That's nothing. I wonder what you'll say presently, when they let the Dead loose. Fifteen years ago, to a day, Agamemnon was murdered. And what a change has come over the light-hearted folk of Argos since that day; how near and dear to me they are at present!

ORESTES: Dear to *you*?

ZEUS: Pay no heed, young man. That was a slip of the tongue. Near and dear to the gods, I meant.

ORESTES: You surprise me. Then those blood-smeared walls, these swarms of flies, this reek of shambles and the stifling heat, these empty streets and yonder god with his gashed face, and all those creeping, half-human creatures beating their breasts in darkened rooms, and those shrieks, those hideous, blood-curdling shrieks – can it be that Zeus and his Olympians delight in these?

ZEUS: Young man, do not sit in judgement on the gods. They have their secrets – and their sorrows.

[*A short silence.*]

ORESTES: Am I right in thinking Agamemnon had a daughter? A daughter named Electra?

ZEUS: Yes. She lives there, in the Palace – that building yonder.

ORESTES: So that's the Palace? . . . And what does Electra think of – all this?

ZEUS: Oh, she's a mere child. There was a son, too, named Orestes. But he's dead, it seems.

ORESTES: Dead? Well, really . . .

THE TUTOR: Of course he's dead, young master. I thought you knew it. Don't you remember what they told us at Nauplia – about Aegistheus having him murdered, soon after Agamemnon's death?

ZEUS: Still, some say he's alive. The story goes that the men ordered to kill the child had pity on him and left him in the forest. Some rich Athenians found him there and took him home. For my part, I'd rather he were dead.

ORESTES: Pray, why?

ZEUS: Suppose that one day he appeared in this city, and . . .

ORESTES: Continue, please.

ZEUS: As you wish. . . . Well, I'd say this to him. 'My lad . . .' I'd say 'My lad,' as he's your age or thereabouts – if he's alive, of course. By the way, young lord, may I know your name?

ORESTES: 'Philebus' is my name, and I hail from Corinth. I am travelling to improve my mind, and this old slave accompanying me used to be my tutor.

ZEUS: Thank you. Well, I'd say something like this. 'My lad, get you gone! What business have you here? Do you wish to enforce your rights? Yes, you're brave and strong and spirited. I can see you as a captain in an army of good fighters. You have better things to do than reigning over a dead-and-alive city, a carrion city plagued by flies. These people are great sinners but, as you see, they're working out their atonement. Let them be, young fellow, let them be; respect their sorrowful endeavour, and begone on tiptoe. You cannot share in their repentance, since you did not share their crime. Your brazen innocence makes a gulf between you and them. So if you have any care for them, be off! Be off, or you will work their doom. If you hinder them on their way, if even for a moment you turn their thoughts from their remorse, all their sins will harden on them – like cold fat. They have guilty consciences, they're afraid – and fear and guilty consciences have a good savour in the nostrils of the gods. Yes, the gods take pleasure in such poor souls. Would you oust them from the favour of the gods? What, moreover, could you give them in exchange? Good digestions, the grey monotony of provincial life, and the boredom – ah, the soul-destroying boredom – of long days of mild content. Go your ways, my lad, go your ways. The repose of cities and men's souls hangs on a thread; tamper with it and you bring disaster. [*Looking him in the eyes*] A disaster which will recoil on you.'

ORESTES: Yes? So that is what you'd say? Well, if I were that young man, I'd answer . . . [*They eye each other truculently. the* TUTOR *coughs.*] No, I don't know how I'd answer you.

Perhaps you're right, and anyhow it's no concern of mine.

ZEUS: Good. I only hope Orestes would show as much sense.... Well, peace be with you, my friend; I must go about my business.

ORESTES: Peace be with you.

ZEUS: By the way, if those flies bother you, here's a way of getting rid of them. You see that swarm buzzing round your head? Right. Now watch! I flick my wrist – so – and wave my arm once, and then I say: Abraxas, galla, galla, tsay, tsay. See! They're falling down and starting to crawl on the ground like caterpillars.

ORESTES: By Jove!

ZEUS: Oh, that's nothing. Just a parlour trick. I'm a fly-charmer in my leisure hours. Good day to you. We shall meet again.

[*Exit* ZEUS].

THE TUTOR: Take care. That man knows who you are.

ORESTES: 'Man', you say. But *is* he a man?

THE TUTOR: What else should he be? You grieve me, my young master. Have all my lessons, all my precepts, the smiling scepticism I taught you, been wasted on your ears? 'Is he a man?' you ask. There's nothing else but men – what more would you have? And that bearded fellow is a man, sure enough; probably one of Aegistheus' spies.

ORESTES: A truce to your philosophy! It's done me too much harm already.

THE TUTOR: Harm? Do you call it doing harm to people when one emancipates their minds? Ah, how you've changed! Once I read you like an open book.... But at least you might tell me your plans. Why bring me to this city, and what's your purpose here?

ORESTES: Did I say I had a purpose? But that's enough. Be silent now. [*He takes some steps towards the Palace.*] That is *my* Palace. My father's birthplace. And it's there a whore and

244

her paramour foully butchered him. I, too, was born there.
I was nearly three when that usurper's bravos carried me
away. Most likely we went out by that door. One of them
held me in his arms. I had my eyes wide open, and no
doubt I was crying. And yet I have no memories, none
whatever. I am looking at a huge, gloomy building, solemn
and pretentious in the worst provincial taste. I am looking
at it, but I *see* it for the first time.

THE TUTOR: No memories, master? What ingratitude, con-
sidering that I gave ten years of my life to stocking you with
them! And what of all the journeys we have made together, all the towns we visited? And the course of archaeo-
logy I composed specially for you? No memories, indeed!
Palaces, shrines and temples – with so many of them is your
memory peopled that you could write a guide-book of all
Greece.

ORESTES: Palaces – that's so. Palaces, statues, pillars – stones,
stones, stones! Why, with all those stones in my head, am I
not heavier? While you are about it, why not remind me of
the three hundred and eighty-seven steps of the temple at
Ephesus? I climbed them, one by one, and I remember
each. The seventeenth, if my memory serves me, was badly
broken. And yet – ! Why, an old, mangy dog, warming
himself at the hearth, and struggling to his feet with a little
whimper to welcome his master home – why, that dog has
more memories than I! At least he recognizes his master.
His master. But what can I call mine?

THE TUTOR: And what of your culture, Lord Orestes? What
of that? All that wise lore I culled for you with loving care,
like a bouquet, matching the fruits of my knowledge with
the finest flowers of my experience? Did I not, from the
very first, set you a-reading all the books there are, so as to
make clear to you the infinite diversity of men's opinions?
And did I not remind you, time and again, how variable

are human creeds and customs? So, along with youth, good looks and wealth, you have the wisdom of far riper years; your mind is free from prejudice and superstition, you have no family ties, no religion and no calling; you are free to turn your hand to anything. But you know better than to commit yourself – and there lies your strength. So, in a word, you stand head and shoulders above the ruck and, what's more, you could hold a chair of philosophy or architecture in a great university. And yet you cavil at your lot!

ORESTES: No, I do not cavil. What should I cavil at? You've left me free as the strands torn by the wind from spiders' webs, that one sees floating ten feet above the ground. I'm light as gossamer and walk on air. I know I'm favoured, I appreciate my lot at its full value. [*A pause.*] Some men are born bespoken; a certain path has been assigned them and at its end there is something they *must* do, a deed allotted. So on and on they trudge, wounding their bare feet on the flints. I suppose that strikes *you* as vulgar – the joy of going somewhere definite. And there are others, men of few words, who bear deep down in their hearts a load of dark imaginings; men whose whole life was changed because one day in childhood, at the age of five or seven . . . Right; I grant you these are no great men. When I was seven, I know I had no home, no roots. I let sounds and scents, the patter of rain on housetops, the golden play of sunbeams, slip past my body and fall round me – and I knew these were for others, I could never make them *my* memories. For memories are luxuries reserved for people who own houses, cattle, fields and servants. Whereas I – ! I'm free as air, thank God. My mind's my own, gloriously aloof. [*He goes nearer to the Palace.*] I might have lived there. I'd not have read any of your books; perhaps I'd not have learned to read. It's rare for a Greek prince to know how to read. But I'd have come in and gone out by that door ten thousand times. As a child I'd have played with its leaves, and when I pushed at them with all my little might, they'd have creaked without yielding, and I'd have taken the measure of my weakness. Later on, I'd have pushed them open furtively by night, and gone out after girls. And, some years later, when I came of age, the slaves would have flung the doors wide open, and I'd have crossed the threshold on horseback. My old wooden door! I'd have been able to find your keyhole with my eyes shut. And that notch there – I might have made it showing off, the first day they let me hold a spear. [*He steps back.*] Let's see. That's the Dorian style, isn't it? And what do you make of that gold inlay? I saw the like at Dodona; a pretty piece of craftsmanship. And now I'm going to say something that will rejoice you. This is not *my* palace, nor *my* door. And there's nothing to detain us here.

THE TUTOR: Ah, that's talking sense. For what would you have gained by living in Argos? By now your spirit would be broken, you'd be wallowing in repentance.

ORESTES: Still, it would be *my* repentance. And this furnace heat singeing my hair would be *mine*. Mine, too, the buzz of all these flies. At this moment I'd be lying naked in some dark room at the back of the Palace, and watching a ribbon of red light lengthen across the floor. I'd be waiting for sundown; waiting for the cool dusk of an Argos evening to rise like perfume from the parched earth; an Argos evening like many a thousand others, familiar yet ever new, another evening that should be *mine*. ... Well, well, my worthy pedagogue, let's be off. We've no business to be luxuriating in others' heat.

THE TUTOR: Ah, my young lord, how you've eased my mind! During these last few months – to be exact, ever since I revealed to you the secret of your birth – I could see you

changing day by day, and it gave me many a sleepless night.
I was afraid . . .

ORESTES: Of what?

THE TUTOR: No, it will anger you.

ORESTES: Speak.

THE TUTOR: Be it so. Well, though from one's earliest years
one has been trained to sceptic irony, one can't help having
foolish fancies now and then. And I wondered if you
weren't hatching some wild scheme to oust Aegistheus and
take his place.

ORESTES [*thoughtfully*]: To oust Aegistheus. Ah . . . [*A pause.*]
No, my good slave, you need not fear; the time for that is
past. True, nothing could please me better than to grip that
sanctimonious ruffian by the beard and drag him from my
father's throne. But what purpose would it serve? These
folk are no concern of mine. I have not seen one of their
children come into the world, nor been present at their
daughters' weddings; I don't share their remorse, I don't
even know a single one of them by name. That bearded
fellow was right; a King should share his subjects' memories. So we'll let them be, and begone on tiptoe. . . . But,
mind you, if there were something I could do, something to
give me the freedom of the city; if, even by a crime, I could
acquire their memories, their hopes and fears, and fill with
these the void within me, yes, even if I had to kill my own
mother –

THE TUTOR: Hush! For heaven's sake, hush!

ORESTES: Yes, these are idle dreams. Let's be off. Now go and
see if we can get some horses here, and we'll move on to
Sparta, where I have good friends.

[ELECTRA *comes forward, carrying a large bin. She goes up to
the statue of Zeus, without seeing them.*]

ELECTRA: Yes, you old swine, scowl away at me with your
goggle eyes and your fat face all smeared with raspberry

juice – scowl away, but you won't scare me, not you! They've been to worship you, haven't they, those pious matrons in black dresses. They've been padding round you in their big creaky shoes. And you were pleased, old bugaboo, it warmed your silly wooden heart. You like them old, of course; the nearer they are to corpses, the more you love them. They've poured their choicest wines out at your feet, because it's your festival today, and the stale smell from their petticoats tickled your nostrils. [*She rubs herself against him.*] Now smell me for a change, smell the perfume of a fresh, clean body. But of course I'm young, I'm alive – and you loathe youth and life. I, too, am bringing you offerings, while all the others are at prayers. Here they are: ashes from the hearth, peelings, scraps of offal crawling with maggots, a chunk of bread too filthy even for our pigs. But your darling flies will love it, won't they, Zeus? A good feast-day to you, old idol, and let's hope it is your last. I'm not strong enough to pull you down. All I can do is to spit at you. But some day he will come, the man I'm waiting for, carrying a long, keen sword. He'll look you up and down, and chuckle, with his hands on his hips, like this, and his head thrown back. Then he'll draw his sword and chop you in two, from top to bottom – like this! So the two halves of Zeus will fall apart, one to the left, one to the right, and everyone will see he's made of common wood. Just a lump of cheap white deal, the terrible God of Death! And all that frightfulness, the blood on his face, his dark green eyes and all the rest – they'll see it was only a coat of paint. *You*, anyhow, you know you're white inside, white as a child's body, and you know, too, that a sword can rip you limb from limb, and you won't even bleed. Just a log of deal – anyhow it will serve to light our fires next winter. [*She notices Orestes.*] Oh!

ORESTES: Don't be alarmed.

ELECTRA: I'm not alarmed. Not a bit. Who are you?

ORESTES: A stranger.

ELECTRA: Then you are welcome. All that's foreign to this town is dear to me. Your name?

ORESTES: Philebus. I've come from Corinth.

ELECTRA: Ah? From Corinth. My name's Electra.

ORESTES: Electra . . . [*To the tutor*] Leave us.
[*Exit the* TUTOR.]

ELECTRA: Why are you looking at me like that?

ORESTES: You're very beautiful. Not at all like the people in these parts.

ELECTRA: I, beautiful? Can you really mean it? As beautiful as the Corinthian girls?

ORESTES: Yes.

ELECTRA: Well, here they never tell me that I'm beautiful. Perhaps they don't want me to know it. Anyhow what use would beauty be to me? I'm only a servant.

ORESTES: What! You, a servant?

ELECTRA: The least of the servants in the Palace. I wash the King's and the Queen's underlinen. And how dirty it is, all covered with spots and stains! Yes, I have to wash everything they wear next to their skin, the shifts they wrap their rotting bodies in, the nightdresses Clytemnestra has on when the King shares her bed. I shut my eyes and scrub with all my might. I have to wash up, too. You don't believe me? See my hands, all chapped and rough. Why are you looking at them in that funny way? Do they, by any chance, look like the hands of a princess?

ORESTES: Poor little hands. No, they don't look like a princess's hands. . . . But tell me more. What else do they make you do?

ELECTRA: Every morning I've to empty the dustbin. I drag it out of the Palace, and then – well, you saw what I do with the refuse. That big fellow in wood is Zeus. God of Death and

250

Flies. The other day, when the High Priest came here to make his usual bows and scrapings, he found himself treading on cabbage-stumps and rotten turnips and mussel-shells. He looked startled, I can tell you! I say! You won't tell on me, will you?

ORESTES: No.

ELECTRA: Really I don't care if you do. They can't make things much worse for me than they are already. I'm used to being beaten. Perhaps they'd shut me up in one of the rooms in the tower. That wouldn't be so bad; at least I wouldn't have to see their faces. Just imagine what I get by way of thanks at bedtime, when my day's work is done. I go up to a tall, stout lady with dyed hair, with thick lips and very white hands, a queen's hands, that smell of honey. Then she puts her hands on my shoulders and dabs my forehead with her lips and says, 'Good night, Electra. Good night.' Every evening. Every evening. I have to feel that woman slobbering on my face. Ugh! Like a piece of raw meat on my forehead. But I hold myself up. I've never fallen yet. She's my mother, you know. If I was up in the tower, she wouldn't kiss me any more.

ORESTES: Have you never thought of running away?

ELECTRA: I haven't the courage; I daren't face the country roads at night all by myself.

ORESTES: Is there no one, no girl-friend of yours, who'd go with you?

ELECTRA: No, I am quite alone. Ask any of the people here, and they'll tell you I'm a pest, a public nuisance. I've no friends.

ORESTES: Not even an old nurse, who saw you into the world and has kept a little affection for you?

ELECTRA: Not even an old nurse. Mother will tell you; I freeze even the kindest hearts – that's how I am.

ORESTES: Do you propose to spend your life here?

ELECTRA [*excitedly*]: My life? Oh no, no! Of course not! Listen. I'm waiting for . . . for something.

ORESTES: Something, or someone?

ELECTRA: That's my secret. Now it's your turn to speak. You're good-looking, too. Will you be here long?

ORESTES: Well, I'd thought of leaving today. But, as it is –

ELECTRA: Yes?

ORESTES: As it is, I'm not so sure.

ELECTRA: Is Corinth a pretty place?

ORESTES: Very pretty.

ELECTRA: Do you like it? Are you proud of Corinth?

ORESTES: Yes.

ELECTRA: How strange that sounds! I can't imagine myself being proud of my home town. Tell me what it feels like.

ORESTES: Well . . . No, I don't know. I can't explain.

ELECTRA: You can't? I wonder why. [*A short silence.*] What's Corinth like? Are there shady streets and squares? Places where one can stroll in the cool of the evening?

ORESTES: Yes.

ELECTRA: And everyone comes out of doors? People go for walks together?

ORESTES: Almost everyone is out and about at sundown.

ELECTRA: Boys and girls together?

ORESTES: Oh yes, one often sees them going for walks together.

ELECTRA: And they always find something to say to each other? They like each other's company, and one hears them laughing in the streets quite late at night?

ORESTES: Yes.

ELECTRA: I suppose you think I'm very childish. But it's so hard for me to picture a life like that – going for walks, laughing and singing in the streets. Everybody here is sick with fear. Everyone except me. And I –

ORESTES: Yes? And you?

ELECTRA: Oh, I – I'm sick with . . . hatred. And what do they do all day, the girls at Corinth?

ORESTES: Well, they spend quite a while making themselves pretty; then they sing or play on lutes. Then they call on their friends and, at night, they go to dances.

ELECTRA: But don't they have any worries?

ORESTES: Only quite little ones.

ELECTRA: Yes? Now listen well, please. . . . Don't the people at Corinth feel remorse?

ORESTES: Sometimes. Not very often.

ELECTRA: So they do what they like and, afterwards, don't give another thought to it?

ORESTES: That's their way.

ELECTRA: How strange! [*A short silence.*] Please tell me something else; I want to know it because of . . . of someone I'm expecting. Suppose one of the young fellows you've been telling about, who walk and laugh with girls in the evenings – suppose one of these young men came home after a long journey and found his father murdered, and his mother living with the murderer, and his sister treated like a slave – what would he do, that young man from Corinth? Would he just take it for granted and slink out of his father's house, and look for consolation with his girl-friends? Or would he draw his sword and hurl himself at the assassin, and slash his brains out? . . . Why are you silent?

ORESTES: I was wondering . . .

ELECTRA: What? You can't say what he'd do?

CLYTEMNESTRA [*off stage, calling*]: Electra!

ELECTRA: Hush!

ORESTES: What is it?

ELECTRA: That was my mother, Queen Clytemnestra. [CLYTEMNESTRA *enters.*] What's this, Philebus? Are you afraid of her?

ORESTES [*to himself*]: So that's the face I tried to picture, night after night, until I came to see it, really *see* it, drawn and haggard under the rosy mask of paint. But I hadn't counted on those dead eyes.

CLYTEMNESTRA: Electra, hear the King's order. You are to make ready for the ceremony. You must wear your black dress and your jewels. . . . Well, what does this behaviour mean? Why are you pressing your elbows to your hips and staring at the ground? Oh, I know your tricks, my girl, but they don't deceive me any longer. Just now I was watching at the window and I saw a very different Electra, a girl with flashing eyes, bold gestures. . . . Why don't you answer?

ELECTRA: Do you really think a scullery maid would add to the splendour of your festival?

CLYTEMNESTRA: No play-acting. You are a princess, Electra, and the townsfolk expect to see you, as in former years.

ELECTRA: A princess – yes, the princess of a day. Once a year, when this day comes round, you remember who I am; because, of course, the people want an edifying glimpse of our family life. A strange princess, indeed, who herds pigs and washes up. Tell me, will Aegistheus put his arm round my neck as he did last time? Will he smile tenderly on me, while he mumbles horrible threats in my ear?

CLYTEMNESTRA: If you would have him otherwise, it rests with you.

ELECTRA: Yes – if I let myself be tainted by your remorse; if I beg the gods' forgiveness for a crime I never committed. Yes – if I kiss your royal husband's hand and call him 'Father'. Ugh! The mere thought makes me sick. There's dry blood under his nails.

CLYTEMNESTRA: Do as you will. I have long ceased giving you orders in my name. It is the King's command I bring you.

ELECTRA: And why should I obey him? Aegistheus is your husband, mother, your dearly beloved husband – not mine.

CLYTEMNESTRA: That is all I have to say, Electra. Only too well I see you are determined to bring ruin on yourself, and on us all. Yet who am I to counsel you, I who ruined my whole life in a single morning? You hate me, my child, but what disturbs me more is your likeness to me, as I was once. I used to have those clean-cut features, that fever in the blood, those smouldering eyes – and nothing good came of them.

ELECTRA: No! Don't say I'm like you! Tell me, Philebus – you can see us side by side – am I really like her?

ORESTES: How can I tell? Her face is like a pleasant garden that hail and storms have ravaged. And upon yours I see a threat of storm; one day passion will sear it to the bone.

ELECTRA: A threat of storm? Good! So far I welcome the likeness. May your words come true.

CLYTEMNESTRA: And you, young man, who stare so boldly at us, who are you and why have you come here? Let me look at you more closely.

ELECTRA [quickly]: He's a Corinthian, of the name of Philebus. A traveller.

CLYTEMNESTRA: Philebus? Ah!

ELECTRA: You seemed to fear another name.

CLYTEMNESTRA: To fear? If the doom I brought on my life has taught me anything, it is that I have nothing left to fear.... Welcome to Argos, stranger. Yes, come nearer. How young you seem! What's your age?

ORESTES: Eighteen.

CLYTEMNESTRA: Are your parents alive?

ORESTES: My father's dead.

CLYTEMNESTRA: And your mother? Is she about my age? Ah, you don't answer. I suppose she looks much younger; she still laughs and sings when you are with her. Do you love her? Answer me, please. Why did you leave her?

ORESTES: I am on my way to Sparta, to enlist in the army.

CLYTEMNESTRA: Most travellers give our city a wide berth. Some go twenty leagues out of their way, to avoid it. Were you not warned? The people of the Plain have put us in quarantine; they see our repentance as a sort of pestilence, and are afraid of being infected.

ORESTES: I know.

CLYTEMNESTRA: Did they tell you that we bear the burden of an inexpiable crime, committed fifteen years ago?

ORESTES: Yes, they told me that.

CLYTEMNESTRA: And that Queen Clytemnestra bears the heaviest load of guilt; that men shudder at her name?

ORESTES: That, too, I heard.

CLYTEMNESTRA: And yet you've come here! Stranger, I am Queen Clytemnestra.

ELECTRA: Don't pity her, Philebus. The Queen is indulging in our national pastime; the game of public confession. Here, everyone cries his sins on the housetops. On holidays you'll often see a worthy shopkeeper dragging himself along on his knees, covering his hair with dust, and screaming out that he's a murderer, a libertine, a liar, and all the rest of it. But the folk of Argos are getting a little tired of these amusements; everyone knows his neighbour's sins by heart. The Queen's, especially, have lost their interest; they're official – our basic crimes, in fact. So you can imagine her delight when she finds someone like you, somebody raw and young, who doesn't even know her name, to hear her tale of guilt. A marvellous opportunity! It's as if she were confessing for the first time.

CLYTEMNESTRA: Be silent. Anyone has the right to spit in my face, to call me murderess and whore. But no one has the right to speak ill of my remorse.

ELECTRA: Note her words, Philebus. That'a a rule of the game. People will beg you to condemn them, but you must be sure to judge them only on the sins they own to; their other evil deeds are no one's business, and they wouldn't thank you for detecting them.

CLYTEMNESTRA: Fifteen years ago men said I was the loveliest woman in Greece. Look at me now, and judge my sufferings. Let me be frank, young stranger; it is not the death of that old lecher that I regret. When I saw his blood tingeing the water in the bath, I sang and danced for joy. And even now, after fifteen years, whenever I recall it, I have a thrill of pleasure. But – but I had a son; he would be your age now. When Aegistheus handed him over to his bravos, I . . .

ELECTRA: You had a daughter too, my mother, if I'm not mistaken. And you've made a scullion of her. But that crime, it seems, sits lightly on your conscience.

CLYTEMNESTRA: You are young, Electra. It is easy for young people, who have not yet had a chance of sinning, to condemn. But wait, my girl; one day you, too, will be trailing after you an inexpiable crime. At every step you will think that you are leaving it behind, but it will remain as heavy as before. Whenever you look back you will see it there, just at arm's length, glowing darkly like a black crystal. And you will have forgotten what it really is, and murmur to yourself, 'It wasn't I, it could not have been I, who did that.' Yes, though you disown it time and time again, always it will be there, a dead weight holding you back. And then at last you will realize that you staked your life on a single throw of the dice, and nothing remains for you but to drag your crime after you until you die. For that is the Law, just or unjust, of repentance. Ah, then we'll see a change come over your young pride.

ELECTRA: My *young* pride? So it's your lost youth you are regretting, still more than your crime. It's my youth you detest, even more than my innocence.

CLYTEMNESTRA: What I detest in you, Electra, is – myself. Not your youth – far from it! – but my own.

ELECTRA: And I – it's you, it's *you* I hate.

CLYTEMNESTRA: For shame, Electra! Here we are, scolding each other like two women of the same age in love with the same man! And yet I am your mother . . . I do not know who you are, young man, nor what brings you here, but your presence bodes no good. Electra hates me – that, of course, I always knew. But for fifteen years we have kept the peace; only our eyes betrayed our feelings. And now you have come, you have spoken, and here we are showing our teeth and snapping at each other like two curs in the street. An ancient law of Argos compels us to give you hospitality but, I make no secret of it, I had rather you were gone. As for you, my child, too faithful copy of myself, 'tis true I have no love for you. But I had rather cut off my right hand than do you harm. Only too well you know it, and you trade on my weakness. But I advise you not to rear your noxious little head against Aegistheus; he has a short way with vipers. Mark my words, do his bidding – or you will rue it.

ELECTRA: Tell the King that I shall not attend the rite. Do you know what they do, Philebus? Above the town there's a great cavern; none of our young men, not even the bravest, has ever found its end. People say that it leads down to hell, and the High Priest has had the entrance blocked with a great stone. Well – would you believe it? – each year when this anniversary comes round, the townspeople gather outside the cavern, soldiers roll away the stone, and our dead, so they say, come up from hell and roam the city. Places are laid for them at every table, chairs and beds made ready, and the people in the house huddle in corners to make room for them during the night-watches. For the dead are everywhere, the whole town's at their mercy. You can imagine how our townsfolk plead with them. 'My poor dead darling, I didn't mean to wrong you. Please be kind.' Tomorrow, at cock-crow, they'll return underground, the stone will be rolled back, and that will be the end of it until this day next year. Well, I refuse to take part in this mummery. Those dead folk are *their* dead, not mine.

CLYTEMNESTRA: If you will not obey his summons willingly, the King will have you brought to him by force.

ELECTRA: By force? . . . I see. Very well then. My good, kind mother, will you please tell the King that I shall certainly obey. I shall attend the rite and, if the townsfolk wish to see me, they won't be disappointed. . . . Philebus, will you do something for me? Please don't go at once, but stay here for the ceremony. Perhaps some parts of it may entertain you. Now I'll go and make myself ready.

[*Exit* ELECTRA.]

CLYTEMNESTRA [*to Orestes*]: Leave this place. I feel that you are going to bring disaster on us. You have no cause to wish us ill; we have done nothing to you. So go, I beg you. By all you hold most sacred, for your mother's sake, I beg you, go.

[*Exit* CLYTEMNESTRA.]

ORESTES [*thoughtfully*]: For my mother's sake.

[ZEUS *enters and comes up to him.*]

ZEUS: Your attendant tells me you wish to leave. He has been looking for horses all over Argos, but can find none. Well, I can procure for you two sturdy mares and riding gear at a very low figure.

ORESTES: I've changed my mind. I am not leaving Argos.

ZEUS [*meditatively*]: Ah, so you're not leaving, after all. [*A short pause. Then, in a quicker tempo*] In that case I shall stay with you and be your host. I know an excellent inn in the lower town, where we can lodge together. You won't regret my company, I can assure you. But first – Abraxas, galla, galla, tsay, tsay – let me rid you of those flies. A man of my age can often be very helpful to lads like you. I'm old enough to be your father; you must tell me all about yourself and your troubles. So come, young man, don't try to shake me off. Meetings like this are often of more use than one would think. Consider the case of Telemachus – you know who I mean, King Ulysses' son. One fine day he met an old worthy of the name of Mentor, who joined forces with him. Now I wonder if you know who that old fellow Mentor really was . . .

[*He escorts Orestes off the stage, holding him in conversation, while the curtain falls.*]

ACT TWO

SCENE ONE

A mountain terrace, with a cavern on the right. Its entrance is blocked by a large black boulder. On the left is a flight of steps leading up to a temple. A crowd of men and women have gathered for the ceremony.

A WOMAN [*kneeling before her little son, as she straightens the kerchief round his neck*]: There! That's the third time I've had to straighten it for you. [*She dusts his clothes.*] That's better. Now try to behave properly, and mind you start crying when you're told.

THE CHILD: Is that where they come from?

THE WOMAN: Yes.

THE CHILD: I'm frightened.

THE WOMAN: And so you should be, darling. Terribly frightened. That's how one grows up into a decent, god-fearing man.

A MAN: They'll have good weather today.

ANOTHER MAN: Just as well. It seems they still like sunlight, shadows though they are. Last year, when it rained, they were fierce, weren't they?

FIRST MAN: Aye, that's the word. Fierce.

SECOND MAN: A shocking time we had!

THIRD MAN: Once they've gone back to their cave and left us to ourselves, I'll climb up here again and look at that there stone, and I'll say to myself, 'Now we've a year's peace before us.'

FOURTH MAN: Well, I'm not like you, I ain't consoled that easily. From tomorrow I'll start wondering how they'll be next year. Every year they're getting nastier and nastier, and –

SECOND MAN: Hold your tongue, you fool! Suppose one of them has crept out through a crevice and is prowling round us now, eavesdropping, like. There's some of the Dead come out ahead of time, so I've heard tell.

[*They eye each other nervously.*]

A YOUNG WOMAN: If only it would start? What are they up to, those palace folk? They're never in a hurry, and it's all this waiting gets one down, what with the blazing sun and only that big black stone to look at. Just think! They're all there, crowded up behind the stone, gloating over the cruel things they're going to do to us.

AN OLD WOMAN: That's enough, my girl. . . . We all know she's no better than she should be; that's why she's so scared of her ghost. Her husband died last spring, and for ten years she'd been fooling the poor man.

YOUNG WOMAN: I don't deny it. Sure enough I fooled him to the top of his bent; but I always liked him and I led him a pleasant life, that he can't deny. He never knew a thing about the other men and when he died you should have seen the way he looked at me, so tenderly, like a grateful dog. Of course he knows everything now, and it's bitter pain for him, poor fellow, and all his love has turned to hate. Presently I'll feel him coiling round me, like a wisp of smoke, and he'll cling to me more closely than any living man has ever clung. I'll bring him home with me, wound round my neck like a tippet. I've a tasty little meal all ready, with the cakes and honey that he always liked. But it's all no use, I know. He'll never forgive me, and tonight – oh, how I dread it! – he will share my bed.

A MAN: Aye, she's right. What's Aegistheus doing? We can't bear this suspense much longer. It ain't fair to keep us waiting like this.

ANOTHER MAN: Sorry for yourself, are you? But do you think Aegistheus is less afraid than we? Tell me, how'd you like to be in his shoes, and have Agamemnon gibbering at you for twenty-four hours?

YOUNG WOMAN: Oh, this horrible, horrible suspense! Do you know, I have a feeling that all of you are drifting miles and miles away, leaving me alone. The stone is not yet rolled aside, but each of us is shut up with his dead, and lonely as a raindrop.

[ZEUS *enters, followed by* ORESTES *and the* TUTOR.]

ZEUS: This way, young man; you'll have a better view.

ORESTES: So here we have them, the citizens of Argos, King Agamemnon's loyal subjects!

THE TUTOR: What an ugly lot! Observe, young master, their sallow cheeks and sunken eyes. These folk are perishing of fear. What better example could we have of the effects of superstition? Just look at them! And if you need another proof of the soundness of my teaching, look on me and my rosy cheeks.

ZEUS: Much good they do you, your pink cheeks. For all your roses, my good man, you're no more than a sack of dung, like all those others, in the eyes of Zeus. Yes, though you may not guess it, you stink to heaven. These folk at least are wise in their generation; they know how bad they smell.

A MAN [*climbing on to the temple steps, harangues the crowd*]: Do they want to drive us mad? Let's raise our voices all together and summon Aegistheus. Make him understand we will not suffer any more delay.

THE CROWD: Aegistheus! King Aegistheus! Have pity on us!

A WOMAN: Pity, yes, pity, you cry. And will none have pity on me? He'll come with his slit throat, the man I loathed so bitterly, and clammy, unseen arms will maul me in the darkness, all through the night.

ORESTES: But this is madness! Why doesn't someone tell these wretched people . . . ?

ZEUS: What's this, young man? Why this ado over a woman who's lost her nerve? Wait and see; there's worse to come.

A MAN [*falling on his knees*]: I stink, oh how I stink! I am a mass of rottenness. See how the flies are teeming round me, like carrion crows . . . That's right, my harpies; sting and gouge and scavenge me; bore through my flesh to my black heart. I have sinned a thousand times, I am a sink of ordure, and I reek to heaven.

ZEUS: O worthy man!

SOME MEN [*helping him to his feet*]: That's enough. You shall talk about it later, when *they* are out.

[*Gasping, rolling his eyes, the man stares at them.*]

THE CROWD: Aegistheus! Aegistheus! For mercy's sake give the order to begin. We can bear no more.

[AEGISTHEUS *comes on to the temple steps, followed by* CLYTEMNESTRA, THE HIGH PRIEST, *and* BODYGUARDS.]

AEGISTHEUS: Dogs! How dare you bewail your lot? Have you forgotten your disgrace? Then, by Zeus, I shall refresh your memories. [*He turns to Clytemnestra.*] We must start without her, it seems. But let her beware! My punishment will be condign.

CLYTEMNESTRA: She promised to attend. No doubt she is making ready, lingering in front of her mirror.

AEGISTHEUS [*to the soldiers*]: Go, seek Electra in the Palace, and bring her here; by force, if needs be. [SOLDIERS *file out. He addresses the crowd.*] Take your usual places. The men on my right; women and children on my left. Good.

[*A short silence.* AEGISTHEUS *is waiting.*]

HIGH PRIEST: Sire, these people are at breaking-point.

AEGISTHEUS: I know. But I am waiting for . . .

[*The* SOLDIERS *return.*]

A SOLDIER: Your Majesty, we have searched for the princess everywhere. But there is no one in the Palace.

AEGISTHEUS: So be it. We shall deal with her tomorrow. [*To the High Priest*] Begin.

HIGH PRIEST: Roll away the stone.

THE CROWD: Ah!

[*The* SOLDIERS *roll away the stone. The* HIGH PRIEST *goes to the entrance of the cavern.*]

HIGH PRIEST: You, the forgotten and forsaken, all you whose hopes were dupes, who creep along the ground darkling like smoke-wraiths, and have nothing left you but your great shame – you, the dead, arise; this is your day of days. Come up, pour forth like a thick cloud of fumes of brimstone driven by the wind; rise from the bowels of the earth, ye who have died a hundred deaths, ye whom every heartbeat in our breasts strikes dead again. In the name of anger unappeased and unappeasable, and the lust of vengeance, I summon you to wreak your hatred on the living. Come forth and scatter like a dark miasma in our streets, weave between the mother and her child, the lover and his beloved; make us regret that we, too, are not dead. Arise, spectres, harpies, ghouls, and goblins of our nights. Soldiers, arise, who died blaspheming; arise downtrodden victims, children of disgrace; arise all ye who died of hunger, whose last sigh was a curse. See, the living are here to greet you, fodder for your wrath. Arise and have at them like a great rushing wind, and gnaw them to the bone. Arise! Arise! Arise!

[*A tom-tom sounds, and the* PRIEST *dances at the entrance of the cavern, slowly at first, then quickening his gyrations until he falls to the ground, exhausted.*]

AEGISTHEUS: They are coming forth.

THE CROWD: Heaven help us!

ORESTES: I can bear this no longer. I must go . . .

ZEUS: Look at me, young man. In the eyes. Good; you understand. Now, keep quiet.

ORESTES: Who – who are you?

ZEUS: You shall know soon.

[AEGISTHEUS *comes slowly down the temple steps.*]

AEGISTHEUS: They are there. All of them. [*A short silence.*] There he is, Aricië, the husband you used so ill. There he is, beside you, kissing you tenderly, clasping you in his dead arms. How he loves you! And, ah, how he hates you! . . . There she is, Nicias, your mother, who died of your neglect . . . And you there, Segestes, you blood-sucker – they are all round you, the wretched men who borrowed of you; those who starved to death, and those who hanged themselves because of you. In your debt they died, but today they are your creditors. And you, fathers and mothers, loving parents, lower your eyes humbly. They are there, your dead children, stretching their frail arms towards you, and all the happiness you denied them, all the tortures you inflicted, weigh like lead on their sad, childish, unforgiving hearts.

THE CROWD: Have mercy!

AEGISTHEUS: Mercy? You ask for mercy? Do you not know the dead have no mercy? Their grievances are time-proof, adamant; rancour without end. Do you hope, Nicias, to atone by deeds of kindness for the wrong you did your mother? But what act of kindness can ever reach her now? Her soul is like a sultry, windless noon, in which nothing stirs, nothing changes, nothing lives. Only a fierce un-moving sun beats down on bare rocks for ever. The dead have ceased to be – think what that implies in all its ruthless-ness – yes, they are no more, and in their eternal keeping your crimes have no reprieve.

THE CROWD: Mercy!

AEGISTHEUS: Well you may cry mercy! Play your parts, you wretched mummers, for today you have a full house to watch you. Millions of staring, hopeless eyes are brooding darkly on your faces and your gestures. They can see us, read our hearts, and we are naked in the presence of the dead. Ah, that makes you squirm; it burns and sears you, that stern, calm gaze unchanging as the gaze of eyes remembered.

THE CROWD: Mercy!

THE MEN: Forgive us for living while you are dead.

THE WOMEN: Have mercy! Tokens of you are ever with us, we see your faces everywhere we turn. We wear mourning unceasingly, and weep for you from dawn till dusk, from dusk till dawn. But somehow, try as we may, your memory dwindles and slips through our fingers; daily it grows dimmer and we know ourselves the guiltier. Yes, you are leaving us, ebbing away like life-blood from a wound. And yet, know you well – if this can mollify your bitter hatred – that you, our dear departed, have laid waste our lives.

THE MEN: Forgive us for living while you are dead.

THE CHILDREN: Please forgive us. We didn't want to be born, we're ashamed of growing up. What wrong can we have done you? It's not our fault if we're alive. And only just alive; see how small we are, how pale and puny. We never laugh or sing, we glide about like ghosts. And we're so frightened of you, so terribly afraid. Have mercy on us.

THE MEN: Forgive us for living while you are dead.

AEGISTHEUS: Hold your peace! If you voice your sorrow thus, what will be left for me, your king, to say? For my ordeal has begun; the earth is quaking, and the light failing, and the greatest of the dead is coming forth – he whom I slew with my own hand, King Agamemnon.

ORESTES [drawing his sword]: I forbid you to drag my father's name into this mummery.

ZEUS [clutching his arms]: Stop, young fellow! Stop that!

AEGISTHEUS [looking round]: Who dares to . . . ? [ELECTRA, wearing a white dress, comes on to the temple steps. AEGISTHEUS sees her.] Electra!

THE CROWD: Electra!

AEGISTHEUS: What is the meaning of this Electra? Why are you in white?

ELECTRA: It's my prettiest dress. The city holds high festival today, and I thought I'd look my best.

HIGH PRIEST: Would you insult our dead? This day is *their* day, and well you know it. You should be in mourning.

ELECTRA: Why? I'm not afraid of *my* dead, and yours mean nothing to me.

AEGISTHEUS: That is so; your dead are not our dead... Remember the breed she comes of, the breed of Atreus who treacherously cut his nephews' throats. What are you, Electra, but the last survivor of an accursed race? Aye, that whorish dress becomes you. I suffered your presence in the Palace out of pity, but now I know I erred; the old foul blood of the House of Atreus flows in your veins. And, if I did not see to it, you would taint us all. But bide a while, my girl, and you will learn how I can punish. Your eyes will be red with weeping for many a day.

THE CROWD: Sacrilege! Sacrilege! Away with her!

AEGISTHEUS: Hear, miserable girl, the murmurs of these good folk you have outraged. Were I not here to curb their anger, they would tear you in pieces.

THE CROWD: Away with her, the impious wretch!

ELECTRA: Is it impious to be gay? Why can't these good folk of yours be gay? What prevents them?

AEGISTHEUS: She is laughing, the wanton – and her dead father is standing there, with blood on his face.

ELECTRA: How dare you talk of Agamemnon? How can you be so sure he doesn't visit me by night and tell me all his secrets? Ah, if you knew the love and longing that hoarse, dead voice breathes in my ears! Yes, I'm laughing – laughing for the first time in my life; for the first time I'm happy. And can you be so sure my new-won happiness doesn't rejoice my father's heart? More likely, if he's here and sees his daughter in her white dress – his daughter of whom you've made a wretched drudge – if he sees her holding her head high, keeping her pride intact, more likely the last thing he dreams of is to blame me. No, his eyes are sparkling in the havoc of his face, he's twisting his blood-stained lips in the shadow of a smile.

THE YOUNG WOMAN: Can it be true, what she says?

VOICES: No, no. She's talking nonsense. She's gone mad. Electra, go, for pity's sake, or your sins will be visited on us.

ELECTRA: But what is it you're so frightened of? I can see all round you and there's nothing but your own shadows. Now, listen to what I've just been told, something you may not know. In Greece there are cities where men live happily. White, contented cities, basking like lizards in the sun. At this very moment, under this same sky, children are playing in the streets of Corinth. And their mothers aren't asking forgiveness for having brought them into the world. No, they're smiling tenderly at them, they're proud of their motherhood. Mothers of Argos, can't you understand? Does it mean nothing to you, the pride of a mother who looks at her son and thinks, 'It's I who bore him, brought him up?'

AEGISTHEUS: That's enough. Keep silent, or I'll thrust your words down your throat.

VOICES: Yes, yes. Make her stop. She's talked enough.

OTHER VOICES: No, let her speak. It's Agamemnon speaking through her.

ELECTRA: The sun is shining. Everywhere, down in the plains, men are looking up and saying, 'It's a fine day,' and they're happy. Are you so set on making yourselves wretched that you've forgotten the simple joy of the peasant who says as he walks across his fields, 'It's a fine day?' No, there you stand, hanging your heads, moping and mumbling, more dead than alive. You're too terrified to lift a finger, afraid of jolting your precious ghosts if you make any movement. That would be dreadful, wouldn't it, if your hand suddenly went through a patch of clammy mist, and it was your grandmother's ghost! Now, look at me. I'm spreading out my arms freely, and I'm stretching like someone just roused from sleep. I have my place in the sunlight, my full place and to spare. And does the sky fall on my head? Now I'm dancing see, I'm dancing, and all I feel is the wind's breath fanning my cheeks. Where are the dead? Do you think they're dancing with me, in step?

HIGH PRIEST: People of Argos, I tell you that this woman is a profaner of all we hold most holy. Woe to her and to all of you who listen to her words!

ELECTRA: Oh, my beloved dead – Iphigeneia, my elder sister, and Agamemnon, my father and my only king – hear my prayer. If I am an evil-doer, if I offend your sorrowing shades, make some sign that I may know. But if, my dear ones, you approve, let no leaf stir, no blade of grass be moved, and no sound break in on my sacred dance. For I am dancing for joy, for peace amongst men; I dance for happiness and life. My dead ones, I invoke your silence that these people around me may know your hearts are with me.

[*She dances.*]

VOICES IN THE CROWD: Look how she's dancing, light as a flame. Look how her dress is rippling, like a banner in the wind. And the Dead – the Dead do nothing.

THE YOUNG WOMAN: And see her look of ecstasy – oh, no, no, that's not the face of a wicked woman. Well, Aegistheus, what have you to say? Why are you silent?

AEGISTHEUS: I waste no words on her. Does one argue with malignant vermin? No, one stamps them out. My kindness to her in the past was a mistake, but a mistake that can be remedied. Have no fear, I shall make short work of her and end her accursed race.

VOICES IN THE CROWD: Answer us, King Aegistheus. Threats are no answer.

THE YOUNG WOMAN: She's dancing, smiling, oh so happily, and the dead seem to protect her. Oh fortunate, too fortunate Electra! Look, I, too, am holding out my arms, baring my neck to the sunlight.

A VOICE IN THE CROWD: The Dead hold their peace. Aegistheus, you have lied.

ORESTES: Dear Electra!

ZEUS: This is too much. I'll shut that foolish wench's tongue. [*Stretches out his right arm.*] Poseidon, carabou, carabou, roola. [*The big stone which blocked the entrance to the cavern rumbles across the stage and crashes against the temple steps.* ELECTRA *stops dancing.*]

THE CROWD: Ah! . . . Mercy on us!
   [*A long silence.*]

HIGH PRIEST: Forward and fickle race, now you have seen how the Dead avenge themselves. Mark how the flies are beating down on you, in thick, swirling clouds. You have hearkened to the tempter's voice and a curse has fallen on the city.

THE CROWD: It is not our fault, we are innocent. That woman came and tempted us, with her lying tongue. To the river with her! Drown the witch.

AN OLD WOMAN [*pointing to the Young Woman*]: That young huzzy there was lapping up her words like milk. Strip her naked and lash her till she squeals.
   [*The* WOMEN *seize the Young Woman, while the* MEN *surge up the temple steps, towards Electra.*]

AEGISTHEUS [*straightening up*]: Silence, dogs! Back to your places! Vengeance is mine, not yours! [*A short silence.*] Well, you have seen what comes of disobeying me. Henceforth you will know better than to misdoubt your ruler. Disperse to your homes, the Dead will keep you company, and be your guests until tomorrow's dawn. Make place for them at your tables, at your hearths, and in your beds. And see that your good behaviour blots out the memory of what has happened here. As for me – grieved though I am by your mistrust, I forgive you. But you, Electra. . . .

ELECTRA: Yes? What of it? I failed to bring it off this time. Next time I'll do better.

AEGISTHEUS: There shall be no 'next time'. The custom of the city forbids my punishing you on the day the Dead are with us. This you knew, and you took advantage of it. But you are no longer one of us; I cast you out for ever. You shall go hence bare-footed, with nothing in your hands, wearing that shameless dress. And I hereby order any man who sees you within our gates after the sun has risen, to strike you down and rid the city of its bane.

[*He goes out, followed by the* SOLDIERS. *The* CROWD *file past Electra, shaking their fists at her.*]

ZEUS [*to Orestes*]: Well, young master, were you duly edified? For, unless I'm much mistaken, the tale has a moral. The wicked have been punished and the good rewarded. [*He points to Electra.*] As for that woman . . .

ORESTES [*sharply*]: Mind what you say! That woman is my sister. Now go; I want to talk to her.

ZEUS [*observes him for a moment, then shrugs his shoulders*]: Very good.

[*Exit* ZEUS, *followed by the* TUTOR.]

ORESTES: Electra!

ELECTRA [*still standing on the temple steps, she raises her eyes and gazes at him*]: Ah, you're still there, Philebus?

ORESTES: You're in danger, Electra. You mustn't stay a moment longer in this city.

ELECTRA: In danger? Yes, that's true. You saw how I failed to bring it off. It was a bit your fault, you know – but I'm not angry with you.

ORESTES: My fault? How?

ELECTRA: You deceived me. [*She comes down the steps towards him.*] Let me look at your eyes. Yes, it was your eyes that made a fool of me.

ORESTES: There's no time to lose. Listen, Electra! We'll escape together. Someone's getting a horse for me and you can ride pillion.

ELECTRA: No.

ORESTES: What? You won't come away with me?

ELECTRA: I refuse to run away.

ORESTES: I'll take you with me to Corinth.

ELECTRA [*laughing*]: Corinth? Exactly! I know you mean well, but you're fooling me again. What could a girl like me do in Corinth? I've got to keep a level head, you know. Only yesterday, my desires were so simple, so modest. When I waited at table, with meek, downcast eyes, I used to watch the two of them – the handsome old woman with the dead face, and the fat, pale King with the slack mouth and that absurd beard like a regiment of spiders running round his chin. And then I'd dream of what I'd see one day – a wisp of steam, like one's breath on a cold morning, rising from their split bellies. That was the only thing I lived for, Philebus, I assure you. I don't know what you're after, but this I know; that I mustn't believe you. Your eyes are too bold for my liking. . . . Do you know what I used to tell myself before I met you? That a wise person can want nothing better from life than to pay back the wrong that has been done him.

ORESTES: If you come with me, Electra, you'll see there are many, many other things to ask of life – without one's ceasing to be wise.

ELECTRA: No, I won't listen any more; you've done me quite enough harm already. You came here with your kind, girlish face, and your eager eyes – and you made me forget my hatred. I unlocked my hands and I let my one and only treasure slip through them. You lured me into thinking one could cure the people here by words. Well, you saw what happened. They nurse their disease; they've got to like their sores so much that they scratch them with their dirty nails to keep them festering. Words are no use for such as they. An evil thing is conquered only by another evil thing, and only violence can save them. So good-bye, Philebus, and leave me to my bad dreams.

ORESTES: They'll kill you.

ELECTRA: We have a sanctuary here, Apollo's shrine. Often criminals take shelter there, and so long as they are in the temple, no one can touch a hair of their heads. That's where I'll go.

ORESTES: But why refuse my help?

ELECTRA: It's not for you to help me. Someone else will come, to set me free. [*A short silence.*] My brother isn't dead; I know that. And I'm waiting for his coming.

ORESTES: Suppose he doesn't come?

ELECTRA: He *will* come; he's bound to come. He is of our stock, you see; he has crime and tragedy in his blood, as I have – the bad blood of the House of Atreus. I picture him as a big, strong man, a born fighter, with bloodshot eyes like our father's, always smouldering with rage. He, too, is doomed; tangled up in his destiny, like a horse whose belly is ripped open and his legs are caught up in his guts. And now at every step he tears his bowels out. Yes, one day he will come, this city draws him. Nothing can hinder his coming, for it is here he can do the greatest harm, and suffer the greatest harm. I often seem to see him coming, with lowered head, sullen with pain, muttering angry words. He scares me; every night I see him in my dreams, and I wake screaming with terror. But I'm waiting for him and I love him. I must stay here to direct his rage – for I, anyhow, keep a clear head – to point to the guilty and say, 'Those are they, Orestes. Strike!'

ORESTES: And suppose he isn't like that at all?

ELECTRA: How can he be otherwise? Don't forget he's the son of Agamemnon and Clytemnestra.

ORESTES: But mightn't he be weary of all that tale of wickedness and bloodshed; if, for instance, he'd been brought up in a happy, peaceful city?

ELECTRA: Then I'd spit in his face, and I'd say: 'Go away, you cur; go and keep company where you belong, with women. But you're reckoning without your doom, poor fool. You're a grandson of Atreus, and you can't escape the heritage of blood. You prefer shame to crime; so be it. But Fate will come and hunt you down in your bed; you'll have the shame to start with, and then you will commit the crime, however much you shirk it.'

ORESTES: Electra, I am Orestes.

ELECTRA [with a cry]: Oh! . . . You liar!

ORESTES: By the shades of my father, Agamemnon, I swear I am Orestes. [A short silence.] Well? Why don't you carry out your threat, and spit in my face?

ELECTRA: How could I? [She gazes at him earnestly.] So those shining eyes, that noble forehead, are – my brother's! Orestes. . . . Oh, I'd rather you had stayed Philebus, and my brother was dead. [Shyly] Was it true, what you said about your having lived at Corinth?

ORESTES: No. I was brought up by some well-to-do Athenians.

ELECTRA: How young you look! Have you ever been in battle! Has that sword you carry ever tasted blood?

ORESTES: Never.

ELECTRA: It's strange. I felt less lonely when I didn't know you. I was waiting for the Orestes of my dream; always thinking of his strength and of my weakness. And now you're there before me; Orestes, the real Orestes, was you all the time. I look at you and I see we're just a boy and a girl, two young orphans. But, you know, I love you. More than I'd have loved the other Orestes.

ORESTES: Then, if you love me, come away. We'll leave this place together.

ELECTRA: Leave Argos? No. It's here the doom of the Atrides must be played out, and I am of the House of Atreus. I ask nothing of you. I've nothing more to ask of Philebus. But here I stay.

[ZEUS *enters, back stage, and takes cover to listen to them.*]

ORESTES: Electra, I'm Orestes; your brother. I, too, am of the House of Atreus, and my place is at your side.

ELECTRA: No. You're not my brother; you're a stranger. Orestes is dead, and so much the better for him. From now on I'll do homage to his shade, along with my father's and my sister's. You, Philebus, claim to be of our House. So be it! But can you truly say that you are one of *us*? Was *your* childhood darkened by the shadow of a murder? No, more likely you were a quiet little boy with happy, trustful eyes, the pride of your adoptive father. Naturally you could trust people – they always had a smile for you – just as you could trust the solid, friendly things around you: tables, beds, and stairs. And because you were rich, and always nicely dressed, and had lots of toys, you must have often thought the world was quite a nice world to live in, like a big warm bath in which one can splash and loll contentedly. My childhood was quite different. When I was six I was a drudge, and I mistrusted everything and everyone. [*A short pause.*] So go away, my noble-souled brother. I have no use for noble souls; what I need is an accomplice.

ORESTES: How could I leave you all alone; above all, now that you've lost even your last hope? . . . What do you propose to do here?

ELECTRA: That's my business. Good-bye, Philebus.

ORESTES: So you're driving me away? [*He takes some steps; then halts and faces her.*] Is it my fault if I'm not the fierce young swashbuckler you expected? Him you'd have taken by the hand at once, and said, 'Strike!' Of me you asked nothing. But, good heavens, why should I be outcast by my own sister – when I've not even been put to the test?

ELECTRA: No, Philebus, I could never lay such a load upon a heart like yours; a heart that has no hatred in it.

ORESTES: You are right. No hatred; but no love, either. You, Electra, I might have loved. And yet – I wonder! Love or hatred calls for self-surrender. He cuts a fine figure, the warm blooded, prosperous man, solidly entrenched in his well-being, who one fine day surrenders all to love – or to hatred; himself, his house, his land, his memories. But who am I, and what have I to surrender? I'm a mere shadow of a man; of all the ghosts haunting this town today none is ghostlier than I. The only loves I've known were phantom loves, rare and vacillating as will-o'-the-wisps. The solid passions of the living were never mine. Never! [*A short silence.*] But, oh the shame of it! Here I am, back in the town where I was born, and my own sister disavows me. And now – where shall I go? What city must I haunt?

ELECTRA: Isn't there some pretty girl waiting for you – somewhere in the world?

ORESTES: Nobody is waiting for me anywhere. I wander from city to city, a stranger to all others and to myself, and the cities close again behind me like the waters of a pool. If I leave Argos, what trace of my coming will remain, except the cruel disappointment of your hope?

ELECTRA: You told me about happy towns . . .

ORESTES: What do I care for happiness? I want my share of memories, my native soil, my place amongst the men of Argos. [*A short silence.*] Electra, I shall not leave Argos.

ELECTRA: Please, please. Philebus, go away. If you have any love for me, go. It hurts me to think what may come to you here – nothing but evil, that I know – and your innocence would ruin all my plans.

ORESTES: I shall not go.

ELECTRA: How can you think I'd let you stay beside me – you with your stubborn uprightness – to pass silent judgement on my acts? Oh, why are you so obstinate? Nobody wants you here.

ORESTES: It's my one chance, and you, Electra – surely you won't refuse it to me? Try to understand. I want to be a man who belongs to some place, a man amongst comrades. Only consider. Even the slave bent beneath his load, dropping with fatigue and staring dully at the ground a foot in front of him – why, even that poor slave can say he's in *his* town, as a tree is in a forest, or a leaf upon the tree. Argos is all around him, warm, compact and comforting. Yes, Electra, I'd gladly be that slave, and enjoy that feeling of drawing the city round me like a blanket, and curling myself up in it. No, I shall not go.

ELECTRA: Even if you stayed a hundred years amongst us, you'd still be a stranger here, and lonelier than if you were tramping the highroads of Greece. The townspeople would be watching you all the time from the corner of an eye, and they'd lower their voices when you came near.

ORESTES: Is it really so hard to win a place amongst you? My sword can serve the city, and I have gold to help the needy.

ELECTRA: We are not short of captains, or of charitable souls.

ORESTES: In that case ... [*He takes some steps away from her, with lowered eyes.* ZEUS *comes forward and gazes at him, rubbing his hands.* ORESTES *raises his eyes heavenwards.*] Ah, if only I knew which path to take! Oh Zeus, our Lord and King of Heaven, not often have I called on you for help, and you have shown me little favour; yet this you know: that I have always tried to act aright. But now I am weary and my mind is dark; I can no longer distinguish Right from Wrong. I need a guide to point my way. Tell me, Zeus, is it truly your will that a king's son, hounded from his city, should meekly school himself to banishment, and slink away from his ancestral home like a whipped cur? I cannot think it. And yet... and yet you have forbidden the shedding of blood... What have I said? Who spoke of bloodshed?... Oh Zeus, I beseech you, if meek acceptance, the bowed head and lowly heart are what you would have of me, make plain your will by some sign; for no longer can I see my path.

ZEUS [aside]: Ah, that's where I can help you, my young friend. Abraxas, abraxas, tsou, tsou.

[Light flashes out round the stone.]

ELECTRA [laughing]: Splendid! It's raining miracles today! See what comes of being a pious young man and asking counsel of the gods. [She is convulsed with laughter and can hardly get the words out.] Oh noble youth, Philebus darling of the gods! 'Show me a sign,' you asked. 'Show me a sign.' Well, now you've had your sign – a blaze of light round that precious, sacred stone of theirs. So off you go to Corinth! Off you go!

ORESTES [staring at the stone]: So that is the Right Thing. To live at peace... always at perfect peace. I see. Always to say 'Excuse me,' and 'Thank you.' That's what's wanted, eh? [He stares at the stone in silence for some moments.] The Right Thing. Their Right Thing. [Another silence.] Electra!

ELECTRA: Hurry up and go. Don't disappoint your fatherly old friend, who has bent down from Olympus to enlighten you. [She stops abruptly, a look of wonder on her face.] But – but what's come over you?

ORESTES [slowly, in a tone he has not used till now]: There is another way.

ELECTRA [*apprehensively*]: No, Philebus, don't be stubborn. You asked the gods for orders; now you have them.

ORESTES: Orders? What do you mean? Ah yes, the light round that big stone. But it's not for me, that light; from now on I'll take no one's orders, neither man's nor god's.

ELECTRA: You're speaking in riddles.

ORESTES: What a change has come on everything, and, oh, how far away you seem! Until now I felt something warm and living round me, like a friendly presence. That something has just died. What emptiness! What endless emptiness, as far as eye can reach! [*He takes some steps away from her.*] Night is coming on. The air is getting chilly, isn't it? But what was it . . . what was it that died just now?

ELECTRA: Philebus . . .

ORESTES: I say there is another path . . . *my* path. Can't you see it? It starts here and leads down to the city. I must go down – do you understand? – I must go down into the depths, amongst you. For you are living, all of you, at the bottom of a pit. [*He goes up to Electra.*] You are *my* sister, Electra, and that city is *my* city. *My* sister. [*He takes her arm.*]

ELECTRA: Don't touch me. You're hurting me, frightening me – and I'm *not* yours.

ORESTES: I know. Not yet. I'm still too . . . too light. I must take a burden on my shoulders, a load of guilt so heavy as to drag me down, right down into the abyss of Argos.

ELECTRA: But what – what do you mean to do?

ORESTES: Wait. Give me time to say farewell to all the lightness, the aëry lightness that was mine. Let me say good-bye to my youth. There are evenings at Corinth and at Athens, golden evenings full of songs and scents and laughter; these I shall never know again. And mornings, too, radiant with promise. Good-bye to them all, good-bye. . . . Come, Electra, look at our city. There it lies, rose-red in the sun, buzzing with men and flies, drowsing its doom away in the languor of a summer afternoon. It fends me off with its high walls, red roofs, locked doors. And yet it's mine for the taking; I've felt that since this morning. You, too, Electra, are mine for the taking – and I'll take you, too. I'll turn into an axe and hew those walls asunder, I'll rip open the bellies of those stolid houses and there will steam up from the gashes a stench of rotting food and incense. I'll be an iron wedge driven into the city, like a wedge rammed into the heart of an oak-tree.

ELECTRA: Oh, how you've changed! Your eyes have lost their glow; they're dull and smouldering. I'm sorry for that, Philebus; you were so gentle. But now you're talking like the Orestes of my dreams.

ORESTES: Listen! All those people quaking with fear in their dark rooms, with their dear departed round them – supposing I take over all their crimes. Supposing I set out to win the name of 'guilt-stealer', and heap on myself all their remorse; that of the woman unfaithful to her husband, of the tradesman who let his mother die, of the usurer who bled his victims white? Surely, once I am plagued with all those pangs of conscience, innumerable as the flies of Argos – surely then I shall have earned the freedom of your city. Shall I not be as much at home within your red walls as the red-aproned butcher in his shop, amongst the carcasses of flayed sheep and cattle?

ELECTRA: So you wish to atone for us?

ORESTES: To atone? No, I said I'd house your penitence, but I did *not* say what I'd do with all those cackling fowls; may be I'll wring their necks.

ELECTRA: And how can you take over our sense of guilt?

ORESTES: Why, all of you ask nothing better than to be rid of it. Only the King and Queen force you to nurse it in your foolish hearts.

ELECTRA: The King and Queen . . . Oh, Philebus!

ORESTES: The gods bear witness that I had no wish to shed their blood.

[*A long silence.*]

ELECTRA: You're too young, too weak.

ORESTES: Are you going to draw back . . . *now*? Hide me somewhere in the Palace, and lead me tonight to the royal bedchamber – and then you'll see if I am too weak!

ELECTRA: Orestes!

ORESTES: Ah! For the first time you've called me 'Orestes'.

ELECTRA: Yes. I know you now. You are indeed Orestes. I didn't recognize you at first. I'd expected somebody quite different. But this throbbing in my blood, this sour taste on my lips – I've had them in my dreams, and I know what they mean. So at last you have come, Orestes, and your resolve is sure. And here I am beside you – just as in my dreams – on the brink of an act beyond all remedy. And I'm frightened; that, too, was in my dreams. How long I've waited for this moment, dreading and hoping for it! From now on all the moments will link up, like the cogs in a machine, and we shall never rest again until they both are lying on their backs, with faces like crushed mulberries. In a pool of blood. To think it's you who are going to shed it, you with those gentle eyes! I'm sorry now, sorry that never again I'll see that gentleness, never again see Philebus. Orestes, you are my elder brother, and Head of our House; fold me in your arms, protect me. Much suffering, many perils lie ahead of both of us.

[ORESTES *takes her in his arms.* ZEUS *leaves his hiding-place and creeps out on tip-toe.*]

CURTAIN

SCENE TWO

The Throne-Room in the Palace. An awe-inspiring, blood-smeared image of ZEUS *occupies a prominent position. The sun is setting.*
    [ELECTRA *enters: then beckons to Orestes to follow her.*]
ORESTES: Someone's coming.
    [*He begins to draw his sword.*]
ELECTRA: It's the sentries on their rounds. Follow me. I know where to hide.
    [*Two* SOLDIERS *enter.*]
FIRST SOLDIER: I can't think what's come over the flies this evening. They're all crazy-like.
SECOND SOLDIER: They smell the Dead; that's why they're in such a state. Why, I daren't open my mouth to yawn, for fear they all come teeming down my throat and start a round-dance in my gullet. [ELECTRA *peeps from her hiding-place; then quickly withdraws her head.*] Hear that? Something creaked yonder.
FIRST SOLDIER: Oh, it's only Agamemnon, sitting down on his throne.
SECOND SOLDIER: And the seat creaked when he planted his fat bottom on it? No, it couldn't be that; a dead man's light as air.
FIRST SOLDIER: That goes for common folk like you and I. But a king, he's different. Mind you, Agamemnon always did himself proud at table. Why, he weighed seventeen stone or more, if he weighed a pound. It'd be surprising if there wasn't some pounds left of all that flesh.
SECOND SOLDIER: So – so you think he's here, do you?
FIRST SOLDIER: Where else should he be? If I was a dead king and I had twenty-four hours' leave each year, you may be sure I'd spend them squatting on my throne, just to remind me of the high old times I had when I was His

Almighty Majesty. And I'd stay put; I wouldn't run round pestering folks in their houses.

SECOND SOLDIER: Ah, wouldn't you? You say that because you're alive. But if you were dead, you'd be just as nasty as the others. [FIRST SOLDIER *smacks his face*.] Hey! What are you up to?

FIRST SOLDIER: I'm doing you a good turn. Look, I've killed seven of 'em, all at a go.

SECOND SOLDIER: Seven what? Seven dead 'uns?

FIRST SOLDIER: O' course not. *Flies*. Look, I've made my hand all bloody. [*He wipes it on his pants*.] Ugh, the filthy brutes!

SECOND SOLDIER: Pity you can't swot the lot of them while you're about it. The dead men now – they don't do nothing, they know how to behave. If the flies were all killed off, we'd have some peace.

FIRST SOLDIER: Peace, you say? No, if I thought there were ghost-flies here as well, that'd be the last straw.

SECOND SOLDIER: Why?

FIRST SOLDIER: Don't you see? They die by millions every day, the little buzzers. Well, if all the flies that have died since last summer were set loose in the town, there'd be three hundred and sixty-five dead flies for every one that's here. The air'd be laced with flies, we'd breathe flies, eat flies, sweat flies; they'd be rolling down our throats in clusters and bunging up our lungs. . . . I wonder now? Maybe that's why there's such a funny smell in this room.

SECOND SOLDIER: No, no, it ain't that. They say our dead men have foul breaths, you know. And this room's not so big as it looks – a thousand square feet or so, I should say. Two or three dead men would be enough to foul the air.

FIRST SOLDIER: That's so. Fussing and fuming, like they do.

SECOND SOLDIER: I tell you there's something amiss here. I heard a floorboard creak over there.

[*They go behind the throne to investigate*. ORESTES *and*

284

ELECTRA *slip out on the left, and tiptoe past the steps of the throne, returning to their hiding-place just as the soldiers emerge on the left.*]

FIRST SOLDIER: You see, there ain't nobody. It's only that old sod Agamemnon. Like as not, he's sitting on them cushions, straight as a poker. I shouldn't be surprised if he's watching you and me, for want of anything else to do.

SECOND SOLDIER: Aye, and we'd better have a good look round, I ain't easy in my mind. These flies are something wicked, but it can't be helped.

FIRST SOLDIER: I wish I was back in the barracks. At least the dead folk there are old chums come back to visit us, just ordinary folk like us. But when I think that His Late Lamented Majesty is there, like as not counting the buttons missing on my tunic, well it makes me dithery, like when the General's doing an inspection.

[*Enter* AEGISTHEUS *and* CLYTEMNESTRA, *followed by* SERVANTS *carrying lamps.*]

AEGISTHEUS: Go, all of you.

[*Exeunt* SOLDIERS *and* SERVANTS.]

CLYTEMNESTRA: What is troubling you tonight?

AEGISTHEUS: You saw what happened? Had I not played upon their fear, they'd have shaken off their remorse in the twinkling of an eye.

CLYTEMNESTRA: Is that all? Then be reassured. You will always find a way to freeze their courage when the need arises.

AEGISTHEUS: I know. Oh, I'm only too skilful in the art of false pretence. [*A short silence.*] I am sorry I had to rebuke Electra.

CLYTEMNESTRA: Why? Because she is my daughter? It pleased you to so do, and all you do has my approval.

AEGISTHEUS: Woman, it is not on your account that I regret it.

285

CLYTEMNESTRA: Then – why? You used not to have much love for Electra.

AEGISTHEUS: I am tired. So tired. For fifteen years I have been upholding the remorse of a whole city, and my arms are aching with the strain. For fifteen years I have been dressing a part, playing the scaremonger, and the black of my robes has seeped through to my soul.

CLYTEMNESTRA: But, sire, I, too . . .

AEGISTHEUS: I know, woman, I know. You are going to tell me of your remorse. I wish I shared it. It fills out the void of your life. *I* have no remorse – and no man in Argos is sadder than I.

CLYTEMNESTRA: My sweet lord. . . .

[*She goes up to him affectionately.*]

AEGISTHEUS: Keep off, you whore! Are you not ashamed – under his eyes?

CLYTEMNESTRA: Under his eyes? Who can see us here?

AEGISTHEUS: Why, the King. The Dead came forth this morning.

CLYTEMNESTRA: Sire, I beg you. . . . The dead are underground, and will not trouble us for many a long day. Have you forgotten it was you yourself who invented that fable to impress your people?

AEGISTHEUS: That's so. Well, it only shows how tired I am, how sick at heart. Now leave me to my thoughts. [*Exit* CLYTEMNESTRA.] Have you in me, Lord Zeus, the king you wished for Argos? I come and go amongst my people, I speak in trumpet tones, I parade the terror of my frown, and all who see me cringe in an agony of repentance. But I – what am I but an empty shell? Some creature has devoured me unawares, gnawed out my inner self. And now, looking within, I see I am more dead than Agamemnon. Did I say I was sad? I lied. Neither sad nor gay is the desert; a boundless waste of sand under a burning waste of sky. Not sad, nor gay, but... sinister. Ah, I'd give my kingdom to be able to shed a tear.

[ZEUS *enters.*]

ZEUS: That's right. Complain away! You're only a king, like every other king.

AEGISTHEUS: Who are you? What are you doing here?

ZEUS: So you don't recognize me?

AEGISTHEUS: Begone, stranger, or I shall have you thrown out by my guards.

ZEUS: You don't recognize me? Still, you have seen me often enough, in dreams. It's true I looked more awe-inspiring. [*Flashes of lightning, a peal of thunder.* ZEUS *assumes an awe-inspiring air.*] And now do you know me?

AEGISTHEUS: Zeus!

ZEUS: Good! [*Affable again, he goes up to the statue.*] So that's meant to be me? It's thus the Argives picture me at their prayers? Well, well, it isn't often that a god can study his likeness, face to face. [*A short silence.*] How hideous I am! They cannot like me much.

AEGISTHEUS: They fear you.

ZEUS: Excellent! I've no use for love. Do you, Aegistheus, love me?

AEGISTHEUS: What do you want of me? Have I not paid heavily enough?

ZEUS: Never enough.

AEGISTHEUS: But it's killing me, the task I have undertaken.

ZEUS: Come now! Don't exaggerate! Your health is none too bad; you're fat. Mind, I'm not reproaching you. It's good, royal fat, yellow as tallow – just as it should be. You're built to live another twenty years.

AEGISTHEUS: Another twenty years!

ZEUS: Would you rather die?

AEGISTHEUS: Yes.

ZEUS: So, if anyone came here now, with a drawn sword, would you bare your breast to him?

AEGISTHEUS: I – I cannot say.

ZEUS: Now mark my words. If you let yourself be slaughtered like a dumb ox, your doom will be exemplary. You shall be King in Hell for all eternity. That's what I came here to tell you.

AEGISTHEUS: Is someone planning to kill me?

ZEUS: So it seems.

AEGISTHEUS: Electra?

ZEUS: Not only Electra.

AEGISTHEUS: Who?

ZEUS: Orestes.

AEGISTHEUS: Oh! . . . Well, that's in the natural order of things, no doubt. What can I do against it?

ZEUS [*mimicking his tone*]: What can I do? [*Imperiously*] Bid your men arrest a young stranger going under the name of Philebus. Have him and Electra thrown into a dungeon – and if you leave them there to rot, I'll think no worse of you. Well? What are you waiting for? Call your men.

AEGISTHEUS: No.

ZEUS: Be good enough to tell me why that 'No.'

AEGISTHEUS: I am tired.

ZEUS: Don't stare at the ground. Raise your big, bloodshot eyes and look at me. That's better. Yes, you're majestically stupid, like a horse; a kingly fool. But yours is not the stubbornness that vexes me; rather, it will add a spice to your surrender. For I know you will obey me in the end.

AEGISTHEUS: I tell you I refuse to fall in with your plans. I have done so far too often.

ZEUS: That's right. Show your mettle! Resist! Resist! Ah, how I cherish souls like yours! Your eyes flash, you clench your fists, you fling refusal in the teeth of Zeus. None the less, my little rebel, my restive little horse, no sooner had I warned you than your heart said 'Yes'. Of course you'll obey. Do you think I leave Olympus without good reason? I wished to warn you of this crime because it is my will to avert it.

AEGISTHEUS: To warn me! How strange!

ZEUS: Why 'strange'? Surely it's natural enough. Your life's in danger and I want to save it.

AEGISTHEUS: Who asked you to save it? What about Agamemnon? Did you warn *him*? And yet *he* wished to live.

ZEUS: Oh miserable man, what base ingratitude! You are dearer to me than Agamemnon, and when I prove this, you complain!

AEGISTHEUS: Dearer than Agamemnon? I? No, it's Orestes whom you cherish. You allowed me to work my doom, you let me rush in, axe in hand, to King Agamemnon's bath – and no doubt you watched from high Olympus, licking your lips at the thought of another damned soul to gloat over. But today you are protecting young Orestes against himself; and I, whom you egged on to kill his father – you have chosen me to restrain the young man's hand. I was a poor creature, just qualified for murder; but for Orestes, it seems, you have higher destinies in view.

ZEUS: What strange jealousy is this! But have no fear; I love him no more than I love you. I love nobody.

AEGISTHEUS: Then see what you have made of me, unjust God that you are. And tell me this. If today you hinder the crime Orestes has in mind, why did you permit mine of fifteen years ago?

ZEUS: All crimes do not displease me equally. And now, Aegistheus, I shall speak to you frankly, as one King to another. The first crime was mine; I committed it when I made man mortal. Once I had done that, what was left for you, poor human murderers, to do? To kill your victims? But they already had the seed of death in them; all you could do was to hasten its fruition by a year or two. Do you know what would have befallen Agamemnon, if you had not killed him? Three months later he'd have died of apoplexy in a pretty slave-girl's arms. But your crime served my ends.

AEGISTHEUS: What ends? For fifteen years I have been atoning for it – and you say it served your ends!

ZEUS: Exactly. It's because you are atoning for it that it served my ends. I like crimes that *pay*. I like yours because it was a clumsy, boorish murder, a crime that did not know itself, a crime in the antique mode, more like a cataclysm than an act of man. Not for one moment did you defy me. You struck in a frenzy of fear and rage. And then, when your frenzy had died down, you looked back on the deed with loathing, and disowned it. Yet what a profit I have made on it! For one dead man, twenty thousand living-men wallowing in penitence. Yes, it was a good bargain I struck that day.

AEGISTHEUS: I see what lies behind your words. Orestes will have no remorse.

ZEUS: Not a trace of it. At this moment he is thinking out his plan, coolly, methodically, cheerfully. What good to me is a carefree murder, a shameless, sedate crime, that lies light as thistledown on the murderer's conscience? No, I won't allow it. Ah, how I loathe the crimes of this new generation; thankless and sterile as the wind! Yes, that nice-minded young man will kill you as he'd kill a chicken; he'll go away with red hands and a clean heart. In your place I should feel humiliated. So – call your men!

AEGISTHEUS: Again, I tell you, I will *not*. The crime that is being hatched displeases you enough for me to welcome it.

ZEUS: Aegistheus, you are a king, and it's to your sense of kingship I appeal; for you enjoy wielding the sceptre.

AEGISTHEUS: Continue.

ZEUS: You may hate me, but we are akin; I made you in my image. A king is a god on earth, glorious and terrifying as a god.

290

AEGISTHEUS: You, terrifying?

ZEUS: Look at me. [*A long silence.*] I told you you were made in my image. Each keeps order; you in Argos, I in heaven and on earth – and you and I harbour the same dark secret in our hearts.

AEGISTHEUS: I have no secret.

ZEUS: You have. The same as mine. The bane of gods and kings. The bitterness of knowing men are free. Yes, Aegistheus, they are free. But your subjects do not know it, and you do.

AEGISTHEUS: Why, yes. If they knew it, they'd send my Palace up in flames. For fifteen years I've been playing a part to mask their power from them.

ZEUS: So you see we are alike.

AEGISTHEUS: Alike? A god likening himself to me – what freak of irony is this? Since I came to the throne, all I said, all my acts, have been aimed at building up an image of myself. I wish each of my subjects to keep that image in the foreground of his mind, and to feel, even when alone, that my eyes are on him, severely judging his most private thoughts. But I have been trapped in my own net. I have come to see myself only as they see me. I peer into the dark pit of their souls and there, deep down, I see the image that I have built up. I shudder, but I cannot take my eyes off it. Almighty Zeus, who am I? Am I anything more than the dread that others have of me?

ZEUS: And I – who do you think *I* am? [*Points to the statue.*] I, too, have my image, and do you suppose it doesn't fill me with confusion? For a hundred thousand years I have been dancing a slow, dark ritual dance before men's eyes. Their eyes are so intent on me that they forget to look into themselves. If I forgot myself for a single moment, if I let their eyes turn away . . .

AEGISTHEUS: Yes?

ZEUS: Enough. That is *my* business. Aegistheus, I know that you are weary of it all; but why complain? You'll die one day – but I shall not. So long as there are men on earth, I am doomed to go on dancing before them.

AEGISTHEUS: Alas! But who has doomed us?

ZEUS: No one but ourselves. For we have the same passion. You, Aegistheus, have, like me, a passion for order.

AEGISTHEUS: For order? That is so. It was for the sake of order that I wooed Clytemnestra, for order that I killed my king; I wished that order should prevail, and that it should prevail through me. I have lived without love, without hope, even without lust. But I have kept order. Yes, I have kept good order in my kingdom. That has been my ruling passion; a godlike passion, but how terrible!

ZEUS: We could have no other, you and I; I am God, and you were born to be a king.

AEGISTHEUS: Aye, more's the pity!

ZEUS: Aegistheus, my creature and my mortal brother, in the name of this good order that we serve, both you and I, I ask you – nay, I command you – to lay hands on Orestes and his sister.

AEGISTHEUS: Are they so dangerous?

ZEUS: Orestes knows that he is free.

AEGISTHEUS [eagerly]: He knows he's free? Then, to lay hands on him, to put him in irons, is not enough. A free man in a city acts like a plague-spot. He will infect my whole kingdom and bring my work to nothing. Almighty Zeus, why stay your hand? Why not fell him with a thunderbolt?

ZEUS [slowly]: Fell him with a thunderbolt? [A pause. Then, in a muffled voice.] Aegistheus, the gods have another secret. . . .

AEGISTHEUS: Yes?

ZEUS: Once freedom lights its beacon in a man's heart, the gods are powerless against him. It's a matter between man and man, and it is for other men, and for them only, to let him go his gait, or to throttle him.

AEGISTHEUS [*observing him closely*]: To throttle him? Be it so. Well, I shall do your will, no doubt. But say no more, and stay here no longer – I could not bear it.

[*As* ZEUS *departs,* ELECTRA *leaps forward and rushes to the door.* ORESTES *comes forward.*]

ELECTRA: Strike him down! Don't give him time to call for help. I'll bar the door.

AEGISTHEUS: So you, young man, are Orestes?

ORESTES: Defend yourself.

AEGISTHEUS: I shall not defend myself. It's too late for me to call for help, and I am glad it is too late. No, I shall not resist. I *wish* you to kill me.

ORESTES: Good. Little I care how it is done. . . . So I am to be a murderer.

[ORESTES *strikes him with his sword.*]

AEGISTHEUS [*tottering*]: Ah! You struck well, Orestes. [*He clings to Orestes.*] Let me look at you. Is it true you feel no remorse?

ORESTES: Remorse? Why should I feel remorse? I am only doing what is right.

AEGISTHEUS: What is right is the will of God. You were hidden here and you heard the words of Zeus.

ORESTES: What do I care for Zeus? Justice is a matter between men, and I need no God to teach me it. It's right to stamp you out, like the foul brute you are, and to free the people of Argos from your evil influence. It is right to restore to them their sense of human dignity.

AEGISTHEUS [*groaning*]: Pain! What agony!

ELECTRA: Look! Look! He's swaying; his face has gone quite grey. What an ugly sight's a dying man!

ORESTES: Keep silent! Let him carry with him to the grave no other memory than the memory of our joy.

AEGISTHEUS: My curse on you both.

ORESTES: Won't you have done with dying?

[*He strikes again.* AEGISTHEUS *falls.*]

AEGISTHEUS: Beware of the flies, Orestes, beware of the flies. All is not over.

[*Dies.*]

ORESTES [*giving the body a kick*]: For him, anyhow, all is over. Now lead me to the Queen's room.

ELECTRA: Orestes!

ORESTES: What?

ELECTRA: She – she can do us no more harm.

ORESTES: What of it? What has come over you? This is not how you spoke a little while ago.

ELECTRA: Orestes! You, too, have changed. I hardly recognize you.

ORESTES: Very well. I'll go alone.

[*Exit.*]

ELECTRA [*to herself*]: Will she scream? [*Silence. She is listening.*] He's walking down the passage. When he opens the fourth door. . . . Oh, I wanted this to happen. And I – I want it now, I *must* want it. [*She looks at Aegistheus.*] That one – yes, he's dead. So *this* is what I wanted. I didn't realize how it would be. [*She comes closer to the body.*] A hundred times I've seen him, in my dreams, lying just where he is now, with a sword through his heart. His eyes were closed, he seemed asleep. How I hated him, what joy I got from hating him! But he doesn't seem asleep; his eyes are open, staring up at me. He is dead, and my hatred is dead, too. And I'm standing here; waiting, waiting. That woman is still alive, she's in her bedroom, and presently she'll be screaming. Screaming like an animal in pain. No, I can't bear those eyes any longer. [*Kneeling, she lays a mantle over the King's face.*] What was it, then, I wanted? What? [*A short silence.* CLYTEMNESTRA *screams.*] He's struck her. She was our mother – and he's struck her. [*She rises to her feet.*] It's done; my enemies are dead. For years and years I've revelled in the thought of this and, now it's happened, my heart is like a lump of ice. Was

I lying to myself all those years? No, that's not true, it can't be true. I'm not a coward. Only a moment ago I wanted it, and I haven't changed. I'm glad, glad, to see that swine lying at my feet. [*She jerks the mantle off the dead King's face.*] Those dead-fish eyes goggling up at nothing – why should they trouble me? That's how I wanted to see them, dead and staring, and I'm glad, glad . . . [CLYTEMNESTRA'S *screams are weakening.*] Let her scream! Make her scream, Orestes. I want her to suffer. [*The screams cease.*] Oh joy, joy! I'm weeping for joy; my enemies are dead, my father is avenged.

[ORESTES *returns, his sword dripping blood.* ELECTRA *runs to him and flings herself into his arms.*]

ELECTRA: Orestes! . . . Oh! . . .

ORESTES: You're frightened. Why?

ELECTRA: I'm not frightened. I'm drunk. Drunk with joy. What did she say? Did she beg for mercy long?

ORESTES: Electra, I shall not repent of what I have done, but I think fit not to speak of it. There are some memories one does not share. It is enough for you to know she's dead.

ELECTRA: Did she die cursing us? That's all I want you to tell me. Did she curse us?

ORESTES: Yes. She died, cursing us.

ELECTRA: Take me in your arms, beloved, and press me to your breast. How dark the night is! I never knew such darkness; those torches have no effect on it. . . . Do you love me?

ORESTES: It is not night; a new day is dawning. We are free, Electra. I feel as if I'd brought you into life, and I, too, had just been born. Yes, I love you, and you belong to me. Only yesterday I was empty-handed, and today I have *you*. Ours is a double tie of blood; we two come of the same race and we two have shed blood.

ELECTRA: Let go your sword. Give me that hand, your strong right hand. [*She clasps and kisses it.*] Your fingers are short and square; made to grasp and hold. Dear hand! It's whiter than mine. But how heavy it became to strike down our father's murderers! Wait! [*She takes a torch and holds it near Orestes.*] I must light up your face; it's getting so dark that I can hardly see you. And I *must* see you; when I stop seeing you, I'm afraid of you. I daren't take my eyes off you. I must tell myself again and again that I love you. But – how strange you look!

ORESTES: I am free, Electra. Freedom has crashed down on me like a thunderbolt.

ELECTRA: Free? But I – I don't feel free. And you – can you undo what has been done? Something has happened and we are no longer free to blot it out. Can you prevent our being the murderers of our mother . . . for all time?

ORESTES: Do you think I'd wish to prevent it? I have done *my* deed, Electra, and that deed was good. I shall bear it on my shoulders as a carrier at a ferry carries the traveller to the farther bank. And when I have brought it to the farther bank I shall take stock of it. The heavier it is to carry, the better pleased I shall be; for that burden is my freedom. Only yesterday I walked the earth haphazard; thousands of roads I tramped that brought me nowhere, for they were other men's roads. Yes, I tried them all; the haulers' tracks along the riverside, the mule-paths in the mountains, and the broad, flagged highways of the charioteers. But none of these was mine. Today I have one path only, and heaven knows where it leads. But it is *my* path. . . . What is it, Electra?

ELECTRA: I can't see you any more. Those torches give no light. I hear your voice, but it hurts me, it cuts like a knife. Will it always be as dark as this; always, even in the daytime? . . . Oh, Orestes! There they are!

ORESTES: Who?

ELECTRA: There they are! Where have they come from? They're hanging from the ceiling like clusters of black grapes; the walls are alive with them; they're swirling down across the torchlight and it's their shadows that are hiding your face from me.

ORESTES: The flies . . .

ELECTRA: Listen! The sound of their wings is like a roaring furnace. They're all round us, Orestes, watching, biding their time. Presently they'll swoop down on us and I shall feel thousands of tiny clammy feet crawling over me. Oh, look! They're growing bigger, bigger; now they're as big as bees. We'll never escape them, they'll follow us everywhere in a dense cloud. Oh God, now I can see their eyes, millions of beady eyes all staring at us!

ORESTES: What do the flies matter to us?

ELECTRA: They're the Furies, Orestes, the goddesses of remorse.

VOICES [*from behind the door*]: Open! Open! . . . If you don't we'll smash the door in.

[*Heavy thuds. They are battering at the door.*]

ORESTES: Clytemnestra's cries must have brought them here. Come! Lead me to Apollo's shrine. We will spend the night there, sheltered from men and flies. And tomorrow I shall speak to my people.

ACT THREE

The temple of Apollo. Twilight. A statue of Apollo in the centre of the stage.

> [ELECTRA *and* ORESTES *are sleeping at the foot of the statue, their arms clasped round its legs. The* FURIES *ring them round. They sleep standing, like cranes. At the back is a huge bronze door.*]

FIRST FURY [*stretching herself*]: Aaaah! I slept the night out standing, stiff with rage, and my sleep was glorious with angry dreams. Ah, how lovely is the flower of anger, the red flower in my heart! [*She circles round Orestes and Electra.*] Still sleeping. How white and soft they are! I'll roll on their breasts and bellies, like a torrent over stones. And I shall polish hour by hour their tender flesh; rub it, scour it, wear it to the bone. [*She comes a few steps forward.*] Oh clear, bright dawn of hate! A superb awakening. They're sleeping, sweating, a smell of fever rises from them. But I am awake; cool and hard and gemlike. My soul is adamant – and I feel my sanctity.

ELECTRA [*sighing in her sleep*]: No! No!

FIRST FURY: She's sighing. Wait, my pretty one, wait till you feel our teeth. Soon you'll be screaming with the agony of our caresses. I'll woo you like a man, for you're my bride, and you shall feel my love crushing your life out. You, Electra, are more beautiful than I; but you'll see how my kisses age you. Within six months I'll have you raddled like an old hag; but I stay young for ever. [*She bends over Orestes and Electra.*] Ah, this lovely human carrion, what a tasty meal we have in store! As I gaze down at them and breathe their breath, I choke with rage. Nothing is sweeter, nothing, than to feel a dawn of hatred spreading like quickfire in one's veins; teeth and talons ready for their task. Hatred is flooding through me, welling up in my breasts like milk. Awake, sisters, awake. The day has come.

SECOND FURY: I dreamt I was biting them.

FIRST FURY: Be patient. Today they are protected by a god, but soon hunger and thirst will drive them out of sanctuary. And then you shall bite them to your heart's content.

THIRD FURY: Aaah! How I want to claw them!

FIRST FURY: Your turn will come. In a little while your iron talons will be ribboning the flesh of those young criminals with angry red. Come closer, sisters, come and look at them.

A FURY: How young they are!

ANOTHER FURY: And how beautiful!

FIRST FURY: Yes, we are favoured. Only too often criminals are old and ugly. Too seldom do we have the joy, the exquisite delight, of ruining what's beautiful.

THE FURIES: Heiah! Heiahah!

THIRD FURY: Orestes is almost a child. I shall mother him, oh so tenderly, with my hatred; I shall take his pale head on my knees and stroke his hair.

FIRST FURY: And then?

THIRD FURY: Then, when he least expects it, I shall dig these two fingers into his eyes.

[*All laugh.*]

FIRST FURY: See, they're stretching, sighing, on the brink of waking. And now my sisters, flies my sisters, let's sing the sinners from their sleep.

THE FURIES [*together*]: Bzz. Bzz. Bzz. Bzz.
We shall settle on your rotten hearts like flies on butter;
Rotten hearts, juicy, luscious hearts.
Like bees we'll suck the pus and matter from your hearts,
And we'll turn it into honey, rich, green honey.
What love could ravish us as hatred does?

Bzz. Bzz. Bzz. Bzz.
We shall be the staring eyes of the houses,
The growls of the kennelled mastiff baring his fangs as you
    go by,
A drone of wings pulsing in high air,
Sounds of the forest,
Whistlings, whinings, creakings, hissings, howlings,
We shall be the darkness,
The clotted darkness of your souls.
Bzz. Bzz. Bzz. Bzz.
Heiah, heiah, heiahah!
Bzz. Bzz. Bzz. Bzz.
We are the flies, the suckers of pus,
We shall have open house with you,
We shall gather our food from your mouths,
And our light from the depths of your eyes.
All your life we will be with you,
Until we make you over to the worms.
    [*They dance.*]

ELECTRA [*still half asleep*]: Was someone speaking? Who –
who are you?

THE FURIES: Bzz. Bzz. Bzz.

ELECTRA: Ah, yes. There you are. Well? Have we really killed
them?

ORESTES [*waking*]: Electra!

ELECTRA: You, who are you? Ah, yes. Orestes. Go away.

ORESTES: But – what's wrong, Electra?

ELECTRA: You frighten me. I had a dream. I saw our mother
lying on her back. Blood was pouring from her, gushing
under the doors. A dream. . . . Feel my hands. They're icy.
No, don't. Don't touch me. Did she really bleed much?

ORESTES: Don't!

ELECTRA [*waking up completely*]: Let me look at you. You
killed them. It was you, you who killed them. You are here

beside me, you have just woken up, there's nothing written on your face, no brand. . . . And yet you killed them.

ORESTES: Why, yes, I killed them. [*A short silence.*] You, too, make me afraid. Yesterday you were so beautiful. And now you look as if some wild beast had clawed your face.

ELECTRA: No beast. Your crime. It's tearing off my cheeks and eyelids; I feel as if my eyes and teeth were naked. . . . But what are those creatures?

ORESTES: Take no notice of them. They can do you no harm.

FIRST FURY: No harm? Let her dare to come amongst us, and you'll see if we can do no harm!

ORESTES: Keep quiet. Back to your kennel, bitches! [*The* FURIES *growl*.] Is it possible that the girl who only yesterday was dancing in a white dress on the temple steps – is it possible you were that girl?

ELECTRA: I've grown old. In a single night.

ORESTES: You have not lost your beauty, but . . . Where, now, have I seen dead eyes like those? Electra . . . you are like *her*. Like Clytemnestra. What use, then, was it killing her? When I see my crime in those eyes, it revolts me.

FIRST FURY: That is because *you* revolt *her*.

ORESTES: Is that true, Electra? Do I revolt you?

ELECTRA: Oh, let me be!

FIRST FURY: Well? Can you still have any doubt? How should she not hate you? She lived in peace, dreaming her dreams; and then you came, bringing murder and impiety upon her. So now she has to share your guilt and hug that pedestal, the only scrap of earth remaining to her.

ORESTES: Do not listen.

FIRST FURY: Away! Away! Make him go, Electra; don't let him touch you! He's a butcher. He reeks of fresh, warm blood. He used the poor old woman very foully, you know; he killed her piecemeal.

ELECTRA: Oh no! That's a lie, surely?

FIRST FURY: You can believe me; I was there all the time, buzzing in the air around them.

ELECTRA: So he struck her several times?

FIRST FURY: Ten times at least. And each time the sword squelched in the wound. She tried to shield her face and belly with her hands, and he carved her hands to ribbons.

ELECTRA: So it wasn't a quick death. Did she suffer much?

ORESTES: Put your fingers in your ears, do not look at them, and, above all, ask no questions. If you question them, you're lost.

FIRST FURY: Yes, she suffered – horribly.

ELECTRA [*covering her face with her hands*]: Oh!

ORESTES: She wants to part us, she is building up a wall of solitude around you. But beware; once you are alone, alone and helpless, they will fling themselves upon you. Electra, we planned this crime together and we should bear its brunt together.

ELECTRA: You dare to say I planned it with you?

ORESTES: Can you deny it?

ELECTRA: Of course I deny it. Wait! Well, perhaps ... In a way ... Oh, I don't know. I dreamt the crime, but you carried it out, you murdered your own mother.

THE FURIES [*shrieking and laughing*]: Murderer! Murderer! Butcher!

ORESTES: Electra, behind that door is the outside world. A world of dawn. Out there the sun is rising, lighting up the roads. Soon we shall leave this place, we shall walk those sunlit roads, and these hags of darkness will lose their power. The sunbeams will cut through them like swords.

ELECTRA: The sun ...

FIRST FURY: You will never see the sun again, Electra. We shall mass between you and the sun like a swarm of locusts; you will carry darkness round your head, wherever you go.

ELECTRA: Oh, let me be! Stop torturing me!

ORESTES: It's your weakness gives them their strength. Mark how they dare not speak to me. A nameless horror has descended on you, keeping us apart. And yet why should this be? What have you lived through that I have not shared? Do you imagine that my mother's cries will ever cease ringing in my ears? Or that my eyes will ever cease to see her great sad eyes, lakes of lambent darkness in the pallor of her face? And the anguish that consumes you – do you think it will ever cease ravaging my heart? But what matter? I am free. Beyond anguish, beyond remorse. Free. And at one with myself. No, you must not loathe yourself, Electra. Give me your hand. I shall never forsake you.

ELECTRA: Let go of my hand! Those hell-hounds frighten me, but you frighten me more.

FIRST FURY: You see! You see! . . . That's quite true, little doll; you're less afraid of us than of that man. Because you need us, Electra. You are our child, our little girl. You need our nails to score your skin, our teeth to bite your breast, and all our savage love to save you from your hatred of yourself. Only the suffering of your body can take your mind off your suffering soul. So come and let us hurt you. You have only those two steps to come down, and we will take you in our arms. And when our kisses sear your tender flesh, you'll forget all in the cleansing fires of pain.

THE FURIES: Come down to us! Come down!

[*Slowly they dance round her, weaving their spell.* ELECTRA *rises to her feet.*]

ORESTES [*gripping her arm*]: No, no, for pity's sake. Don't go to them. Once they get you, all is lost.

ELECTRA [*freeing herself violently*]: Let go! Oh, how I hate you! [*She goes down the steps, and the* FURIES *fling themselves on her.*] Help!

[ZEUS *enters.*]

ZEUS: Kennel up!

FIRST FURY: The master!

[*The* FURIES *slink off reluctantly, leaving* ELECTRA *lying on the ground.*]

ZEUS: Poor children. [*He goes up to Electra.*] So to this you've come, unhappy pair? My heart is torn between anger and compassion. Get up, Electra. So long as I am here, my Furies will not hurt you. [*He helps her to rise, and gazes at her face.*] Ah, what a cruel change! In a night, a single night, all the wild-rose bloom has left your cheeks. In one night your body has gone to ruin, lungs, gall, and liver all burnt out. The pride of headstrong youth – see what it has brought you to, poor child.

ORESTES: Stop talking in that tone, fellow. It is unbecoming for the King of the Gods.

ZEUS: And you, my lad, drop that haughty tone. It's unbecoming for a criminal atoning for his crime.

ORESTES: I am no criminal, and you have no power to make me atone for an act I don't regard as a crime.

ZEUS: So you may think, but wait a while. I shall cure you of that error before long.

ORESTES: Torture me to your heart's content; I regret nothing.

ZEUS: Not even the doom you have brought upon your sister?

ORESTES: Not even that.

ZEUS: Do you hear, Electra? And this man professed to love you!

ORESTES: She is dearer to me than life. But her suffering comes from within, and only she can rid herself of it. For she is free.

ZEUS: And you? You, too, are free, no doubt?

ORESTES: Yes, and well you know it.

ZEUS: A pity you can't see yourself as you are now, you fool, for all your boasting! What a heroic figure you cut there, cowering between the legs of a protecting god, with a pack of hungry vixen keeping guard on you! If *you* can brag of freedom, why not praise the freedom of a prisoner languishing in fetters, or a slave nailed to the cross?

ORESTES: Certainly. Why not?

ZEUS: Take care. You play the braggart now because Apollo is protecting you. But Apollo is my most obedient servant. I have but to lift a finger and he will abandon you.

ORESTES: Then do so. Lift a finger, lift your whole hand, while you are about it.

ZEUS: No, that is not my way. Haven't I told you that I take no pleasure in punishment. I have come to save you both.

ELECTRA: To save us? No, it is too cruel to make sport of us. You are the lord of vengeance and of death but, god though you are, you have no right to delude your victims with false hopes.

ZEUS: Within a quarter of an hour, you can be outside that door.

ELECTRA: Safe and sound?

ZEUS: You have my word for it.

ELECTRA: And what do you want from me in return?

ZEUS: Nothing, my child. Nothing.

ELECTRA: Nothing? Did I hear right? Then you are a kind god, a lovable god.

ZEUS: Or next to nothing. A mere trifle. What you can give most easily – a little penitence.

ORESTES: Take care, Electra. That trifle will weigh like a millstone on your soul.

ZEUS [*to Electra*]: Don't listen to him. Answer me, instead. Why hesitate to disavow that crime? It was committed by someone else; one could hardly say even that you were his accomplice.

ORESTES: Electra! Are you going to go back on fifteen years of hope and hatred?

ZEUS: What has she to go back on? Never did she really wish that impious deed to be accomplished.

ELECTRA: If only that were true!

ZEUS: Come now! Surely you can trust my word. Do I not read in men's hearts?

ELECTRA [*incredulously*]: And you read in mine that I never really desired that crime? Though for fifteen years I dreamt of murder and revenge?

ZEUS: Bah! I know you nursed bloodthirsty dreams – but there was a sort of innocence about them. They made you forget your servitude, they healed your wounded pride. But you never really thought of making them come true. Well, am I mistaken?

ELECTRA: Ah Zeus, dear Zeus, how I long to think you are not mistaken!

ZEUS: You're a little girl, Electra. A mere child. Most little girls dream of becoming the richest or the loveliest woman on earth. But you were haunted by the cruel destiny of your race, you dreamt of becoming the saddest, most criminal of women. You never willed to do evil; you willed your own misfortune. At an age when most children are playing hopscotch or with their dolls, you, poor child, who had no friends or toys, you toyed with dreams of murder, because that's a game to play alone.

ELECTRA: Yes, yes! I'm beginning to understand.

ORESTES: Listen, Electra! It's *now* you are bringing guilt upon you. For who except yourself can know what you really wanted? Will you let another decide that for you? Why distort a past that can no longer stand up for itself? And why disown the firebrand that you were, that glorious young goddess, vivid with hatred, that I loved so much? Can't you see this cruel god is fooling you?

ZEUS: No, Electra, I'm not fooling you. And now hear what I offer. If you repudiate your crime, I'll see that you two occupy the throne of Argos.

ORESTES: Taking the places of our victims?

ZEUS: How else?

ORESTES: And I shall put on the royal robe, still warm from the dead king's wearing?

ZEUS: That or another. What can it matter?

ORESTES: Nothing of course – provided that it's black.

ZEUS: Are you not in mourning?

ORESTES: Yes, I was forgetting; in mourning for my mother. And my subjects – must I have them, too, wear black?

ZEUS: They wear it already.

ORESTES: True. We can give them time to wear out their old clothes. . . . Well, Electra, have you understood? If you shed some tears, you'll be given Clytemnestra's shifts and petti-coats – those dirty, stinking ones you had to wash for fifteen years. And the part she played is yours for the asking. Now that you have come to look so much like her, you will play the part superbly; everyone will take you for your mother. But I – I fear I am more squeamish – I refuse to wear the breeches of the clown I killed.

ZEUS: You talk big, my boy. You butchered a defenceless man and an old woman who begged for mercy. But, to hear you speak, one would think you'd bravely fought, one against a crowd, and were the saviour of your city.

ORESTES: Perhaps I was.

ZEUS: You, a saviour! Do you know what's afoot behind that door? All the good folk of Argos are waiting there. Waiting to greet you with stones and pikes and pitchforks. Oh, they are very grateful to their saviour! . . . You are lonely as a leper.

ORESTES: Yes.

ZEUS: So you take pride in being an outcast, do you? But the solitude you're doomed to, most cowardly of murderers, is the solitude of scorn and loathing.

ORESTES: The most cowardly of murderers is he who feels remorse.

ZEUS: Orestes, I created you, and I created all things. Now see! [*The walls of the temple draw apart, revealing the firmament, spangled with wheeling stars.* ZEUS *is standing in the background. His voice becomes huge – amplified by loud-speakers – but his form is shadowy.*] See those planets wheeling on their appointed ways, never swerving, never clashing. It was I who ordained their courses, according to the law of Justice. Hear the music of the spheres, that vast, mineral hymn of praise, sounding and resounding to the limits of the firmament. [*Sounds of music.*] It is my work that living things increase and multiply, each according to his kind. I have ordained that man shall always beget man, and dog give birth to dog. It is my work that the tides with their innumerable tongues creep up to lap the sand and draw back at the appointed hour. I make the plants grow, and my breath fans round the earth the yellow clouds of pollen. You are not in your own home, intruder; you are a foreign body in the world, like a splinter in flesh, or a poacher in his lordship's forest. For the world is good; I made it according to my will, and I am Goodness. But you, Orestes, you have done evil, the very rocks and stones cry out against you. The Good is everywhere, it is the coolness of the well-spring, the pith of the reed, the grain of flint, the weight of stone. Yes, you will find it even in the heart of fire and light; even your own body plays you false, for it abides perforce by my Law. Good is everywhere, in you and about you; sweeping through you like a scythe, crushing you like a mountain. Like an ocean it buoys you up and rocks you to and fro, and it enabled the success of your evil plan, for it was in the brightness of the torches, the temper of your blade, the strength of your right arm. And that of which you are so vain, the Evil that you think is your creation, what is it but a reflection in a mocking mirror, a phantom thing that would have no being but for Goodness. No, Orestes, return to your saner self; the universe refutes you, you are a mite in the scheme of things. Return to Nature, Nature's thankless son. Know your sin, abhor it, and tear it from you as one tears out a rotten, noisome tooth. Or else – beware lest the very seas shrink back at your approach, springs dry up when you pass by, stones and rocks roll from your path and the earth crumbles under your feet.

ORESTES: Let it crumble! Let the rocks revile me, and flowers wilt at my coming. Your whole universe is not enough to prove me wrong. You are the king of gods, king of stones and stars, king of the waves of the sea. But you are not the king of man.

[*The walls draw together.* ZEUS *comes into view, tired and dejected, and he now speaks in his normal voice.*]

ZEUS: Impudent spawn! So I am not your king? Who, then, made you?

ORESTES: You. But you blundered; you should not have made me free.

ZEUS: I gave you freedom so that you might serve me.

ORESTES: Perhaps. But now it has turned against its giver. And neither you nor I can undo what has been done.

ZEUS: Ah, at last! So this is your excuse?

ORESTES: I am not excusing myself.

ZEUS: No? Let me tell you it sounds much like an excuse, this freedom whose slave you claim to be.

ORESTES: Neither slave nor master. I *am* my freedom. No sooner had you created me than I ceased to be yours.

ELECTRA: Oh, Orestes! By all you hold most holy, by our father's memory, I beg you do not add blasphemy to your crime!

ZEUS: Mark her words, young man. And hope no more to win her back by arguments like these. Such language is somewhat new to her ears – and somewhat shocking.

ORESTES: To my ears, too. And to my lungs which breathe

the words, and to my tongue, which shapes them. In fact I can hardly understand myself. Only yesterday you were still a veil on my eyes, a clot of wax in my ears; yesterday, indeed, I had an excuse. *You* were my excuse for being alive, for you had put me in the world to fulfil your purpose, and the world was an old pandar prating to me about your goodness, day in, day out. And then you forsook me.

ZEUS: *I* forsook you? How?

ORESTES: Yesterday, when I was with Electra, I felt at one with Nature, this Nature of your making. It sang the praises of the Good – *your* Good – in siren tones, and lavished intimations. To lull me into gentleness, the fierce light mellowed and grew tender as a lover's eyes. And, to teach me the forgiveness of offences, the sky grew bland as a pardoner's face. Obedient to your will, my youth rose up before me and pleaded with me like a girl who fears her lover will forsake her. That was the last time, the last, I saw my youth. Suddenly, out of the blue, freedom crashed down on me, and swept me off my feet. Nature sprang back, my youth went with the wind, and I knew myself alone, utterly alone in the midst of this well-meaning little universe of yours. I was like a man who's lost his shadow. And there was nothing left in heaven, no Right or Wrong, nor anyone to give me orders.

ZEUS: What of it? Do you want me to admire a scabby sheep that has to be kept apart; or the leper mewed in a lazar-house? Remember, Orestes, you once were of my flock, you fed in my pastures amongst my sheep. Your vaunted freedom isolates you from the fold; it means exile.

ORESTES: Yes, exile.

ZEUS: But the disease can't be deeply rooted yet; it began only yesterday. Come back to the fold. Think of your loneliness; even your sister is forsaking you. Your eyes are big with anguish, your face is pale and drawn. The disease you're suffering from is inhuman, foreign to my nature, foreign to yourself. Come back. I am forgetfulness, I am peace.

ORESTES: Foreign to myself – I know it. Outside nature, against nature, without excuse, beyond remedy, except what remedy I find within myself. But I shall not return under your Law; I am doomed to have no other law but mine. Nor shall I come back to Nature, the Nature you found good; in it are a thousand beaten paths all leading up to you – but I must blaze my own trail. For I, Zeus, am a man, and every man must find out his own way. Nature abhors man, and you too, god of gods, abhor mankind.

ZEUS: That is true; men like you I hold in abhorrence.

ORESTES: Take care; those words were a confession of your weakness. As for me, I do not hate you. What have I to do with you, or you with me? We shall glide past each other, like ships in a river, without touching. You are God, and I am free; each of us is alone, and our anguish is akin. How can you know I did not try to feel remorse in the long night that has gone by? And to sleep? But no longer can I feel remorse, and I can sleep no more.

[*A short silence.*]

ZEUS: What do you propose to do?

ORESTES: The folk of Argos are my folk. I must open their eyes.

ZEUS: Poor people! Your gift to them will be a sad one; of loneliness and shame. You will tear from their eyes the veils I had laid on them, and they will see their lives as they are, foul and futile, a barren boon.

ORESTES: Why, since it is their lot, should I deny them the despair I have in me?

ZEUS: What will they make of it?

ORESTES: What they choose. They're free; and human life begins on the far side of despair.

[*A short silence.*]

ZEUS: Well, Orestes, all this was foreknown. In the fullness of time a man was to come, to announce my decline. And you're that man, it seems. But seeing you yesterday – you with your girlish face – who'd have believed it?

ORESTES: Could I myself have believed it? . . . The words I speak are too big for my mouth, they tear it; the load of destiny I bear is too heavy for my youth, and has shattered it.

ZEUS: I have little love for you, yet I am sorry for you.

ORESTES: And I, too, am sorry for *you*.

ZEUS: Good-bye, Orestes. [*He takes some steps forward.*] As for you, Electra, bear this in mind. My reign is not yet over – far from it! – and I shall not give up the struggle. So choose if you are with me or against me. Farewell.

ORESTES: Farewell. [ZEUS *goes out.* ELECTRA *slowly rises to her feet.*] Where are you going?

ELECTRA: Leave me alone. I'm done with you.

ORESTES: I have known you only for a day, and must I lose you now for ever?

ELECTRA: Would to God that I had never known you!

ORESTES: Electra! My sister, dear Electra! My only love, the one joy of my life, do not leave me. Stay with me.

ELECTRA: Thief! I had so little, so very little to call mine; only a few weak dreams, a morsel of peace. And now you've taken my all; you've robbed a pauper of her mite! You were my brother, the head of our House, and it was your duty to protect me. But, no, you needs must drag me into carnage; I am red as a flayed ox, these loathsome flies are swarming after me, and my heart is buzzing like an angry hive.

ORESTES: Yes, my beloved, it's true, I have taken all from you, and I have nothing to offer in return; nothing but my crime. But think how vast a gift that is! Believe me, it weighs on my heart like lead. We were too light, Electra; now our feet sink into the soil, like chariot-wheels in turf. So come with me; we will tread heavily on our way, bowed beneath our precious load. You shall give me your hand, and we will go . . .

ELECTRA: Where?

ORESTES: I don't know. Towards ourselves. Beyond the rivers and mountains are an Orestes and an Electra waiting for us, and we must make our patient way towards them.

ELECTRA: I won't hear any more from you. All you have to offer me is misery and squalor. [*She rushes out into the centre of the stage. The* FURIES *slowly close in on her.*] Help! Zeus, King of gods and men, my King, take me in your arms, carry me from this place, and shelter me. I will obey your Law, I will be your creature and your slave, I will embrace your knees. Save me from the flies, from my brother, from myself. Do not leave me lonely and I will give up my whole life to atonement. I repent, Zeus. I bitterly repent.

[*She runs off the stage. The* FURIES *make as if to follow her, but the* FIRST FURY *holds them back.*]

FIRST FURY: Let her be, sisters. She is not for us. But that man is ours, and ours, I think, for many a day. His little soul is stubborn. He will suffer for two.

[*Buzzing, the* FURIES *approach Orestes.*]

ORESTES: I am alone, alone.

FIRST FURY: No, no, my sweet little murderer, I'm staying with you, and you'll see what merry games I'll think up to entertain you.

ORESTES: Alone until I die. And after that . . .?

FIRST FURY: Take heart, sisters, he is weakening. See how his eyes dilate. Soon his nerves will be throbbing like harp-strings, in exquisite arpeggios of terror.

SECOND FURY: And hunger will drive him from his sanctuary before long. Before nightfall we shall know how his blood tastes.

ORESTES: Poor Electra!

[*The* TUTOR *enters.*]

THE TUTOR: Master! Young master! Where are you? It's so dark one can't see a thing. I'm bringing you some food. The townspeople have surrounded the temple; there's no hope of escape by daylight. We shall have to try our chance when night comes. Meanwhile, eat this food to keep your strength up. [*The* FURIES *bar his way.*] Hey! Who are these? More of those primitive myths! Ah, how I regret that pleasant land of Attica, where reason's always right.

ORESTES: Do not try to approach me, or they will tear you in pieces.

THE TUTOR: Gently now, my lovelies. See what I've brought you, some nice meat and fruit. Here you are! Let's hope it will calm you down.

ORESTES: So the people of Argos have gathered outside the temple, have they?

THE TUTOR: Indeed they have, and I can't say which are the fiercer, the thirstier for your blood: these charming young creatures here, or your worthy subjects.

ORESTES: Good. [*A short silence.*] Open that door.

THE TUTOR: Have you lost your wits? They're waiting behind it, and they're armed.

ORESTES: Do as I told you.

THE TUTOR: For once permit me, sir, to disobey your orders. I tell you, they will stone you. It's madness.

ORESTES: Old man, I am your master, and I order you to unbar that door.

[*The* TUTOR *opens one leaf of the double doors a few inches.*]

THE TUTOR: Oh dear! Oh dear!

ORESTES: Open both leaves.

[*The* TUTOR *half opens both leaves of the door and takes cover behind one of them. The* CROWD *surges forward, thrusting the doors wide open; then stops, bewildered, on the threshold.*

The stage is flooded with bright light. Shouts rise from the CROWD. 'Away with him!' 'Kill him!' 'Stone him!' 'Tear him in pieces!']

ORESTES [*who has not heard them*]: The sun!

THE CROWD: Murderer! Butcher! Blasphemer! We'll tear you limb from limb. We'll pour molten lead into your veins.

A WOMAN: I'll pluck out your eyes.

A MAN: I'll eat your gizzard!

ORESTES [*drawing himself up to his full height*]: So here you are, my true and loyal subjects? I am Orestes, your King, son of Agamemnon, and this is my coronation day. [*Exclamations of amazement, mutterings amongst the crowd.*] Ah, you are lowering your tone? [*Complete silence.*] I know; you fear me. Fifteen years ago to the day, another murderer showed himself to you, his arms red to the elbows, gloved in blood. But him you did not fear; you read in his eyes that he was of your kind, he had not the courage of his crimes. A crime which its doer disowns becomes ownerless – no man's crime; that's how you see it, isn't it? More like an accident than a crime?

So you welcomed the criminal as your King, and that crime without an owner started prowling round the city, whimpering like a dog that has lost its master. You see me, men of Argos, you understand that my crime is wholly mine; I claim it as my own, for all to know, it is my glory, my life's work, and you can neither punish me nor pity me. That is why I fill you with fear.

And yet, my people, I love you, and it was for your sake that I killed. For your sake. I had come to claim my kingdom, and you would have none of me because I was not of your kind. Now, I am of your kind, my subjects; there is a bond of blood between us, and I have earned my kingship over you.

As for your sins and your remorse, your night-fears, and the crime Aegistheus committed – all are mine, I take them all upon me. Fear your Dead no longer; they are *my* Dead. And, see, your faithful flies have left you, and come to me. But have no fear, people of Argos. I shall not sit on my victim's throne or take the sceptre in my blood-stained hands. A god offered it to me, and I said 'No'. I wish to be a king without a kingdom, without subjects.

Farewell, my people. Try to reshape your lives. All here is new, all must begin anew. And for me, too, a new life is beginning. A strange life . . .

Listen now to this tale. One summer there was a plague of rats in Scyros. It was like a foul disease; they soiled and nibbled everything, and the people of the city were at their wits' end. But one day a flute-player came to the city. He took his stand in the market-place. Like this. [ORESTES *rises to his feet.*] He began playing on his flute and all the rats came out and crowded round him. Then he started off, taking long strides – like this. [*He comes down from the pedestal.*] And he called to the people of Scyros, 'Make way!' [*The* CROWD *makes way for him.*] And all the rats raised their heads and hesitated – as the flies are doing. Look! Look! at the flies! Then all of a sudden they followed in his train. And the flute-player, with his rats, vanished for ever. Thus.

[*He strides out into the light. Shrieking, the* FURIES *fling themselves after him.*]

CURTAIN

MORE ABOUT PENGUINS

Penguin Book News, an attractively illustrated magazine which appears every month, contains details of all the new books issued by Penguins as they are published. Every four months it is supplemented by *Penguins in Print*, which is a complete list of all books published by Penguins which are still available. (There are well over two thousand of these.)

A specimen copy of *Penguin Book News* can be sent to you free on request, and you can become a regular subscriber at 3s. for twelve issues (with the complete lists). Just write to Dept EP, Penguin Books Ltd, Harmondsworth, Middlesex, enclosing a cheque or postal order, and your name will be added to the mailing list.

Other books published by Penguins are described on the following pages.

Note: *Penguin Book News* and *Penguins in Print*
are not available in the U.S.A. or Canada

NAUSEA

Jean-Paul Sartre

A new translation of Sartre's celebrated first novel. Written in 1938, *Nausea* remains one of the peaks of Sartre's achievement. It is a novel of the alienation of personality and the mystery of being, and presents us with the first full-length essay in the philosophy for which Sartre has since become famous. *Nausea* is a novel of brilliant observation, wit, and psychological penetration by one of the world's front-rank intellectuals.

THE AGE OF REASON

Jean-Paul Sartre

This novel by one of France's greatest post-war writers covers two days in the life of Mathieu Delarue, a teacher of philosophy, and in the lives of his acquaintances and friends. Mathieu is trying to raise money for an abortion for a woman with whom he has been living for seven years, and at the same time he is obsessed with a desire for personal freedom. Individual tragedies and happiness are etched against the Paris summer of 1938, with its night clubs, galleries, students, and café society.

But behind it all there is a threat, only half realized at the time, of the coming catastrophe of the Second World War.

'There is a wonderful feeling of suspense about the book' – Henry Reed in the *Listener*

'Constantly delights with its brilliance' – *Spectator*

'A dynamic, deeply disturbing novel' – Elizabeth Bowen

The other two volumes of Sartre's trilogy, 'Roads to Freedom', are also in Penguins:

THE REPRIEVE
IRON IN THE SOUL